Jean Laffite

Prince of Pirates

Jean Laffite
Prince of Pirates

by
Jack C. Ramsay, Jr.

EAKIN PRESS   Austin, Texas

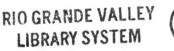

Published in the United States of America
By Eakin Press
An Imprint of Sunbelt Media, Inc.
P.O. Drawer 90159 ★ Austin, TX 78709-0159

3   4   5   6   7   8   9

ISBN 1-57168-029-2

Library of Congress Cataloging-in-Publication Data

Ramsay, Jack C., Jr., 1922–
   Jean Laffite : prince of pirates / by Jack C. Ramsay, Jr.
     p.   cm.
   Includes bibliographical references and index.
   ISBN 1-57168-029-2
   1. Laffite, Jean. 2. Pirates — Louisiana — Biography. 3. Pirates — Texas — Biography. 4. New Orleans (LA), Battle of, 1815. 5. Privateering — Mexico, Gulf of— History — 19th Century. I. Title.
F374.L176   1995
973.5'239'092–dc20
   [B]   95-5782
                                                                    CIP

This work is dedicated to

KARIN K. RAMSAY,

my companion in unraveling the mystery of Jean Laffite.

The American battle line at Chalmette. A few hundred yards down from this position, Laffite's men under Dominique Youx manned an artillery battery during the legendary battle of January 8, 1815. Most of the New Orleans battlefield is part of the Chalmette National Military Park.

— Photo by Kevin Young

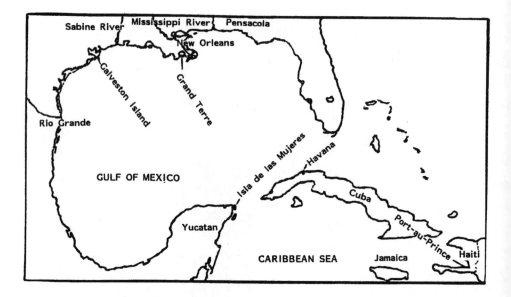

Laffite's Islands:

Grande Terre

Galveston

Cuba

Isla de las Mujeres

Contents

Preface	The Mysterious Jean Laffite	vii
Chapter 1	A City in Confusion	1
Chapter 2	The Lady New Orleans	5
Chapter 3	The Louisiana Connection	9
Chapter 4	A Mistress in the City	15
Chapter 5	In Serious Straits	20
Chapter 6	A Seaward Island	23
Chapter 7	Kingdom by the Sea	28
Chapter 8	A Nation Goes to War	34
Chapter 9	A Bold Gesture	38
Chapter 10	The British Menace	42
Chapter 11	The Stray Sheep	47
Chapter 12	A Bloodless Conquest	53
Chapter 13	Hellish Banditti	58
Chapter 14	Beyond the Fog	63
Chapter 15	Desperate Need	67
Chapter 16	Hardships and Fatigues	73
Chapter 17	The Celebration	78
Chapter 18	A Restless Yearning	84
Chapter 19	Mistresses and Espionage	89
Chapter 20	Immune from Attack	93
Chapter 21	Suspicion	98
Chapter 22	Blatant Misrepresentation	103
Chapter 23	A Balancing Act	110
Chapter 24	A Body Left Dangling	116
Chapter 25	Sails in the Sunrise	120
Chapter 26	An Isolated Cove	124
Chapter 27	The Last Island	130
Epilogue	The Lure of the Sea	135
Appendix A	The Journal of Jean Laffite	147
Appendix B	Capt. Dominique Youx's Company	153
Endnotes		155
Bibliography		187
Index		203

At the peak of Jean Laffite's notoriety, the English romantic, Lord Byron, wrote his epic poem, *The Corsair.* Byron's "Chief of Pirates" possessed "a glance of fire" and he commanded his followers with "a smooth voice and calm . . . mien." His deeds were "link'd with one virtue and a thousand crimes."

*Cecil B. DeMille resurrected his **Buccaneer** script, and featured the dashing Yul Brynner as Laffite.*
— Courtesy Institute of Texan Cultures

Preface:
The Mysterious Jean Laffite

Death stalked the Louisiana coast.

A young woman in her mid-twenties huddled in a violently pitching yawl next to her husband and children. Gale-force winds had swamped their sailing craft. All had survived a nighttime storm, but there was little chance of staying alive. Without provisions or knowledge of the area, they could not maneuver the open boat through heavy seas to safety.

The young father wrestled with the oars as he rowed for shore. Ahead he could see the outline of a tall masted ship. The grey light of early morning displayed what he most feared: an armed brig under the command of the notorious Jean Laffite. He had no choice but to allow crewmen to assist his family in boarding.

Martha Martin later wrote her memoirs in which she recorded the event: "Laffite the Pirate . . . treated [us] with all kindness possible." She was taken "aboard his vessel" and given "a bountiful breakfast." Laffite then "ordered a schooner" to assure a safe homeward journey for her family "even supplying a hat for her husband who had lost his own hat in the sinking."[1]

There were others who gave similar accounts of Laffite's gallantry. A woman who knew him declared he was "very handsome" and a "very, very polite gentleman."[2]

Another contemporary described Laffite as "graceful and elegant in manners . . . accomplished in conversation."[3]

And yet, this was the man who was often described in very different terms: "the Prince of Pirates,"[4] or the "ferocious" head of "desperadoes."[5] One widely accepted source declared that

Laffite "had no more regard for innocent lives than a butcher has for his victims."[6]

Some considered him a rapacious rogue, a man of unmitigated violence. Others, many of whom were young women, regarded him as a charming person. He was seductive, perhaps deceptive, but always elegantly gracious.

In spite of divergent appraisals of the man, a president of the United States once considered him a trustworthy ally. When British forces attacked New Orleans, Laffite played the role of patriot. He won the confidence of Andrew Jackson who, after the battle, officially commended him for his "courage and fidelity."[7]

Today, a town in Louisiana bears his name. The United States government has named a national park in his behalf. An unlimited mass of legend revolves around his personage and deeds.

One fact is clear: Laffite was a man of mystery whose actions and motives were subject to a variety of interpretations. One authority declared that Laffite deliberately "told many conflicting stories about himself . . . tall tales . . . [which he] never intended people to believe."[8] He consistently denied he was a pirate, yet he relished the notoriety his reputation bestowed upon him.

The nature of his clandestine activity required deception. He encouraged the mysterious using this element to weave around himself a web of delusion. He was successful in blurring the facts relating to his own origin, and during his final years he established circumstances that obscured his own demise.

The spelling of his name furthers the sense of the unknown. His surname was a familiar one in late eighteenth century Louisiana. Yet, there is evidence he insisted upon a different spelling, possibly as a means of disassociating himself from his own kin, adding the element of mystery to his very existence.[9] In spite of this, the spelling he preferred will be used in this volume. With the reputation that has been bestowed upon him, how could one even consider doing otherwise?

But it is far more than fear of ghostly retaliation that has discouraged examination of the life of one of the most intriguing and fascinating characters of modern history. One biographer who did seek to unravel the mystery of Jean Laffite made reference to the fact that there is a monumental task in "sifting truth from legend."[10]

It must be granted that the quest for authentic Laffite data is a complex one. One record that claimed to include information gained from a contemporary declared: "Nobody knows the truth about Laffite."[11]

Perhaps that is so.

Possibly no one knew or will ever know all of the facets of the enigma of Jean Laffite. Contradictory, delusive, mysterious he was, but there is one more certainty: he did make a unique impact upon both history and legend.

It was in Louisiana's wetlands that Laffite first rose to prominence. Even in its beauty, it is a land of illusion. Much of it appears to be a prairie upon which one might walk with ease. What seems to be solid ground may be no more than marsh grass beneath which there is water and mire.

Like the land where he lived for a time, he was both illusionary and mysterious. And yet, the quest for information about Laffite beckons one beyond the emerald isles and uncertain waters.

This is a mystery well worth solving.

Jackson's victory continued to inspire long after most of its participants had passed on. This version of the battle appeared in Harper's Weekly *some forty-six years after the battle on the eve of the American Civil War.*

THE PLACE D'ARMES

The Place D'Armes, New Orleans. Drawing from A History of Louisiana by Harriet Magruder (1909).
— Courtesy Institute of Texan Cultures

x

CHAPTER 1

A City in Confusion

The seaport town of New Orleans was a city in confusion.

In November 1803, the growing village on the banks of the Mississippi was under the dominion of Spain. On the last day of the month, the Spanish flag was lowered and the standard of France was raised over the Place d'Armes. It would fly there for less than three weeks.

On the morning of December 20, the city girded itself for another change of national allegiance. Contemporary accounts suggest that the weather was unusually warm. The sun sparkled upon the broad waters of the river determined to hold in check the damp chill of the winter months.

Suddenly, the quiet was broken by the sound of cannon fire. Merchants in the shops near the river quay paused, listened apprehensively. The noise that reverberated within the walls of the town was no more than the guns of nearby forts announcing the arrival of a new government. Casually the tradesmen resumed their tasks.

On the street, there was the rhythmic sound of marching men. A column of troops carrying a red-striped banner moved through the narrow passageway of Rue Chartres and formed

1

ranks before St. Louis Cathedral. Uniformed militia companies assembled in the Place d'Armes. Local residents filled the nearby balconies. Others watched warily.

All eyes strained to catch a glimpse of the new governor of Louisiana. William C. C. Claiborne, the executive of Mississippi territory, had been appointed to the task of anglicizing New Orleans. As soon as his troops assumed a ceremonial position, he dismounted. Accompanied by Gen. James Wilkinson, commander of the military unit, he entered the Cabildo. The two officials climbed the stairs to the council room. They were greeted by Governor Laussat, who had symbolically ruled the town for twenty days. He gave Claiborne the keys to the city and led him to the balcony. Speaking in French, he absolved the Louisianians of allegiance to the French Republic and declared: "You are now American citizens and will soon take oaths to your new country."[1]

Claiborne spoke in English. His speech was brief, one that could be summed up in a single statement: "The American people receive you as brothers."[2]

When he had finished his address, there was no applause. In somber silence, the flag of the Republic of France was removed from the flagstaff. A French militiaman solemnly took the tricolor, folded it reverently. In silence, he returned to his place in line. A star-studded banner was unfurled. The flag moved slowly up the pole, but stuck midway before suddenly continuing to the top. A few of the newly arrived troops cheered. There was no sound from the crowd.[3]

Two young men were among those who watched. Both were in their early twenties. One was Renato Beluche, who would soon become famous as a privateer captain on the Gulf of Mexico. He would operate in defiance of American law.[4] Another was an individual with striking Gallic features. Slender and well proportioned, he stood out in any crowd. He was later described as "remarkably handsome," one who possessed the marks of "genuine aristocracy . . . smallness of hands . . . brilliancy of teeth."[5] When he walked the streets of the city, he exhibited an air of gentlemanly self-confidence.[6] He shared the feelings of others who regretted the sudden political change.

His name was Jean Laffite.

One fact was apparent to the French population of New Orleans: the territory had been annexed to the United States without previous consultation with the inhabitants of Louisiana. The transfer had taken place, not by virtue of conquest or referendum, but by purchase. For most of the town's residents and for the owners of the upriver plantations, the sight of the new flag flying above the river dock was reason for apprehension. For many, it was cause for anger.

Three of the most powerful nations of the world had, at one time or another, vied for New Orleans: France, Great Britain, and Spain.[7]

Once the United States had established itself as an independent nation, concern over the proprietorship of Louisiana became a major issue. In the fall of 1802, the acting intendant of the territory, Juan Ventura Morales, withdrew the American right of deposit in New Orleans shutting off trading rights in the city. Protests were lodged with the Spanish government that then controlled the territory. This was a violation of treaty. Morales defended his action as necessary because of the extensive smuggling of goods into New Orleans by citizens of the United States.[8]

Spain had technically returned Louisiana to France in October. This act caused President Thomas Jefferson to declare to Congress that should Napoleon send French troops to occupy the territory, this would produce "a change in the aspect of our foreign relations."[9]

Although this was a strong statement for Jefferson, it did not satisfy the American expansionists. Alexander Hamilton called the president's message "a lullaby." He demanded that the United States annex the territory that included New Orleans.[10]

In the American capital, there was talk of war. By the end of December, more moderate voices were heard. Louisiana would be gained by purchase.

Napoleon's troops were engaged in vicious guerrilla warfare in Santo Domingo. Before a French administration of Louisiana could be put in place, refugees began to arrive from the Caribbean reporting carnage and "white defeat."[11]

On April 8, 1803, James Monroe arrived at Le Havre in the hope that Napoleon's need of American dollars would encourage the emperor to sell Louisiana. Napoleon summoned his advisors. During the discussion, he was reported to have said: "I think of ceding it to the United States . . . I can scarcely say . . . cede . . . for it is not yet in our possession."[12]

On April 14, Monroe was presented to Charles Maurice de Tallyrand-Perigord, the French foreign minister. Tallyrand began work with Monroe and the resident American minister, Robert R. Livingston.[13] By the end of the month, the negotiators had hammered out an agreement. The sale price was set at sixty million francs, approximately $11,250,000 at the existing rate of exchange. Before the first of May, the compact was signed by representatives of both nations.

Livingston, after completing the treaty of cession, stated to Monroe: "This is the noblest work of our whole lives."[14] For the expansionists and for all who believed in the manifest destiny of the American nation, it was precisely that.

Congress moved quickly to ratify the treaty. On July 17, Jefferson ordered Claiborne to New Orleans. One technicality remained before the Americans could legally claim their purchase. The French had to reclaim Louisiana from Spain and possess the province before the sale would be in order. On November 23, a commission from Paris arrived in the river city with a letter from the Spanish Crown authorizing the transfer.

The tricolor was raised on November 30. It would fly near the quay for no more than twenty days and then be replaced by the national emblem of the United States.[15]

Having experienced allegiance to three nations in as many weeks, the proud lady of the Mississippi was, by the beginning of the year 1804, a city in confusion.

Her inhabitants were more than confused; they were angry.

CHAPTER 2

The Lady New Orleans

Once more she had been bartered and sold, this time for yankee dollars.

Although there were some who questioned the exchange, others recognized that the lady New Orleans had no option other than to become intimate with the vigorous young nation that had claimed her.

She had survived many vicissitudes during her long history. She would survive this: she would accept the inevitable and hope that nothing would disrupt her livelihood or disturb her mode of engaging in commerce.

In the years Spain had administered her affairs, she had known only gentle restraints. Recognizing that she was an independent lady, the Spaniards did not integrate her into the imperial administerial system.[1] Open navigation of the lower Mississippi was permitted during most of the years of Spanish rule.[2] During this time, she established her position as a port for all nations, a haven for those who sought refuge from both political and economic distress.

At the beginning of the nineteenth century, the town consisted of a little over thirty carefully laid-out city blocks that ran uniformly along a broad bend in the Mississippi. A waterfront road known as Rue du Quay followed the curve of the levees as it arched, crescent-like, away from the center of the village. Four thoroughfares ran the length of the town. Rue de Chartres formed the far edge of the Place d'Armes. Beyond were three major streets: Rue Royale, Rue Bourbon, and Rue Dauphine. Among the French inhabitants, these routes of travel were still known by the original names as the people of New Orleans clung to their Gallic heritage in spite of decades of Spanish domination.[3]

During the first months of American rule, there were indications the city would maintain her place as the queen of the Gulf. With spring, shipping began to increase as the river's waters swelled within the levees providing greater accessibility for deep-water navigation.

By the time the feasts following Lent had been adequately savored, vessels from distant ports reached quayside bringing with them succulent foodstuffs from more tropical climes, the fineries of Europe, and in some cases, human cargo.

One of the ships that arrived in the spring of 1804 docked under the diminutive feminine name of *La Soeur Cherie*. She flew the flag of Republican France. The master of the vessel, a "Capt. Lafette," had brought his ship into harbor for repairs and provisions. Claiming the right of a ship in distress to put into a safe harbor, he reported his craft had suffered damage in a storm at sea.[4]

The arrival concerned officials of the new government. Governor Claiborne had misgivings about the ship docked only a hundred yards from his official residence. He suspected the vessel was a privateer engaged in the slave trade. He instructed the harbor master to allow only necessary repairs without any additional armaments.[5]

Although there is no evidence the "Lafette" of the mystery ship was related to the Laffite of history, several authorities contend that the master of the vessel was Pierre Laffite, the older brother of Jean Laffite.[6]

There is only one certainty: This was one of a number of similar craft that, for decades, had entered the port with few questions asked. The major significance of the landing was the fact the recently appointed officials viewed the arrival with suspicion.

Vessels of all nationalities continued to arrive at the burgeoning port. Upriver, they came to find harbor and do business of one sort or another with the merchants of Rue de Chartres and Rue Royale.

An auction took place in nearby Baton Rouge, according to one account, soon after the arrival of *La Soeur Cherie*. Pierre Laffite was present. He claimed to be a merchant from Plaza Pancola.[7]

Claiborne initiated measures to regulate shipping on the Mississippi. The merchants of New Orleans countered by asking that their port remain open. In February, Congress passed an act dividing the territory into two sections, "Louisiana" and "Orleans." Article Ten of this bill "prohibited the importation of slaves . . . from places without the limits of the United States." In spite of the protests of the planters of southern Louisiana, President Jefferson signed the bill into law.[8]

Claiborne's task became that of enforcing an unpopular regulation upon a people who had become citizens of the United States against their will. Early in the year, he had written James Madison that he feared "no administration or form of government can give general satisfaction" in the territory.[9]

The governor was determined to uphold the law. As a skillful administrator, he recognized the complexities of his task. He moved slowly. On March 31, he established a register of ships docking at New Orleans that provided for "ship enrollments as well as ship registers" for all vessels arriving at the port.[10] But the wetlands of southern Louisiana were vast, and there were many areas where ships could dock, unload cargoes, and return quickly to sea.

New Orleans was growing, and great masses of people were entering Louisiana. The French-speaking population had increased in numbers even during the years of Spanish rule as persons of Gallic heritage sought a haven in the lands bordering the lower reaches of the Mississippi. Many had fled from the slave uprisings in the Caribbean or had migrated from former colonies of France.

There were others who had found a place in the expanding town: those of Spanish heritage, free blacks, refugees from the islands of the Caribbean, and individuals of mixed ancestry. In his report in early 1804, Claiborne had noted that the city was composed of a "heterogeneous mass" of races and nationalities.[11]

Very few were persons with any allegiance to the new gov-

7

ernment. But the American intrusion was not the only Anglo effort to tame the lady New Orleans. The British had sought her. In the middle years of the eighteenth century, English military power claimed the upper reaches of the Mississippi.[12] Colonials in the south would suffer from a Royal Navy blockade. In the ongoing contest to control her, New Orleans was cut off from supply by sea.

Throughout much of her history, she had been used as an enticement in the ongoing affairs of European politics. When Spain claimed her as a prize and occupied the city with troops, she felt betrayed by France, the nation that had given her birth.

In her cafes on Rue Bourbon and Rue Royale, there was talk of establishing the city as an independent republic. She had proven herself to be self-sufficient and had survived in near independence for a century and a half.

She was now strong, and she was mature. Perhaps news had come by way of the ships docked at her quay of independence in other colonial territories. Possibly words such as *liberte* and *egaltie,* which could then only be whispered in the streets of Paris, were spoken in the courtyards of Rue St. Louis and Rue Dumaine.

But the spirited lady was not to gain her full freedom. She was allowed only to speak of liberty and to hope for some degree of equality with those who would control her. In July 1769, the Spanish Crown sent a force of 2,000 men into the city to cool her fever. There would be no more freedom talk. Those who had declared themselves in favor of a republic were imprisoned.[13]

Once all thought of rebellion had ceased, Spain loosened its tenuous grip upon the territory. She was too important a prize to be allowed to slip away, a valuable pawn in the continuing game of international politics.

In 1793, Spain and France again went to war. New Orleans braced herself against a possible attack by the French. The attack never came. Spanish power was in decline. For a time, New Orleans enjoyed a measure of independence with almost total freedom of trade.

In 1803, when the star-spangled banner was raised over the Place d'Armes, the lady of the southern Mississippi wondered whether those who claimed her would woo her or exploit her.

CHAPTER 3

The Louisiana Connection

*I*t was as though he came from nowhere.

Even the origin of Jean Laffite is shrouded in mystery, for the exact circumstances of his birth are as illusive as solid soil in the swamps and bayous where he first gained prominence.

Beginning only a few miles beyond the environs of New Orleans, Louisiana's wetlands stretch southward to the Gulf of Mexico. In the early nineteenth century, this was an isolated land, virtually inaccessible to those who did not know the intricacies of the territory's bays and bayous. Many portions could only be entered by skilled boatmen with a lifelong knowledge of the delta country.[1]

No recent arrival would have been able to assume leadership of a smuggling base dependent upon transport between the coast and the city. This fact alone requires reconsideration of the assumption that the brothers Laffite landed on the Gulf Coast at about the time of annexation.

If they came to New Orleans no sooner than the early 1800s, a related question is how they gained access to the upper levels of French Louisiana's closed-caste structure. The town served as the cultural and economic center for a centuries-old sociological system bound loosely together by a common linguistic heritage within which there were intricate strata. Newcomers did not move easily from one level of society to another.

There is no acceptable evidence for the tradition that the two brothers first came to American shores from France at about the year 1804.[2] Jean, on one occasion, gave what would appear to be a clear answer to the question of his place of birth. One of the few documents that can be traced to him with confidence declared he was thirty-two years of age in 1813 and was from the French city of Bordeaux.[3] But this was a convenient time to be a native of France, a claim that provided protection from the enforcement of American law.

Another document, based on information he originated, gave his place of birth as Bayonne,[4] the same city Pierre claimed as his natal site in registering the baptism of his daughter, Marie Josephe.[5]

Other contemporary sources provide conflicting information. Two additional cities in France were named as the home of the Laffites — St. Malo[6] and Brest.[7] Orduna, in the Basque province of Spain,[8] was also among the possible natal sites. One curious work, published in 1828, gave Westchester, New York, as Jean's place of birth.[9]

The claim that both Laffites were natives of France was no more than a deceptive device, a convenience, one that would add to their mystique. In the absence of any acceptable documentary proof, the parents of Jean and Pierre must have been, along with the others who bore similar surnames, a part of the Caribbean island colonial system known in the seventeenth century as St. Dominique.

Both logic and geography would indicate that the Laffites of Louisiana were a part of the colonialism that flourished in the eighteenth century on the island known earlier as Santo Domingo or Hispanola. In the final decades of that century, the French-speaking residents of St. Dominque were forced to maintain close ties with persons of a similar heritage who had established themselves in the Mississippi Delta country.

This was the Louisiana connection.

Jean and Pierre were a part of this milieu. For this reason they could call themselves French. When convenient, they claimed to be natives of France. As late as 1815, many residents of New Orleans registered with Louis de Tousard, the French consul, declaring themselves subject only to the laws of France in order to escape what they believed was unjust regimentation.[10] One did not have to prove birth in continental France to be French.

Of even greater importance, they thought and acted as persons of French colonial descent, a heritage that accepted privateering as necessary for survival in the Caribbean.[11] France had adopted the practice as a method of containing the rapidly developing English naval power.[12] In the early nineteenth century, Napoleon declared that "every vessel to whatever nation it may belong . . . [which] shall have submitted to a voyage to England . . . shall be captured by our privateers and shall be adjudged to the captors."[13]

Since Britain was a major center of commercial shipping, any shipmaster who could obtain a license from a French official could legally capture a ship upon a sea lane that would eventually lead toward the English coast. Other nations besides France, including the United States, recognized the practice. Privateering played a major role in both the American Revolution and the War of 1812.[14]

When ships arrived at New Orleans in the early years of annexation, officials had no reason to deny harborage solely because they suspected privateering. To do so would have been a repudiation of an institution that continued to have legal status in the Caribbean for years and was not outlawed in the United States until the middle of the nineteenth century.[15]

French colonialism determined the economics of St. Dominique,[16] established as a colony in 1665.[17] By the year 1790, the island had become a prosperous outpost of France that could boast 792 sugar estates and 2,810 coffee plantations. Due to the strenuous labor of blacks, St. Dominique outproduced all of the British Caribbean holdings.[18]

But the rapacious greed of the island's taskmasters would end in disaster. In 1791, an army of escaped slaves attacked Port-au-Prince. Plantation homes were burned, and many of the white overlords who lived in luxury at the expense of the island's laborers died violently.[19] The French retaliated with military force, but Napoleon's European armies were no match for the revolutionists. The island's former name was declared accursed and was

11

replaced by the Arawak name of Haiti.[20] The social upheaval that followed sent the last of the colonists to Louisiana.

But this mainland connection with St. Dominique existed long before actual insurrection. For years, sons of plantation owners sought opportunities beyond the restricted social and economic structure of the colony. The more adventurous went to sea. Some entered the profession of the privateer. Many found land in the Mississippi Delta where daughters of colonists were willing to join them. Whole families took part in the migration. Among them there were several families of Lafittes.

By the time of annexation, the surname was a familiar one in southern Louisiana. There were Lafittes, Lafettes, or Lafites who had been living in the area for decades, a name that occurred frequently in records in New Orleans during this period of migration. A Jean Lafitte, Sr., was listed in the Cabildo records of 1766.[21] A Juan Lafitte was listed in a document dated February 16, 1775, during the Spanish period.[22] Similar references appeared after the year 1765 and continued with regularity through the end of the century.[23]

As the century drew to a close, the name Lafitte appeared in official papers indicating that, by this time, persons with this surname were well established in the economic structure of French Louisiana. A Bruno Lafitte and a P. Lafitte were engaged in business, according to records dated 1787 in the Natchitoches area. There are several references to a Pierre Lafitte and to a Baptiste Lafitte in the Red River area. A "Bayou Pierre" appears on a late eighteenth century map of Louisiana adjacent to a land claim by Pierre Lafitte.[24] A Pierre Lafitte, Jr. claimed a land grant by right of inheritance from his father in the year 1795, and a Sylvestre Lafitte established property "near the Pierre Lafitte claim" in 1810.[25]

Documents among the Cabildo records provide additional clues that lead toward unraveling the Laffite riddle. A Don Pedro Aubry was a merchant in New Orleans during the 1780s.[26] On April 1, 1786, he filed a will that declared nineteen months earlier he had married a widow, a recent refugee from Santo Domingo,[27] who had brought to the marriage a son whose name was "Juan Enrico, hijo legitimo de Juan Lafitte."[28]

12

Although it is impossible to trace a direct relationship between any of these names and the Laffites of privateering fame, one fact is clear: a number of persons with this surname entered Louisiana from St. Dominique during this time.[29] Among them were widows who sought haven in New Orleans and who lived for a time with friends or relatives until suitable marriages could be arranged. Some married merchants of the city.

Jean, Pierre, and their widowed mother arrived in the southern Mississippi country during the 1780s. The older son, Pierre, was sent to live with one of the several households of Lafittes who lived in other parts of Louisiana. Jean, still a young child, would have remained with his mother when she married a member of New Orleans' mercantile class. As a youth, he spent his maturing years in the city and participated in the town's social activities along with members of other merchant families.

Pierre was raised elsewhere in the territory, possibly on a plantation or near a community on the Mississippi or the Red River. He later gained possession of a small trading schooner and established himself as either a privateer or a seagoing trader. Possibly he operated from Santo Domingo for a few years and left when French colonials were no longer tolerated. After annexation, the two brothers united in efforts to take advantage of the merchandising potential that Louisiana offered as a territory of the United States.

Jean Laffite was knowledgeable about the wetlands south of New Orleans and the bayou country. This fact is evidence that he spent a portion of his early years in the region. One record stated that he had "a more accurate knowledge of every inlet from the Gulf than any other man," and declared that because of his "acquaintance with all the secret passages of the Mississippi," he was able to lead the Baratarians in their smuggling operations. This was the reason he "was courted by . . . the British" prior to the Battle of New Orleans.[30]

During his youth, Jean visited the wetlands south of New Orleans, explored the bayous, the inlets, the waterways, and the illusionary islands. He knew the area's isolation, its potential. His maturing years in New Orleans not only provided him with a knowledge of the lands south of the city, but of the town and its people. As a resident, he had contact with the sons of plantation owners who were a part of the social milieu of New Orleans, generally ranking, according to the size and success of their plantations, either as peers or superiors to the merchant class.

One of these youths was Renato Beluche, the scion of a planter family, who lived on a 714-acre establishment served by sixteen slaves. Renato was born in New Orleans in 1780, about the same year as Jean's birth. The Beluche family owned property in the city and had lived at a residence at the corner of Dumaine and Rue Royale until the year 1783.[31] Another family that lived in the area were the Laportes.[32] Both the Laportes and the Beluches produced sons who became privateers on the Gulf of Mexico.[33]

Jean knew both families. He was an associate of Renato Beluche, a relationship that would extend beyond their youthful years. Jean knew other French-speaking families including the Blanques. He was on familiar terms with some of the newcomers to New Orleans. One of these was Edward Livingston, who took up residence in the port town when Laffite was in his early twenties. His brother, Robert Livingston, had negotiated the purchase of Louisiana. A year after his arrival, Edward gained access to the French-speaking community by marrying a Caribbean refugee, Louise Moreau de Lassy.[34]

Another newcomer to the area was a young lawyer named John Randolph Grymes, who later served as the United States district attorney for New Orleans and, after Claiborne's death, married his widow.[35]

Not only did Jean Laffite know both Grymes and Livingston, but he would have known the American governor who arrived in the city late in 1803. When Claiborne assumed responsibility for guiding New Orleans into accepting United States law, he was twenty-eight years of age, only five years older than Jean.[36] He knew Laffite, but he considered him a man who should be watched. Possibly he sensed in twenty-three-year-old Jean a potential for leadership, but a leadership that would be contrary to all that he represented as a governor appointed to the territory of Orleans by the United States of America.

CHAPTER 4

A Mistress in the City

She had about her an aura of sensuous lethargy.

Even summer's warmth dealt gently with the Lady New Orleans. When oppressive humidity crept into her streets and courtyards, refreshing rain would soon cool her fever. Sparkling sunlight on slate roofs followed, renewing verdancy behind iron grill work. It was only late in the season with no breeze upon the river that the heat became unbearable. Then it was that swarms of mosquitoes settled upon the city.

In the early fall of 1804, as New Orleans braced herself for the influx of new inhabitants, there was an outbreak of yellow fever. Blaming the disease on swamp air and uncleanliness, many longtime inhabitants sought refuge outside the immediate area.

A later visitor complained of the town's filthiness: "It is improbable that a residence in New Orleans in the autumn months can ever be less hazardous than a battle of Waterloo."[1] But in 1804, no such comparison could be made, for Napoleon had not yet met his final defeat, nor was the cause of the annual threat to health fully understood.

Efforts were made to keep the town clear of accumulating

garbage. Refuse ditches within the narrow streets were cleared periodically, generally by forced labor from the lowest level of society.[2]

Many of the problems were caused by rapid growth. When the territory was annexed to the United States, New Orleans was a village with less than 8,000 inhabitants. As Americans entered Louisiana, they were joined by a steady stream of immigrants from Caribbean islands. Most were seeking resident status. Two years after annexation, the city doubled her population.

Longtime residents such as the Beluches, the Laportes, and the Blanques fled the city before the yellow fever season. They found refuge in river homes where coastal winds banished all swamp air. Jean Laffite was among them. He, and others of his caste, spent the late summer at sites where the pestiferous drone of the mosquito was not heard.

But there were many who had no choice.

Governor Claiborne dutifully remained in his official residence at the corner of Rue du Quay and Toulouse Street. In early summer, his wife, Eliza, and his two-year-old daughter, Cornelia Tennessee, arrived in New Orleans. At first, they reveled in the spacious courtyard that stretched to Chartres. Carondelet oil lamps swung from projecting arms attached to wooden posts. Outside the enclosure, where street lighting had not yet been installed, passersby could be seen carrying hand-held lanterns. But by the end of September, swamp air settled upon the town. Both mother and daughter contracted the dread disease. They were buried in St. Louis Cemetery.[3]

Other newcomers suffered a similar fate. As the population of the city increased, the vacant areas within the town's cemeteries decreased.

Still, they came.

Some arrived at the river dock from upstream. A few reached the quay on seagoing vessels from the eastern United States. Many came from the still troubled islands of the Caribbean. Over 5,000 refugees landed at the city's wharves in a single season. Housing was already in short supply, and for a time there was a serious shortage of food.[4]

Within a half dozen years, the population of the town more than tripled. By the end of the century's first decade, the city was

16

housing nearly 25,000 persons, who at first crowded the residential areas and then spilled over into the muddy flats upriver.[5]

Once Claiborne had overcome his initial grief, he continued the policy of Americanization. He proposed the establishment of a bank in the city that would issue paper money as an aid to commercial development. This met with resistance from the French-speaking community who feared that the currency in circulation would be depreciated. But the change was inevitable. Soon it was evident that the increasing population would provide a vigorous boost to merchandising regardless of the mode of exchange. Many residents reacted by investing funds in saleable goods.[6] Others sought to enlarge their land holdings to meet the demand for marketable crops.

The city's social life flourished. Balls and masquerades were frequently scheduled in the hall on Rue Chartres. Along the sides of the building's open area, boxes had been built on ascending tiers. There young Creole belles, chaperoned by their mothers, sat to view and be viewed.

On the floor, gentlemen chose dance partners from the ladies seated on the level beneath the boxes. The young men wore long coats of bright colors and boots with elaborate stitching. Each carried a sword-cane, known as a *colchemarde,* a weapon that was sometimes used in dueling. Continued Americanization of the city eventually caused the blade to be outlawed; the instrument often served as a means of settling quarrels between those who sought the attentions of the women who frequented the hall.[7]

Jean Laffite was in his early twenties when the Chartres Street ballroom was at the height of its popularity. Both he and Pierre were present for social events. They wore the *colchemarde.* They attended the dances, socialized with the scions of other New Orleans families, and viewed the attractive young belles on display. Jean did more than view these women. His practiced charm attracted members of the opposite sex both on and off the dance floor.

In addition to the Chartres street hall, two other social centers served as rendezvous sites for the town's elite: the St. Philip Theater and the Theater d'Orleans. Both catered to a French-speaking clientele.[8]

Laffite attended the performances and participated in the

dances, but his social life extended beyond the ballroom and theater. New Orleans had produced a class of persons who were a
significant component of the city's social structure — the mulatto
offsprings of free men and women of color. Their existence as a
caste was recognized in official reports as early as the mid-eigh-
teenth century. During the Spanish period, their numbers increased. After annexation, there was an additional influx of free
blacks who had taken no part in the insurrections. Like their
French counterparts, they sought refuge in Louisiana from turmoil in the Caribbean.

Several social levels were identifiable. The griffe, the offspring of a mulatto and a black, looked down on the pure-
blooded Negro. The mulatto was one step above the griffe.
Above the mulatto were the quadroons and the octoroons. Men
belonging to these two castes occupied a respected position in
society. They were often musicians, merchants, or artisans. Their
sisters were regarded as the most attractive and beautiful of all
women, and were sought after, and sometimes fought over, by
the upper-class white men who wanted them as mistresses.[9]

Balls were held at regular intervals where the young women
of the quadroon and octoroon castes were presented for display,
not as potential prostitutes, but as unwed mates for well-to-do
men. While female members of Creole families generally clad
themselves in relatively drab attire, the quadroon woman was
noted for the elegance of her raiment. Silks, satins, plumes, and
jewelry were skillfully used to bedeck their sleek and sensuous
bodies. A young woman of this caste recognized the fact that at-
tracting an upper-class male was essential to her social standing
and was dependent, at least in part, upon her ability to skillfully
display her physique. Quadroons were aware that the security of
their position required more than a display of physical attractive-
ness. Most had been groomed since childhood in the arts of coquettish charm.

Jean Laffite found these women much to his liking. During
the Spanish period, an effort had been made to suppress the quadroon balls. Governor Miro issued an order designed at severely
limiting the libertinism that accompanied the ballroom events.[10]

With American annexation, the balls again blossomed.

In the early 1800s, the hall on Chartres became the usual site
for an uppercaste male to seek a vivacious and attractive mis-

tress.[11] Creole gentlemen came, viewed, and danced with prospective sexual partners. A mate was chosen from those who were available. The male made arrangements with the woman's parent or guardian. If she accepted him as a lover, he would become obligated to provide a place for her to live, often in one of the small houses beyond the city's residential area. He then became responsible for supporting her as long as the relationship existed. If he later married, he might end the relationship, or he could continue to provide for her and maintain visitation privileges. Often the quadroon remained a mistress to a particular lover for life.

No records were kept of those who participated in this distinctive institution. Little mention was made in official documents or in newspaper accounts of either the quadroon balls or the resulting relationships. Yet the institution continued to flourish into the early years of the nineteenth century.

Pierre Laffite took a mistress who was the daughter of a quadroon mother whose mother had danced at the traditional balls.[12] Jean attended the quadroon balls. In his early maturity, he chose a mistress, a charming and voluptuous beauty who excelled in the subtle art of sensuous seduction. He found living quarters for her, and there he journeyed from time to time to enjoy his own sexuality and develop his ability to charm and be charmed.

The quadroon institution was suited to a person of Laffite's temperament. It provided him with companionship and sexual satisfaction, but did not confine him within the bonds of formal marriage.

He was of that class of men who was unable to accept a lifetime commitment to any mate.

CHAPTER 5

In Serious Straits

*A*s French New Orleans reveled in the social life of Rue de Chartres, ships docked and sailed from the nearby quay. The task of supplying the city's growing population with goods would continue.

In February 1805, a two-masted schooner, *The Two Sisters*, registered at the city's port. On March 5, Renato Beluche, master of the ship, sailed from the quay declaring he was bound for Vera Cruz. In July, he cleared for Havana, quickly returned with a valuable cargo, and in August sailed again for Havana. At least one more voyage by Beluche, ostensibly to Vera Cruz, was recorded before the end of the year.[1]

Beluche's schooner was but one of the continual stream of vessels that docked at the quay. Merchandise quickly found its way into the city's emporiums. In 1805, few questions were asked about ports of origin. Whether these goods had been purchased at a foreign wharf or were the dividends of privateering was of little concern to the city's merchants who desperately needed saleable importations. In this second year of annexation, New Orleans would maintain her position as the principal port of the Gulf.

Many of the new arrivals came with impressive credentials.

One was Aaron Burr, who reached New Orleans in June 1805. As if his fame and former position were not enough, he brought with him letters of introduction from General Wilkinson, governor of the territory. Burr was a man who was comfortable in the circumambience of the city. He moved freely about the town, met with public officials, and was wined and dined by leading residents. During this time, he made plans to establish New Orleans as a base for an invasion of the west.

His scheme failed to materialize,[2] but for a time Burr was a flamboyant figure on the city's social scene. He must have met and at least conversed with Laffite, for Jean possessed a unique ability to move in the most sophisticated of circles.[3]

Laffite was in contact with the leading merchants and traders of the city. By this time, according to one account, he operated a warehouse in New Orleans.[4] Another recorded that he kept a store on Royal Street.[5] A source, originally written in French, referred to the Laffite mart as one located on "Rue Royale."[6]

Merchandise was transported from the nearby quay to Royal Street, a wholesale distribution center. From this warehouse, merchants could select articles for retail on Chartres and Bourbon. Each time a ship made port, the inventory was replenished. Renato Beluche was one of several captains who transferred cargoes directly to Royal Street.

The goods that Laffite provided his customers came from cities and islands throughout the Caribbean. Some had come from Europe, but much came only indirectly from foreign ports. A well-manned schooner could intercept a ship upon the high seas, claim her cargo, and deliver the choice portion to the port that would bring the highest prices. The New Orleans of the early 1800s was such a port.

As Laffite worked as a middleman supplying merchants, he continued to develop his contacts with the town's leading citizens. In the meantime, he made regular visits to the house of his mistress.

Well aware of the rapid changes taking place about him, he sought avenues for expanding his operation. By this time, he had been to sea. Possibly he had monitored the seamanship of Renato Beluche. Jean had not yet sailed as master of a ship, but he had mastered the business techniques essential to the success of an entrepreneur in the Louisiana of the early nineteenth century.

21

New Orleans had long been the mercantile queen of the Gulf. She would continue in this role. Not only was the volume of trade on the increase, but the plantations were prospering. Planters were breaking new ground, increasing their tillable acreage in order to meet the expanding market for produce, cotton, and sugar cane.

Claiborne toured the plantations in 1806. He had dined with one planter whose "sugars bring him near thirty thousand dollars per annum."[7]

The demand for blacks increased, field hands who could withstand the rigors of southern Louisiana's heat, men capable of clearing new land for lucrative crops. But the expectation of expanding prosperity for plantation owners was about to suffer a serious setback. On January 1, 1808, a law became effective that strengthened the earlier ban on the importation of slaves into Louisiana.

New Orleans' merchants soon faced an even greater problem: an embargo was placed on all overseas shipping. Congress "forbade any ship to sail from United States ports to any foreign port." Although this legislation was later replaced by one that permitted trade with ports other than those of France and England,[8] even these strictures produced serious difficulties. Both planter and merchant would suffer. The needs of the town's rapidly increasing population could not be met.

Ships continued to sail from the southern Mississippi port during the early days of the year 1808. Thirty-five vessels got underway in January before the Embargo Act could be enforced. One was captained by Renato Beluche.[9]

But much of the river port's trade fell under the ban. The shipping permitted was subject to strict scrutiny. There were inspections. Customs duties were levied with far greater consistency than at any time in the past either under Spanish or French rule. The government of the United States became a substantial barrier to commerce.

New Orleans would suffer under the intricacies of American law generated in a capital half a continent away. Without an open port, she could no longer maintain her position as queen of the Gulf.

The lady was in serious straits.

CHAPTER 6

A Seaward Island

*I*t was a land of seductive peril.

Only an occasional white-water breaker distinguished the shore from the open Gulf. The placidity of Louisiana's wetlands was no more than an illusion. For all unfamiliar with inland waters, danger lurked beneath the surface.

South of New Orleans, two seaward islands marked the boundary of the open sea: Grande Terre and Grande Isle. Between the two, there was a passage. Through this, a nineteenth century sailing vessel could enter a large bay, if the helmsman knew the channel. This was the portal to one of the more isolated sites on the North American continent — Barataria.[1]

An early visitor described Grande Terre as "pretty nearly the level of the sea," yet an island with ample fuel for wood fires and sufficient soil for growing garden vegetables. There was a prevailing sea breeze that protected its inhabitants from annoying insects, gnats, and mosquitoes.[2]

But it was more than idyllic circumstances that lured some to the area.

The island's inaccessibility made it a haunt for persons who sought escape from authority. The pirate Blackbeard was one of those who found haven there. He had anchored in the bay to escape pursuit in 1718.[3]

The origin of the name, Barataria, is a subject for debate. Some believe the word was taken from the French *barraterie*, meaning the "practice of exciting and encouraging lawsuits and quarrels."[4] Others contend the name came from a word meaning "barter" or trade,[5] or possibly named for Don Quixote's unattainable kingdom.[6]

Whatever may have been the source of the name, in the nineteenth century this was a region difficult to enter. Unless approached in a seagoing vessel, there was no means of reaching Grande Terre other than by barge or pirogue.

The pirogue provided the best, and possibly, the only efficient means of travel from the seaward islands to New Orleans. A boat cut or burned from the trunk of a large cottonwood, this was a conveyance adapted from the primitive canoes of the natives of the swamps. Trees nearly fifty-feet-long were sometimes used. From these, pirogues were fashioned capable of carrying twenty to thirty men or several tons of freight.[7]

If the navigator knew the waterways, travel from the bay to the city of New Orleans in such a vessel required at least two days. If he did not, he could become hopelessly lost amid the twists and turns of the bayous.

In spite of its isolation, Barataria had its inhabitants. Some were the fishermen who frequented the coast. Others sought the area and sometimes remained there for far less legitimate reasons.

Within four years of annexation, wholesaling from Jean Laffite's warehouse on Royal Street was no longer practical. He would need a less conspicuous site, one not subject to tariffs. His older brother joined him at about this time. Pierre's experience at sea would aid Jean in plans for expanding his enterprise.

New Orleans tradition claimed that the Laffites used a blacksmith shop at the corner of Bourbon and St. Philip as a front, but there is no evidence that this was a basis for smuggling. The warehouse on Royal was adequate for Jean's earlier enterprise.[8] By 1809, no site within the city was a wise location from which to operate. One was needed that could not be monitored by American officials.

Jean, accompanied by Pierre, revisited the wetlands where traders not willing to submit to the new restrictions on commerce at New Orleans' quay made landings. Merchandise seized on the Gulf could be unloaded and, with some difficulty, transported to inland markets.

One of the raiders who continued to operate during this period was Renato Beluche. He had chosen to sail under the cloak of legality. Letters of marque were available in the Caribbean. French officials had once issued commissions from Guadeloupe. When the British gained possession of the island, privateer papers could still be obtained at both St. Barthélemy and St. Martin, two dependencies under the control of France.[9]

Beluche's biographer described the method by which quasi-legal sea raiding was conducted. The *L'Intrepide* sailed from New Orleans in January 1810 for St. Barthélemy. Upon arrival, the ship was sold to one of the passengers on board, Joseph Sauvinet, who listed his occupation as merchant. The other passengers became the ship's crew. Pierre Brugman, an alias for Renato Beluche, took command of *L'Intrepide*. The ship sailed to St. Martin.

A back-dated commission was issued to Beluche stating he was "duly registered in the Bureau of Maritime Registry of Marigot, St. Martin, to lead or send into the ports of France or its colonies all ships of enemies of the Empire." The letter included an interesting provision: if he should be "forced by bad weather or by enemies to put in at any neutral port," he was "to explain the reasons for putting in and to give full notice . . . of the commission held." Whatever prize he might take could be legally claimed for himself and his crew by reporting to the "Administrative Officer of the Maritime Registry" upon his "return or putting in."[10]

This was the type of commission that gave its holder extraordinary latitude: the privateer could capture almost any prize he wished, take it to a port where he knew he would receive a good price, and then report back to the issuer of his letter at an indefinite time in the future.

This he would do, if convenient.

The records of the voyage of *L'Intrepide* provide insight into Beluche's operation. When he left St. Martin, he was in command of the seventy-ton ship and a crew of eighty men. The registration list gave the place of birth, rank, age, height, and the beard color of the entire crew. Of even greater importance, it stated the number of shares each would receive when prize money was divided, ranging from the captain's eight shares to half a share for the cabin boy.

When sufficient cargo and specie had been captured, the captain would determine the ship was in distress. Under the terms of his commission, he could put into any port. Beluche was but one of several sea raiders who operated under this guise. During the early years of annexation, business as usual was possible at the port of New Orleans. By March 1810, he had accumulated a sizeable cargo, sufficient captured goods to make the eight shares due him well worth the effort.[11]

Two other privateers, the *Duc de Montebello,* Capt. Baptiste Besson, master, and a smaller vessel, *L'Epine,* were also operating in the Gulf. Besson made port with his prize cargo ahead of Beluche. On March 7, he brought the *Duc de Montebello* into the quay. Under the terms of his privateering commission, he requested a berth for his vessel. He gave his reason for this request as "the want of water and the great number of damages that have been caused us by the successive pursuits of various enemy ships of war."[12] Claiborne authorized provisions and repairs. Besson had complied with the law.

But a new component had been added to Louisiana's waterfront: Commodore David Porter was in command of the United States naval station at New Orleans. By 1810, he had a strong force at his disposal. He had good reason for enforcing the custom laws. As commander of an arresting agency, he would receive one-fourth of the profit from the sale of any ship he seized.

Before Besson could dispose of his cargo, Porter brought a fleet of gunboats downriver. On March 20, a detachment of his men inspected the *Duc de Montebello.* Barrels were broken open, the ship's papers and the officer's personal possessions were confiscated. Besson was arrested.

By the time *L'Intrepide* had docked, Porter was ready. Beluche had learned of Porter's activities. Placing his vessel under the command of a lieutenant, he escaped Besson's fate by disappearing before his ship arrived at the quay. Porter's men boarded the vessel, "undid and upset the hold and made a most unpleasant visit and search." They took possession of the ship in the name of the United States.[13]

A few days later, *L'Epine* arrived and received similar treatment. All three vessels were libeled for violation of United States law. Porter boasted openly that the three prizes would be condemned and sold. The proceeds would be divided among the captors.

The commodore was only partly right. The *Duc de Montebello* was forfeited to the American government, and its appurtenances and cargo were sold. Porter received $25,000 as his share and his lawyer, Edward Livingston, received a legal fee of $1,250.

Beluche's ship and *L'Epine* avoided the fate of Besson's vessel. Both escaped forfeiture. *L'Epine*, a fifty-two-ton schooner, evaded legal process with the help of the French consulate. Her captain put out to sea for another raiding voyage. *L'Intrepide*, although libeled by the district attorney, was ordered liberated by a local judge. New Orleans was prepared to protect her own. Jean Blanque declared himself to be the ship's owner. He paid the bond of $1,500, a pittance when such substantial profits were at stake. The ship was released, and although customhouse officials refused to give her clearance, on May 29, she was once more underway.[14]

Besson did not have friends in New Orleans.

Beluche did. He again assumed command of his ship. Within days, she was back on the high seas. He captured two Spanish vessels. One was looted and burned as having but little value as a prize. The other, *La Invecta España*, was saved, for she carried a cargo of iron, wine, and dry goods valued at $600,000. Beluche had no intention of allowing either *L'Intrepide* or his prize to face legal entanglements in the port of New Orleans. This time he put in to the seaward island of Grande Terre.[15]

Laffite was there ahead of him.

The island suddenly became an efficient ocean port. Landing a cargo on the bay side was far less difficult than the long voyage upriver to the city. For a pilot who knew the deep-water passage, it was both convenient and safe. But far more important, it was a long way from the United States naval base and the gunboats of the commodore.

Merchandise could be landed at Barataria, safely secured until ready for disposition, and then transported by barge or pirogue to wherever there was a demand for saleable goods.

There were no customs inspections, no bureaucratic registrations. Merchandise was not subject to tariffs. No overly zealous officials would libel ships for forfeiture.[16]

CHAPTER 7

Kingdom by the Sea

$\mathcal{B}$y spring of 1810, Barataria was a seaport that could rival legitimate harbors on the Gulf of Mexico. Independent of all authority, it was a kingdom by the sea.

The two Laffite brothers assumed complementary roles for its operation. Both had been involved in the initial establishment of the base. Pierre was familiar with Caribbean trading and knew the needs of Louisiana planters. Jean was experienced in merchandising. He was known as an effective provider of saleable goods.

While Pierre acted as the mainland agent, Jean used his organizational ability to improve the port's efficiency.[1] It was the kind of entrepreneurial challenge he liked. He developed docking procedures, provided warehousing for goods, and organized transport to sites where merchandise could be sold.

Before the end of the year, Pierre's participation in the enterprise became less apparent. This was a role he preferred, a silent partner who would operate from within the city. Perhaps it was Jean's extroverted style that thrust him into the forefront. The younger Laffite was a natural leader, one who was able to provide leadership for men who needed direction.[2]

Pierre's preference to remain in New Orleans added respectability to the activities of his younger brother. He supported Jean's management, receiving shipments and sharing the profits of smuggling.

Jean's role was the more adventuresome one. Many of those who worked with him were veterans of multiple voyages on the high seas, men of all races and nationalities.[3] Some had sailed under privateer captains such as Beluche. Others had raided Caribbean shipping without papers. No questions were asked. All able-bodied seamen willing to work the docks and the warehouses while waiting for a berth on a raider were welcome. Privateer captains with quasi-legal commissions cooperated with men who were outright pirates. As the movement to suppress violence on the world's oceans gained momentum, those who had sailed as buccaneers on distant seas found their way to the island community. This was a diverse band of men who brought with them women willing to join a colony with a singular goal: that of seeking the highest possible gain from the capture and sale of merchandisable goods.

The amazing feature of the Grande Terre enterprise was the fact one man could mold this diverse mass of individuals into an effective organization. Only a person with Jean's charisma could have done so.

The Laffite name became increasingly popular in New Orleans. Once it was learned that the goods that filled the shops on Royal and Bourbon reached the city by way of Grande Terre, the two brothers became local heroes. New Orleans had experienced privation in the past from arbitrary government regulation. French Louisiana resented American annexation. Anyone who could successfully bypass the hated tariff collections and, at the same time, provide the city with needed merchandise was nothing less than a candidate for canonization.

The plantation aristocracy was especially enthusiastic about Barataria. In March 1810, the territorial legislature met and took note of the fact slaves were being imported into Louisiana. But rather than take action that supported national law, an act was passed that required American officials to place captured slaves on auction. The proceeds were then turned over to the territory.[4] Even when slave smugglers were caught, their human merchandise would still reach plantations on the Mississippi.

The American navy was charged with halting the flow of

29

black labor into Louisiana. Occasionally a ship carrying slaves was brought in by the navy. The cargo of one slaver was sold at public auction for $45,000 and resold to planters at even higher prices.[5]

But raiding captains could easily slip through the navy's blockade. Rather than risk a confrontation with American gunboats on the long passage upriver, most made harbor on Barataria Bay.

In June 1810, an event occurred that provided an additional cloak of legality for those who claimed to be privateers. Cartagena expelled its royal governor. Soon after declaring independence, the new nation issued letters of marque. Cartagenan commissions were easily obtained. Condemnation procedures were liberal: a ship could dock at Grande Terre, put prize cargoes on sale, and report to the issuer of the commission only if it was convenient to do so.[6]

In September, Governor Claiborne took a leave of absence. Thomas Robertson assumed temporary control of the territory. As acting governor, he denounced Laffite's operation. He called the Baratarians "brigands who infest our coast and overrun our country" who are acting "in the very teeth of the most positive laws."[7]

This was not an attitude shared by all. Lacarriere Latour, a member of Louisiana's French aristocracy, called Robertson's charges "a calumny." He defended Laffite's operation: "I am persuaded they all had commissions either from Cartagena or from France of the validity of which it would seem the government of those respective countries were alone competent judge."[8]

But, in spite of the acting governor's efforts, the flow of illicit goods continued to enter Louisiana. Merchandise came into the city by barge and pirogue. Through the Baratarian lakes, the Bayous Lafourche and Teche, it came. When there was the possibility of detection, other routes were chosen. The importations of both field hands and expensive goods could not be stopped.[9]

When Claiborne returned to New Orleans and resumed his duties, he knew he could do little to halt illicit trade. He was aware that an important citizen of New Orleans, Jean Blanque, had paid the bond on Beluche's ship. The governor described Blanque as a man who "possesses considerable influence in the city and vicinity of New Orleans." He was a director of the Louisiana bank and a member of the House of Representatives of the territory.[10]

By the early months of 1811, Barataria was a flourishing seaport, outranking the river quay in volume of commerce. Several hundred persons were inhabitants of the island. As ships continued to land, the colony became a mecca for sea raiders.

Dominique Youx was one of those who came to Grande Terre. Described as "an expert artillerist under Napoleon [who had been] privateering on his own,"[11] he had sailed as a French corsair in the year 1806.[12] As captain of the privateer *La Superbe*, he had participated in the capture of at least three American ships that were condemned by the prize court in Basseterre, Guadeloupe and sold in Cuba. Later in the year, he reported to authorities in Santo Domingo that his ship had been lost at sea after a naval engagement.[13] Dominique was French. He would become a valuable ally to Jean Laffite.[14]

Others joined the island colony. With each landing, the community grew. A steady stream of ships brought goods and slaves to the port. A relay of barges and pirogues moved the merchandise to inland markets. Ferment in the Caribbean strengthened the Baratarians. Spain was no longer able to protect her commerce. France had no intention of denying the vast fleet of privateers that had served as a buttress for Gallic interests against both Britain and Spain. Until the youthful United States could become a significant sea power, there was little to hamper Laffite's enterprise.

Louisiana was moving toward self-rule. The 1810 census credited the territory with a population of 76,556, enough to seek statehood.[15] French-speaking Louisiana might gain greater control over her destiny by becoming a state of the Union. In the meantime, Laffite's popularity grew as the entrepreneur of Barataria sent load after load of goods inland. But the free port on Grand Terre had problems.

An incident occurred in 1811 that caused many to question the operation, an event that would eventually cost Laffite much of his support. A band of slaves escaped from their owners in St. John the Baptist Parish. The rioters burned five plantations as they marched toward New Orleans. An armed militia confronted the rebels and killed the majority of the escapees. Others were ruthlessly hunted down. Investigation later determined that the rioters had entered Louisiana through Laffite's free port. Since no whites had been killed, the uprising was temporarily forgotten. The Baratarian chief continued to do business.[16]

By the end of the year, he managed a highly successful establishment. He had little overhead, no rent to pay, no lease agreements to be negotiated. The operation was subject to no taxes. Laffite assessed the privateers he serviced a share of the profits. In return, he provided secure harborage and efficient distribution for booty.

Only one problem existed in the supply/demand equation of Barataria's economics: the delivery system. The journey from the bay harbor to the retailer was difficult. Transportation by pirogue or barge through the maze of swamps and bayous could take as much as a week. Unusual weather could cause additional delay. As a merchant, Laffite knew that a rapid turnover was good business. Lengthy warehousing was costly.

He found a solution to the problem. He established a retail outlet.

About halfway between Grande Terre and New Orleans a memorial mound built of shells stands out above the low-lying wetlands. Known as the Temple, there was easy access to the area from the city. Early in 1812, the Baratarians took saleable goods to the site. The auction attracted merchants, dealers, and individual customers from New Orleans.[17]

This was a bold effort at merchandising. But in spite of Laffite's brash sales techniques, Claiborne still remained hesitant to take decisive action against the supply line Louisiana enjoyed. He knew Laffite was popular both in the city and among the area planters. As an able politician, he found it expedient to move with caution.

For over a year, he refrained from making a statement that would support Robertson. It was not until March 1813[18] that he issued a proclamation against Laffite's colony. By then, Louisiana had become a state of the Union and was a part of a nation at war.

In the meantime, Laffite continued his lucrative enterprise. He made regular visits to the city. Some trips were business junkets. Others were for personal reasons.

In July 1812, a daughter was born to Pierre and his quadroon mistress, Marie Villars. The child was christened Marie Louise.[19] Jean was present for this event.

Frequently seen in New Orleans, Jean visited the house near the ramparts. There were other women who entertained him. The remoteness of Barataria could not have satisfied Jean for long. He moved freely through the city and visited nearby plantations.

One account reported an event that may have taken place during this period. After Claiborne had remarried and his wife was living on a plantation downriver, Jean was reported to have spent an evening with her. Described as "the most charming, the most beautiful and most coquettish woman in New Orleans," she extended her hospitality to Laffite. The servants, who knew his identity, introduced him discretely as "Monsieur Clement." Madame Claiborne later recalled that her guest for the evening was the "most remarkable man she had ever met."[20] Legends of this sort can neither be proved nor disproved, but this particular tale illustrates the contemporary conception of Laffite's social prowess.

On May 4, 1812, an item appeared in the French language newspaper of New Orleans, *La Courrier de la Louisiane*. It was an advertisement for the return of a lost pocketbook that contained "un billet de $500 . . . endosse par Pre. Lafite." The owner requested that, if found, it be delivered to the printing office. The note had been drawn on the owner of the *portefeuille*, Jean Laffite.[21]

Laffite walked the streets in confidence. He advertised for lost objects as any other citizen would. He was a respected member of the community.

And why shouldn't he be?

He was a merchant to merchants, a supplier of needed merchandise. He had reason to believe he had done much to save the city from deprivation. There were others who believed the same, that he may have spared New Orleans from the vicissitudes she had experienced in the past. He had superintended the effort to meet the city's material needs and provided her with the luxuries considered necessary to sustain a traditional way of life.

In the early days of the year 1812, Jean Laffite was a hero in the city of New Orleans.

He was even more.

He was the uncrowned prince of a kingdom by the sea.

CHAPTER 8

A Nation Goes to War

*I*n 1812, Louisiana became a state, and the nation went to war.

In February, Congress approved the proposal for admission of the southernmost portion of the annexed territory. The year would be almost over before all formalities for statehood could be completed.

During the intervening months, the United States declared war. Although it was a war that would be fought largely at sea against the most powerful naval force on the face of the globe, the American nation, for all practical purposes, had no navy. Congress was bitterly divided over the question of whether war should be declared. A substantial minority in the House of Representatives opposed the war. When the bill that established Great Britain as the enemy reached the upper house, the Senate passed the measure by only six votes. The next day, June 18, 1812, President James Madison signed the document that declared war on the kingdom from which the colonies had won their independence.

In the Louisiana of 1812, the causes of war were little understood. It was not that the French inhabitants of the territory had any objection to doing battle with the British. Their Gallic forebears had long considered the English as their chief antagonists. The leaders of Kentucky, Ohio, and Tennessee had joined the representatives from the South Atlantic states in seeking a declaration of war. But their grievances were of little concern to the inhabitants of the lower Mississippi.

Jefferson had sought to deal with the British through sanctions. The Embargo Act and the nonimportation laws might win concessions without resorting to war. But his strictures produced extreme hardship for Americans engaged in overseas commerce. Ships rotted at the wharves, and farmers and plantation owners were unable to sell produce. Even after the embargo was replaced by less severe regulation, trade continued to be stifled. Both merchant and planter suffered.[1]

For those on the Atlantic seaboard, there was no Barataria.

They had no Jean Laffite.

In November 1811, the Twelfth Congress of the United States took office. Many newly elected members were committed to war, but an incident was needed to bring the United States into open conflict with Great Britain. The necessary spark reached the powder keg in May 1812: an American ship, the *Jenny*, was detained in Plymouth harbor.[2] By the end of the following month, the nation was at war.

French Louisiana had difficulty understanding these events, particularly the self-imposed trade restrictions. A July issue of *The Louisiana Gazette* reported the vote of Congress, but gave little explanation for the reason war was declared. One item of interest in the news report did gain the attention of New Orleans readers: the president was authorized "to issue to private armed vessels . . . commissions or letters of marque and general reprisal."[3]

Officials began to seek captains capable of harassing British trade. Letters of marque would be issued at ports wherever qualified seafaring commanders could be found. Thirteen privateers were commissioned at Charleston.[4] All along the Atlantic seaboard and at Gulf ports, letters were available to the masters of armed vessels.

In September, a corsair was inventoried in New Orleans under the name *Francais le Pandoure*, a ship registration that sought raiding status. The captain was listed as Frederick Youx,[5] the Dominique Youx who had allied himself with Laffite's Baratarians.

35

Six letters of marque were eventually issued in New Orleans. United States officials were cautious in selecting only responsible shipowners who could secure able privateer captains. Stephen Debon qualified for one of the letters for the schooner, *Spy*. Debon chose an experienced commander of the ship: Renato Beluche.

Although Beluche had originally sailed under a French commission, in 1812 he held a letter of marque from Cartagena. On the authority of Debon's letter, he sailed from New Orleans with a crew of 100 men under the American flag. Before the end of the year, he captured a 322-ton ship out of Greenock, Scotland, the *Jane*, laden with mahogany and logwood. Early in 1813, he docked the vessel at New Orleans' quay. *The Louisiana Gazette* declared this to be "the first valuable prize that has been brought into this port."[6]

On January 11, 1813, Beluche filed his claim in behalf of his crew for the ship that was duly "adjudged a lawful prize of libelant under authority of letter of marque."[7]

But Beluche had not brought all of his conquests upriver to the city. Since he sailed under multiple letters, when he captured a ship other than one of British registry, he claimed it as a prize under his Cartagenan letter, a commission that would not be honored at the port of New Orleans. At least one Spanish ship was captured while Beluche was sailing under the American flag. This he brought into Barataria Bay, landing his prize cargo at Laffite's improvised dock.

Stephen Debon protected himself by claiming Beluche had acted against instructions, filing a declaration on November 20, 1812, nearly two months before Beluche brought the *Jane* into New Orleans.[8] The disposition of the Scottish ship was little more than a gesture toward the American war effort. Beluche continued to raid the Gulf using whichever flag best suited his purpose.

Other raiders did the same.

But a nation at war needed to do more than seek sea raiders to fight its battles at sea. For the first time, a serious attempt would be made to enforce American revenue laws. Ships that unloaded cargoes at any point other than the river quay were costing the United States in revenue, money necessary for fighting a rich empire. Importations at Barataria Bay would have to be stopped.

Even before the declaration of war, customs officers had attempted to neutralize the port on Grande Terre. On January 30, 1812, a gun vessel from the New Orleans naval base gave chase to two ships believed to be French privateers. In March, the collector of tariffs asked for assistance from Washington. On June 16, only two days before Congress declared war, the same gun ship exchanged fire with vessels engaged in illegal landings, the first shots fired against Laffite's smugglers.[9] These were but futile gestures, no more than token actions against the heavily armed Baratarians. What navy the United States did possess would need be used in the greater war against the British. Customs officers would be left with limited resources for containing Laffite.

Realizing the popularity of duty-free Baratarian goods, official New Orleans began an attempt to stem the illicit tide through the courts. On November 10, 1812, John R. Grymes, United States district attorney, filed a petition against Jean Laffite charging him with "violation of the revenue law."[10]

This action provided a legal basis for a government challenge to smuggling. Three days later, Capt. Andrew Holmes took forty men into the wetlands to ambush the Laffites. On the night of November 16, Holmes intercepted several thousand dollars worth of contraband and arrested twenty-five smugglers. Both Jean and Pierre were members of the unarmed band. They offered no resistance and went peacefully with the custom's officials into New Orleans.

On November 19, the prisoners were formally charged. Holmes testified against his captives, declaring that they had "unlawfully put ashore from a certain vessel . . . a large quantity of foreign goods."[11]

Bond was set by a New Orleans judge and the prisoners were immediately released. At a hearing on November 29, Holmes gave further testimony against the Laffites. None of those charged appeared in court. The bonds were forfeited. For Jean and Pierre, the forfeiture was merely the cost of doing business.

The Laffites still had friends in high places, but by this time they were more than residents of a new state that had some control over its own destiny. They and all other Louisianians had become citizens of a nation suddenly thrust into a deadly contest with the British Empire.

CHAPTER 9

A Bold Gesture

*T*all masts towered above New Orleans' quay.

Cannon on the brig's port gunwale menaced the city. Armed men guarded the deck. This was no ordinary merchantman.

The river was at its lowest ebb. Late February warmth had not penetrated the upper reaches of the river. There would be no increase in the stream's flow until northern snows melted. Seagoing vessels made the upstream journey between mud banks with apprehension. Heavy weaponry added to navigational difficulties, a fact that made it obvious the armed brig was piloted by a helmsman who knew the channel.

Port authorities received a request for registration.

The ship's master gave his name as Jean Laffite.[1]

On March 2, 1813, a certificate was issued for *Le Brig Goelette la Diligente* with armament that included a "douze canons" as well as an array of smaller arms. Pierre Laffite, the ship's "appartenant," claimed ownership.[2] Jean Laffite, still under indictment, listed himself as the captain of a crew of ninety-one. Like the rosters of most sailing vessels of the time, the roll included the surnames of men from several nations. Although there were both Spanish and English names on the list, most of the ship's officers claimed to be natives of France. Laffite gave his age as thirty-two and his place of birth as Bordeaux. The registration certificate listed New York as the port of destination.[3]

This was an attempt to comply with the law, the first step toward gaining a United States letter of marque.[4] The ship's arrival at New Orleans' quay was even more: it was a declaration that Jean Laffite would not be denied access to the city. It was a bold gesture, one that was typical of the man. He had no intention of accepting the role of a hunted fugitive.

Although formal charges had been entered against the two brothers, the Laffites continued to walk New Orleans' streets. Charles Gayarre's account explained why they could do so: "In those days, smuggling was considered but a very venial sin, if a sin at all and men who were looked upon as the soul of honor . . . did not hesitate to avail themselves of the services of the denounced outlaws." He expressed the popular point of view of French New Orleans: "The revenue laws were regarded as oppressive, or at least too restrictive [and] it was thought that the general prosperity of the State needed free trade."[5]

But in spite of Laffite's bold act, in some quarters his popularity was on the decline. Tales of atrocities on the high seas filtered into the city. A man named Williams arrived in New Orleans late in 1812. He claimed he had survived a pirate attack on an American merchant vessel. Those who had been responsible for what was described as "a tale of horror and bloodshed"[6] operated out of Barataria.

Prior to this, according to one account, Gen. Jean Robert Marie Humbert celebrated his birthday at a dinner given in his honor. The Laffites were among the guests. After several glasses of table wine, the general arose shakily to respond to toasts in his behalf. Looking toward his guests he said, "I must not remain here as an associate of outlaws and pirates."[7]

Whether or not the public accusation of piracy was directed toward the Laffites, after the legal proceedings that followed Holmes' testimony, both Jean and Pierre were technically outlaws.

When Laffite sailed down the river in command of a registered ship, it is doubtful he had any intention of ordering the helmsman to steer eastward toward New York. Possibly the primary motive for his voyage was that of establishing himself as a privateering captain. A document, dated April 22, 1813, claimed

Laffite held a Cartagenan commission and, by this time, had captured two prizes that would be sent to Cartagena.[8] With the *Diligente's* armament and crew, such conquests were possible during the seven weeks that followed registration.

Whatever may have been the circumstances of the raiding voyage of 1813, Laffite had no American commission. Even if he had possessed quasi-legal documents, he could have been prosecuted for piracy under United States law.

Laffite sent no prizes to Cartagena. Captures in which he was directly or indirectly involved would be landed at Grande Terre. In spite of this and the questionable legality of any papers he held, there were no indictments of the brothers other than that of smuggling. The accessibility of the bay continued to make Barataria an attractive port of arrival, not only for Laffite and Beluche, but for the masters of other vessels.

A March 17, 1813, report to the British admiralty stated the condition of the Mississippi: "Vessels drawing more than 14 feet of water can not enter" until melting snow upstream raised the level of the river. The banks were "soft . . . for several leagues from the entrance," not practical for making landings.[9] The difficulties that deterred the British from sailing upriver to New Orleans were not found at the seaward islands.

Barataria continued to be a major port of arrival. Privateer and pirate both entered the pass between Grande Terre and Grand Isle and docked at the makeshift landings. With the increasing success of the Baratarian operation, the governor's tacit silence was no longer appropriate.

On March 15, Governor Claiborne issued a proclamation denouncing the "banditti" who "commit depredations and piracies against the vessels of nations at peace with the United States." He described the Baratarians as those "who act in contravention of the laws of the United States . . . to the evident prejudice of the revenue of the federal government." The governor concluded by urging all officers "to seize and apprehend every individual engaged in these criminal practices." The proclamation was publicized in the columns of the nationally read *Niles' Weekly Register.*[10]

On April 7, the government took further legal action. Case number 573 was filed against Jean in the U.S. District Court, and case number 574 named Pierre as a defendant for having "unloaded 26 bales of cinnamon, 54 linen shirts, 3 pieces of Russian sheeting, seven pieces of canvass, one bundle of handkerchiefs of the value of $4,400.89." [11]

Official New Orleans would continue to prosecute the charge of smuggling against the Laffites. It was following this that Jean may have considered leaving Louisiana. On April 22, he wrote to a Captain Garrison declaring "my intention is fixed to leave this country and to proceed to Cartagena." [12] But whatever his true intent may have been, he still had business in Louisiana.

Barataria was flourishing. The demand for duty-free merchandise had not decreased. Laffite's establishment on the seaward island was stronger than ever. No American naval vessel dared venture into his domain.

The kingdom by the sea would stand, at least, for a time.

But its foundations rested on shifting sand.

CHAPTER 10

The British Menace

British warships prowled the Gulf of Mexico in the early summer of 1813.

On June 23, a Royal Navy sloop-of-war approached two privateers anchored off Cat Island. Shots were exchanged. Charles Gayarre's account of the firefight concluded with these words: the Baratarians "showed no disposition to avoid an armed collision, as they generally did . . . and they beat off the English who suffered considerable loss."[1]

But Laffite had enemies who were other than those on the high seas. Again his arrest was ordered. On July 24, officers of the court of New Orleans were "commanded as you have been often commanded that you take the body of Jean Lafite that he be and appear before the District Court."[2]

Customs officials had to do more than issue warrants: They would need to halt a shipment of contraband and seize the smuggler chief. On October 14, a revenue officer, Walker Gilbert, attempted to intercept goods en route from Barataria to the city. This time Laffite's men were armed. The smuggling party halted when challenged. When the demand was made that they surrender their merchandise, there was gunfire. One of Gilbert's men was wounded.

The contraband continued on its way.

On November 24, the governor issued a second proclamation that reflected the frustration of the revenue officers:

> It has been officially known to me that, on the 14th of last month a quantity of smuggled goods, seized by Walter Gilbert, an officer of the revenue of the United States, were forcibly taken from him in open day, at no great distance from the city of New Orleans, by a party of armed men under the orders of a certain John Lafitte, who fired upon and grievously wounded one of the assistants of the said Walter Gilbert; and although process has issued for the apprehension of him, the said John Lafitte, yet such is the countenance and protection afforded him, or the terror excited by the threats of himself and his associates, that the same remains unexecuted.[3]

Claiborne's statement included a practical means of facilitating Laffite's arrest:

> I offer a reward of five hundred dollars . . . to any person delivering the said John Lafitte to the sheriff of the Parish of Orleans . . . so that the said John Lafitte may be brought to justice.[4]

The offer was posted in the city.

Two days later, another handbill appeared in the town's public places calling for the apprehension of the governor. Although the counter offer was made in Laffite's name, it is unlikely it originated with him. Perhaps the second posting was no more than a bit of Louisianian humor affirming that, in New Orleans, an artful smuggler was no more believed worthy of arrest than was the governor.[5]

Laffite wrote Claiborne soon after this defending himself against the governor's proclamations. Laffite declared that he was not a pirate, and that he only "sails under the flag of Cartagena." Aware of the fact that the British were prowling the seas, he was willing to "tender my services to defend [Louisiana]."[6]

The Baratarian chief had enough problems without antagonizing the governor by making a rash offer for his capture. There were signs of discontent among his own men. Laffite had discouraged raids on American shipping. A dispute erupted over the question of whether or not vessels flying the flag of the United

States should be subject to attack. An Italian named Vincent Gambi challenged Jean's authority. When faced with mutiny, he shot one of the insurrectionists,[7] an action that settled the issue.

It was difficult to maintain order on the island. Stories handed down in the bayou country from generation to generation told of violence among those who had served on the vessels that anchored in Barataria Bay. "The horror tales are but fragments," wrote Saxon, "a strangled scream, a woman, nude and bloodstained, dragged by her hair across the sandy beach." Female victims would simply "disappear into the black shadows which lay beyond the flaring torchlight . . . A mutilated corpse [would be] buried before daylight in a shallow grave in the sand."[8]

Many of the men who joined the colony risked their lives to gain the merchandise sold in the shops of New Orleans. They could not enter the city to reap the fruits of their efforts without fear of apprehension. For them life was cheap. Rape, murder, and the vilest of crimes occurred on the seaward islands. Although Laffite could maintain a degree of order when the welfare of the operation required it, he had no control over the private deportment of his associates.

He continued his clandestine journeys into the city. If crimes against women occurred on the island or were perpetrated by the men who sailed ships in and out of Barataria, such deeds were not to his liking. Along with the reports of sexual violence among the Baratarians, there were equally believable tales of lovemaking by both Jean and Pierre in New Orleans. Pierre's quadroon mistress, Marie Louise Villars, had a sister named Catherine, who was, at least for a time, a mistress to Jean.[9]

Jean had other women, both among the quadroons and the French. His charm drew them to him. His sexuality demanded that he seek them even when he risked arrest to enter the city.

Laffite still had a loyal following in French-speaking Louisiana: Merchants welcomed his duty-free goods, and plantation owners needed laborers. The success of the retail outlet at the Temple led to a similar effort at merchandising, one held outside the city in January 1814. A wide variety of merchandise was offered, along with 415 black field hands. Officials sought to break up the auction. Once more, there was armed resistance resulting in the death of one of the revenue officers and the wounding of two others.[10]

Laffite's venture into direct sales antagonized some of the very merchants his duty-free merchandise had once aided. It was particularly annoying to those outside the New Orleans area. A St. Louis publication complained that because of "smuggling at Barataria . . . a great variety of goods are very cheap here."[11]

The governor felt compelled to take further action. Claiborne appealed to the Legislature, which, by this time, was sitting in regular sessions and had assumed a measure of control of the new state. He asked that "a detachment of militia" be provided to "disperse those desperate men on Lake Barataria whose piracies have rendered our shores a terror to neutral flags." He asked for authority to raise a company "by voluntary enlistment" with officers, a drummer, a fifer, and 100 privates "to serve for six months unless sooner discharged."[12]

The Legislature included men such as Jean Blanque who were openly sympathetic to Laffite. This was not a forum that would approve a military unit made up of newcomers who might destroy a portion of Louisiana's centuries-old heritage and, in the process, limit the importation of goods and field hands.

The solons simply did what most legislative bodies do when a controversial request is made: a committee was appointed. No militia was raised. Gayarre explained the reason for inaction: "Most of the members of that body were aware that their constituents thought themselves benefitted by the illicit trade which the Governor wished to suppress." The lawmakers "did not care to be put to the expense and trouble of collecting revenue for a government which could not make itself respected by a handful of desperados."[13]

But the American government was determined to make itself respected. New charges were filed against the Laffites. The summer term of the United States district court received testimony against the Baratarians that resulted in a grand jury indictment. This time one of the principal merchants of the city testified, an act that represented a break in the ranks of the mercantile class.[14] Some, at least, realized that the future of the area was dependent upon an acceptance of American law.

Jean continued his clandestine visits to New Orleans. Pierre was less cautious than Jean. Perhaps the frequency of his visits to his mistress was his undoing. He was arrested and placed in prison. This time the charge was more serious than that of smuggling. He was accused of "having knowingly and wittingly aided and assisted, procured, commanded, counselled, and advised" persons to commit acts of piracy.[15]

The Laffites still had friends in New Orleans. The city's best legal talents were approached in an effort to secure an adequate defense for Pierre should his case come to trial. Gayarre claimed that John R. Grymes agreed to assist even though Grymes held the office of district attorney, a position he would have had to relinquish in order to do so.[16]

Grymes could not take the case, but Edward Livingston did. Possibly friends of the Laffites such as Sauvinet, who had provided financial backing for earlier privateering enterprises, and men like Blanque, were willing to see that Jean's brother received not only a fair hearing, but ample opportunity for release. Substantial funds were available to assist his defense.[17]

Throughout the month of August, Pierre remained in his cell at the Cabildo. A petition in his behalf was filed on the grounds that his health would be impaired by continued confinement. But two doctors testified his imprisonment was not dangerous to his well-being. He remained incarcerated.[18]

Jean continued to operate the establishment on the seaward island.

A whimsical item appeared in the August 18 issue of the *Louisiana Gazette* that spoke of "rich prizes" that "have lately been brought to Grande Isle . . . the arrival of these prizes has been kept pretty much a secret by a certain class of monopolizing gentry." The article was signed "Napoleon Junior" and was accompanied by an editorial comment: "Would it not be *pro bono publico* to establish a press in the Empire of Barataria?"[19]

But the empire was in serious straits.

One of its leaders was in prison. Jean was subject to arrest should he be caught in New Orleans. Even the strongest supporters of Barataria could do little to bring her aid.

But there was yet another force on the horizon. Ships of His Majesty's Navy were cruising the Gulf. An attack upon Louisiana was likely.

With increasing opposition on land and a powerful fleet at sea, Laffite's Barataria could be caught between two colliding nations at war.

CHAPTER 11

The Stray Sheep

*I*n the summer of 1814, the British presence on the Gulf became a significant threat to the nation's southernmost states. In August, Royal Marines landed at Pensacola and established a base. A major invasion was imminent, one that could strike at any point, near Mobile, along the Alabama or Mississippi coasts, or at New Orleans.

On the morning of September 3, a sail was sighted off Grande Terre.

A gentle breeze swept the seaward islands. Sun sparkled upon rhythmically rolling waves. The sea was calm. Only an occasional white cap broke the shore's uniformity.

When the vessel's hull came into view, those on watch recognized her as one of their own. But another sail was in sight: a tall masted sloop, bearing down upon the first.

A cannon boomed.

The makeshift huts beyond the beach emptied. Two hundred or more of the inhabitants of Grande Terre moved toward the shore. Among them were the few women who dared live with the raucous men who made up Laffite's colony.

All gazed seaward. The sloop was a warship flying the Union Jack.

At the sound of naval artillery, the privateer headed toward shallow water and grounded at a point at which no deep-sea helmsman would dare follow.

The British vessel gave no further indication of hostility. The cannon shot was a signal gun. The sloop dropped anchor off-shore, and a dinghy was placed in the water. The prow was turned toward the island as a mast was rigged displaying a white flag.[1]

The Baratarians were willing to meet their potential opponents halfway. A boat was readied, and several members of the privateering community climbed aboard. Among them was Jean Laffite.

Intercepting the British before they could reach the beach, Laffite's men demanded an explanation. The warship was the *Sophia*, dispatched by the senior officer of His Majesty's Navy in the Gulf, Capt. William Henry Percy. Their mission was that of contacting the "Commandant at Barataria."[2]

Both the British army and the navy were represented: Captain McWilliams, under orders from Col. Edward Nicholls, and the commander of the *Sophia*, Capt. Nicholas Lockyer. McWilliams carried a packet that he had been instructed to deliver to Laffite. Both officers asked for a conference with the community's leader.

Latour's account, written in 1815, stated that although Laffite went out to meet the British officers, he did not make himself known until onshore where he had them "in his power." It was there he "dissuaded the multitude from making the British prisoners."[3]

The deputation was not welcome. There was mumbling in the crowd and talk of lynching. The Royal Navy was the enemy.

Members of the community watched sullenly as Jean Laffite led the visitors to his personal dwelling. Guards were posted outside to assure that the conference would not be interrupted. The precaution may have had another purpose: that of preventing the visitors from scrutinizing the entrance to the island port.

Captain Lockyer later reported to his superiors that although he had been temporarily imprisoned, he had carried out his instructions by contacting the Baratarian chief.[4]

Once inside Laffite's residence, the contents of the packet were displayed.

A letter dated August 13 from Lt. Col. Edward Nicholls was addressed to Laffite declaring "I call on you with your brave following to enter into the service of Great Britain."[5]

A document, dated August 30, was written on paper watermarked with the seal of George III. The commander of the king's forces in the Gulf had ordered Lockyer "to proceed in His Majesty's Sloop under your command without a moment's loss of time for Barataria [and] on your arrival . . . communicate with the chief persons there." The Baratarians were offered the status of British subjects. "At the conclusion of the war, lands in His Majesty's colonies in America, will be allotted to them." Two conditions were outlined: "Their naval force [must be put] into the hands of the Senior Officer," and any "Spanish property not disposed of" was to be returned to Spain.[6]

Another document had been prepared by Percy: Lockyer was instructed to "enquire into the circumstances" of any British merchantmen who "have been detained . . . and sold by the inhabitants of Barataria." In case they refused, he had the authority to call upon the full force of the Royal Navy "to destroy . . . the whole place." But, should the Baratarians cooperate, they would receive both pardon and property.[7]

The packet included a letter directed personally to Jean Laffite. It was signed by Nicholls. Dated August 31, the communication urged Laffite to "enter the service of Great Britain in which you shall have the rank of Captain." He would receive land, and "property shall be guaranteed to you and your person protected."[8]

A copy of Nicholls' proclamation to the citizens of Louisiana was enclosed: French residents of the lower Mississippi were urged to assist in "liberating from a faithless, imbecile government, your paternal soil."[9]

The officers of the Crown had been mistaken in a major assumption: that resentment over annexation had reached the level of insurrection. The British had not counted on French Louisiana's ability to adapt to one more change of allegiance, nor were they aware of the effectiveness of the supply lines for bringing goods into the city that bypassed American bureaucratic restrictions.

The British believed Laffite could render valuable assistance in determining an invasion route. Officers of the Crown had scouted the territory. Their intelligence had indicated that expert guidance would be necessary for moving troops toward New Orleans.[10]

Although Latour stated that a sizeable sum was offered Laffite, none of the extant documents hint of a cash gift. It is unlikely Nicholls would have had authorization for such a proposition.[11] The offer of land, citizenship, and rank were sufficient enticements. The Royal Navy would secure Laffite's aid or neutralize his base.[12]

This placed Laffite in a dilemma. If he accepted, few of the Baratarians would follow him into British service. His written reply to Lockyer made mention of this fact.[13]

But there were other reasons for Laffite to hesitate. He had ties with New Orleans far stronger than any bonds of which his visitors were aware. The British knew nothing of the depth of his roots in Louisiana soil.

If Laffite refused the offer, his establishment could be totally destroyed. Grande Terre was much more vulnerable to British naval artillery than it was to the gunboats of the United States customs service. Laffite knew that an American flotilla was being readied for an attack, but he believed this was a force with which he could contend. Placating the British could stave off assault. In any case, he was confident that the United States would eventually triumph in the war with England.

Lockyer wanted an immediate answer. He was under orders from Nicholls to return as quickly as possible. Laffite responded by displaying his mastery of the art of strategic deception.

On September 4, after having detained the representatives of the Crown overnight, Laffite prepared a letter asking for fifteen days to consider the proposition. He would then give the *"satisfaction que vous desirer,"* a delay that would be necessary to put his affairs in order.[14]

A copy of this letter was later discovered by Daniel Patterson, Laffite's nemesis, and used against him as evidence that he was in "correspondence . . . [with] the English commanders in the Gulf of Mexico."[15] But the reply Lockyer and McWilliams received was one that would do little other than buy time for Laffite.

Laffite began immediate work on his response, one different

50

from that he had led his visitors to expect. A packet was prepared for persons in New Orleans he could trust that included either the original documents or copies of the papers brought to Grande Terre. It would also contain a cover letter to Jean Blanque.[16]

Blanque was a man of influence, a member of the state legislature. In addition, he possessed an attribute that would qualify him to receive the information: He was an investor in the privateer operation.[17] The communication requested he become "the depository" of the documents received from the British. Blanque was to use these as he saw fit. Pierre was still a prisoner. The younger brother noted the importance of his early release.

There was another letter in the packet addressed to "Monsieur Wm. C. C. Clayborne," that was a masterpiece of diplomacy. Laffite assured the governor he held the office of "first magistrate of this state" because of "the esteem of your fellow-citizens [which] was conferred on merit." He offered the service of "several citizens who perhaps, in your eyes have lost that sacred title" who are "ready to exert their utmost efforts in defence of the country." As for himself, he assured Claiborne, "I am the stray sheep, wishing to return to the sheepfold . . . If you were thoroughly acquainted with the nature of my offenses, should appear to you much less guilty, and still worthy to discharge the duties of a good citizen."[18] The dispatch pouch was on its way before the end of daylight on September 4.

Three days later, another communication was en route to the Louisiana legislator. In this, Laffite declared that the British would soon attack "to the possession of this place."[19]

On the night of September 6, Pierre mysteriously escaped. An issue of *La Courrier de la Louisiane* perfunctorily published the offer of a reward of $1,000 for the apprehension of the older Laffite. He was described as "5 feet 10 inches high . . . stout, cross eyed . . . Further description is unnecessary as he is very well known in this city." J. H. Holland, keeper of the prison, signed the offer of reward that was published three weeks after the alleged escape.[20]

Possibly Blanque engineered the release of Pierre.[21] The legislator would have received Laffite's packet by September 6. He could have convinced some who were in authority, perhaps Claiborne, that it would be wise to relax security long enough for

Jean's brother to leave. Charles Gayarre simply commented that Pierre "found the means . . . not to remain long in the jail." [22]

Pierre tarried in New Orleans only long enough to urge that the attack against Barataria be aborted. He wrote Blanque a note commending "my brother's conduct under such difficult circumstance," and thanking the legislator for acting as "depository of the papers that were sent to us." [23]

Niles' Weekly Register later reported Laffite's offer from the British commenting "their impudence is equalled only by their folly." [24]

On September 16, the British under Percy and Nicholls attacked Fort Bowyer on the Gulf Coast. Determined defenders resisted the assault, and the invaders returned to their base at Pensacola. Reinforcements from England would be necessary before another landing could be attempted. This turn of events delayed any immediate threat to the Louisiana coast. [25]

CHAPTER 12

A Bloodless Conquest

Britain dominated the waters of the Gulf.

During the final months of 1814, no fighting force afloat could dare confront the power of the Royal Navy, certainly not the fledgling navy of the United States. But there was one fleet of ships that American authorities would challenge.

For several weeks, preparations had been underway for neutralizing Barataria. Commodore Daniel Patterson coordinated the assault. Washington believed the report that the inhabitants of Grande Terre might side with the British. Patterson was commissioned to destroy the privateering base.

Laffite's contacts in New Orleans had apprised him of Patterson's plans. It was for this reason he made haste to communicate the British offer to Blanque. He believed he might still stave off the assault if he could gain the attention of the proper persons in Louisiana.

Laffite's efforts were too late.

Blanque had little time to react to the contents of the packet sent him. On September 11, Patterson's flagship was readied for a voyage downriver. Seventy men of the Forty-fourth Infantry

Regiment boarded the schooner, *Carolina*, prepared to serve as assault troops.[1]

The *Carolina* was joined by six gun vessels and a tender at Balize. On September 13, the fleet sailed from the Southwest Pass and began to move cautiously toward the seaward islands. The last leg of the journey was timed to take place at night. On the morning of September 16, the invasion force sighted Grande Terre. Not knowing the narrow channel into the bay, Patterson anchored his flagship offshore. He ordered the gunboats to attack. Two of the six ran aground. By mid-morning, the assault appeared doomed. Ten armed privateers formed a battle line in the bay. The four remaining gunboats moved forward cautiously. Infantry waited on board the *Carolina*.

By eleven o'clock, there was a dramatic turn of events. In his official report to the navy, the commodore later declared: "To my great disappointment I perceived that the pirates had abandoned their vessels and were flying . . . in all directions."[2]

Patterson ordered his regiment ashore. There was no resistance. Believing they were faced with a potential defending force of 1,000,[3] the troops moved warily toward the Baratarian huts. By the time the area had been secured, two of the vessels in the harbor were ablaze, set afire by fleeing privateer crews. Six schooners, one of which was armed, one felucca, and a brig were salvaged.[4] Some of the vessels flew the Cartagenian flag.[5]

Patterson's troops rounded up as many of the Baratarians as possible. Dominique Youx, who had been placed in charge, allowed himself to be captured. Jean Laffite could not be found. The privateer chief had arranged to be conveniently absent.

Colonel Ross, who commanded the infantry contingent, later reported the systematic destruction of the community. Forty houses of different sizes were burned. Goods valued at half a million dollars, brought to Grande Terre by sea raiders, were carefully removed from storehouses. Eighty prisoners were forced to sort the wares and load Patterson's barges. Of even greater importance, twenty cannon were found and claimed as property of the United States government.[6]

On September 20, another sail was sighted. This was the privateer, *General Bolivar*, commanded by Joseph Clement. The *Carolina* gave chase, and after a two-hour contest, Clement hauled down his colors as his vessel was forced to ground in shallow water. Patterson was able to add a long brass eighteen-pounder, a brass six-pounder, two twelve-pound carronades, and a variety of smaller weapons to his armament inventory.[7]

On September 23, the commodore's fleet, enlarged by the captured vessels, began the return journey to New Orleans. On board the barges were the imprisoned Baratarians, a substantial array of armaments, and a rich load of confiscated merchandise. Jane De Grummond commented that it required a full seven days for the conquerors to return, a journey that should have taken no more than three days, since Patterson did not know the Baratarian route "which the British wanted for their approach to the city."[8]

An October edition of the nationally read *Niles' Weekly Register* reported the raid as a major conquest for the United States.[9] The nation was in desperate need of a victory. Details of the bloodless conquest appeared in later editions of *Niles' Weekly Register*. A mid-November issue included the commodore's report to the secretary of the navy describing the landing on Grande Terre.[10]

Another issue of the *Register* reflected popular opinion beyond the bounds of French-speaking Louisiana. Laffite was described as "a man who, for about two years past, has been famous for crimes that the civilized world wars against." This was the most serious indictment of the privateer chieftain yet to appear in print. Although he had been charged with no crime other than that of smuggling, he was described in the national media as one "who is supposed to have captured one hundred vessels of all nations, and certainly murdered the crews of all that he took, for no one has ever escaped him."[11]

Where was Laffite at the time of the raid and during the days that followed? Probably, as one source claimed, he and Pierre were both "safe at a plantation home in St. Charles Parish."[12] Since Jean had advance information about Patterson's plans, he commissioned Dominique Youx to assume command of the colony. Youx was the one person who could restrain the more impulsive members of the community from doing battle with the American flotilla. Laffite was determined not to fight the United States.

In the meantime, both brothers were enjoying the comforts of plantation life. Most of the planters were still suspicious of the bureaucracy imposed on French Louisiana. The larger plantations were small kingdoms in themselves. Accessible only from the river, escape from a Mississippi villa, should it be necessary, was easier than access. Many were manned by sizeable armies of slaves who were responsible only to a single overlord. Jean and Pierre could have remained on a river plantation as long as they wished, secure from the customs authorities who sought their capture.

Jean Blanque owned a home in the center of New Orleans on Royal Street, but he lived most of the year at a villa fronting on the Mississippi below the city.[13] Possibly both Laffites took refuge on the Blanque plantation. But Blanque was not the only aristocrat who would have been willing to grant protection to Jean and Pierre Laffite. Almost every overlord on the river would have welcomed them as members of their own exclusive caste and would have provided them with both security and entertainment.

There is no record of the incarceration of the captured Baratarians. The town did not possess sufficient prison space for such a sizeable company.

The battle of Barataria Bay was not over. The contest moved to the courtrooms of New Orleans. The law required that the conquerors file suit in district court in order to gain the profits from the confiscated merchandise. The case was heard soon after their return to New Orleans. Patterson and Ross petitioned for the monetary returns from the proposed sale of the schooners. They had a legal claim for the market value of the goods brought to the city from Grande Terre.

The claim was answered in court by attorneys representing Laffite, probably employed by Jean Blanque and Joseph Sauvinet. The defense argued that "all of the ships and goods had been captured by the schooner *General Bolivar* under Cartagenan colors, a regularly commissioned privateer at peace with the United States."[14]

The case in behalf of the Baratarians focused upon Laffite's loyalty to the United States prior to Patterson's raid. John Oliver was placed on the stand. He had been present when "the expedition of Commander Patterson arrived." When questioned about Laffite's national allegiance, he testified: "Lafitte has always said that he never intend[ed] to fight the Americans." Oliver was asked by attorney Grymes: "When they heard of the expedition, was there any intention manifested by any of the Commanders of vessels to fight?" Oliver replied firmly: "No, their object was escape."[15] The participation of "Captain Dominique" was brought into question. Oliver declared "Dominique had no command of any armed vessel at Barataria at the time the expedition arrived, he was considered tho' as a commander under Laffite."[16]

The government's case was based on the contention that both merchandise and vessels had been confiscated from those who "appeared to be sea robbers." Judge Dominick Hall ruled that the proceeds from the goods already sold were to be turned over to the claimants. The case for libel against the ships was yet to be settled.[17] The vessels that Patterson had described as "fine schooners" would remain at the river port under the custody of the United States marshal.

On November 12, "certain vessels and their cargoes . . . taken at Barataria" worth $4,753 were put up for sale.[18]

The captured weaponry was not subject to judication.

CHAPTER 13

Hellish Banditti

Andrew Jackson denounced Laffite and his Baratarians as "Hellish Banditti," but that was before the future president met Jean.

Claiborne's proclamations had influenced Jackson's denunciation. But, by fall 1814, the governor adopted a more temperate appraisal of Barataria. He was no longer the appointed chief of a territory, but an executive responsible to an elected state legislature, some of whom were openly sympathetic to Laffite.

In October, Claiborne wrote United States Attorney General Rush apologizing for the fact "the state government had not sooner been able to put down those banditti." He explained the situation in terms that may have sounded strange to a Washington bureaucrat. Generations of smugglers under Spanish rule were "esteemed honest . . . [and] sympathy for these offenders is certainly more or less felt by many of the Louisianians." He recommended pardons for the majority of those who had been a part of Laffite's colony. "A few hardened ones" might be prosecuted, but men like Dominique Youx, Renato Beluche, and Jean and Pierre Laffite deserved executive leniency. Pardoning these honest privateers would be "an act of clemency [which] would be well received and be attended, at the present moment, with the best effects."[1]

Claiborne was aware of the packet Laffite had sent to Blanque. He believed the privateer chief's profession of loyalty and was willing to welcome back to the fold one who declared himself a penitent "stray sheep."[2]

This was more than political expediency. Claiborne's second wife, Susana, was related to Renato Beluche.[3] Claiborne had gained respect for the opinion of men like Blanque, who had convinced him that Laffite would be of considerable value to the American cause.

The governor had expressed uncertainty about the loyalty of many of the inhabitants of New Orleans in a communication to Jackson in August. It would be wise to take every possible step to avoid offending the sensibilities of French-speaking Louisiana.[4] He had questioned the wisdom of the American raid on Grande Terre. When he learned of Patterson's preparations, he urged that the attack be postponed. Since this was a federal operation, it was beyond the scope of his authority, but he did send copies of Nicholls' proclamation and letters relating to Laffite's dealings with the British to Andrew Jackson.[5]

Soon after the raid, he wrote Jackson he was "vastly solicitous about the Pass of Barataria." He was concerned that there was no naval force in the area, implying Patterson had destroyed a potential first line of defense for Louisiana. He suggested that Jackson take "immediate possession . . . of Grande Terre, the spot from which the pirates were presently expelled, and of occupying the place called 'the Temple.'"[6]

Jackson realized the gravity of the situation on the Louisiana coast, but there was little he could do to bolster the defenses south of New Orleans. After having temporarily repelled the British at Fort Bowyer, he kept a wary eye on enemy operations. He knew the next invasion attempt would be made near the mouth of the Mississippi. Claiborne also believed Nicholls' forces would invade Louisiana. In this same communication to Jackson, the governor enclosed a copy of the British commander's proclamation.

Jackson responded with a statement of his own couched in the forceful language typical of the future president: "I ask you, Louisianians, can we place any confidence in the honor of men who have courted an alliance with pirates and robbers? Have not these Noble Britons . . . dared to insult you?" The word "banditti" had been used in reference to Laffite's men. To this, Jackson added his own touch of linguistics by denouncing the British for associating with "this hellish banditti."[7]

Two months earlier, while Pierre was still imprisoned, the general had written the Spanish governor of Florida, Manique, assuring him that "Monsieur Le Fete" had been arrested. In the same communication, the future president decried the "multifarious crimes" of the "criminals on the Isle of Barataria."[8]

Little did Jackson know he would soon find it expedient to welcome the company of these same "hellish" criminals.

Local opinion of Laffite was much more charitable. Leading citizens of New Orleans and members of the state legislature were among those urging that charges against Laffite's men be dropped.[9]

Claiborne continued to express his concern over the lack of defenses on the coast. In his October letter to the attorney general, he stated that "the Baratarians might be advantageously employed against the enemy."[10]

On November 20, Jackson wrote the secretary of war that he would leave "for New Orleans . . . [and would] . . . travel by land to have a view of the points at which the enemy might effect a landing."[11]

Jackson arrived on the first day of December. He was welcomed by Claiborne and Mayor Nicholas Girod, and escorted to the headquarters prepared for him on Royal Street. A crowd gathered as word of the general's arrival spread through the city. Jackson spoke in English while Edward Livingston, chairman of the citizen's defense committee, translated the general's words into French.[12]

In spite of the continuing threat of British invasion, no American military commander above the rank of colonel had been present in New Orleans since early July when Major General Flournoy had tendered his resignation and left Louisiana.[13] There was no organized defense. The population was still ambivalent about an effort to stave off an invasion.[14] The problem was one of apathy. Another change of political control after centuries of fluctuating allegiances appeared to many to be only a minor inconvenience.[15]

Jackson's first task was that of encouraging the people of

New Orleans to withstand invasion. No one could have been better suited for the task. He had a personal vendetta against the British. As a thirteen-year-old boy, he had refused to clean the boots of an English officer and had suffered a severe wound for his impertinence. He was imprisoned. Upon his release, he was told that the deaths of both his brother and mother were the results of harsh treatment from officers of the Crown.[16]

On the day after his arrival, he reviewed the city's defenders: five companies of Major Plauche's *Battalion d'Orleans*, two militia units of free blacks, and a sixty-two-man rifle company made up largely of lawyers and merchants. In all, this totaled a little more than 1,000 unseasoned troops whose experience in bearing arms was largely ceremonial.

The next day, December 3, he toured the banks of the river noting the difficulty of an effective defense. He conferred with Lacarriere Latour about possible invasion routes. A seafaring force would be essential to any effort to halt the British. Commodore Patterson had plenty of cannon, but only a two-ship navy: the *Carolina* and a sixteen-gun sloop, the *Louisiana*. The schooners captured at Grande Terre were in government custody, but Patterson had only enough sailors to man one ship. Plenty of experienced seamen roamed the town's streets, but these were former followers of Laffite whose ships had been impounded. One source summed up the attitude of the Baratarians. As far as they were concerned, "Patterson could sail his own damn ships."[17]

Jackson's survey convinced him he would be helpless before a determined assault by the Royal Navy. Although he expected reinforcements, even if a sizeable contingent of troops should arrive before the British landed, there would be no time to organize defenses. The strategic placement of artillery would be pointless without experienced cannoneers.

Several persons of influence urged him to meet with Jean Laffite. Claiborne had already suggested that the men of Grande Terre would be needed for any successful defense. Livingston, a man Jackson knew he could trust, recommended that he confer with the former Baratarian chief. Judge Hall agreed to guarantee Laffite's safety in an interview with the general.[18]

Various legends revolve around the initial contact between Laffite and Jackson.[19] The precise circumstances of this meeting

61

are obscure. At some time in mid-December, the two men did meet, probably in the city of New Orleans.[20] Exactly what transpired in that conference will never be known in detail, but one fact is clear: The two men instantly came to a meeting of the minds. A biographer of the future president declared that Jackson "saw in the chief of the sea rovers, a man of remarkable personality, brave, and filled with the war spirit . . . [and was] impressed . . . by his evident honesty."[21]

Laffite had already indicated his willingness to serve the American cause. He was impressed with Jackson. His only condition for service was a recommendation of pardon for all who would fight. The general assured Laffite he would fulfill this request.

Jean believed him and pledged Jackson his support.

It was this conference that provided a measure of hope that lower Louisiana would not become a Crown colony of Great Britain.

CHAPTER 14

Beyond the Fog

*N*othing can hold back the chill that creeps inland from the sea.

In the wetlands of southern Louisiana, the mists of December rise from bayou and inlet to become a fog that crawls relentlessly into the streets and courtyards of New Orleans.

On the river, ships move with caution. On the roadways that lead into the city, passage becomes difficult.

But in the final days of 1814, the inconvenience occasioned by river mists was of little consequence. Retarded visibility and delay of movement were not major concerns.

It was what existed beyond the fog that caused apprehension. A powerful sea and land force would descend upon the city. When Gen. Andrew Jackson arrived in New Orleans, the worst fears of the residents were confirmed: A battle would be fought for the possession of Louisiana, and New Orleans would be at its vortex.

The British had burned Washington. They had attacked another seaport town, Baltimore. But those were English-speaking cities. What might they do to a community long peopled by the French, the traditional enemies of England?

Rumors of a British invasion were heard in the cafes and on the streets. Yet apathy continued to reign. Some refused to believe the ancient foe of France would deign to mount an all-out offensive against a village on the banks of the Mississippi. By late fall, the English effort to seduce Jean Laffite was generally known, but some believed the Baratarian chief may have overstated his case in an attempt to delay Patterson's expedition against his base.

What reason would Royal Britain have for coming to the muddy banks of the Mississippi?

There was one: The British wanted Louisiana.

Whoever controlled the mouth of the Mississippi could dominate mid-America. An ultimate goal for the strategists in London was that of claiming New Orleans as a base for both land and sea operations. Commerce between the river port and Jamaica would become as common as trade had once been between St. Dominique and Louisiana. A permanent foothold on the southern shores of North America would strengthen the empire in the New World. The territorial ambitions of the United States would be thwarted by a well-entrenched Crown colony at the mouth of the great river.[1]

In July of 1814, instructions had been issued to the British peace commissioners: In dealing with the United States the principle of *"uti possidetis"* would be preserved. The royal representatives were to press for the right to retain any land the king's forces occupied at the cessation of hostilities. If they were in New Orleans when the treaty of peace was finally signed, that city was to be, from that time forward, a possession of Great Britain.[2]

Although this provision was not included in the final draft of the treaty, it was no coincidence that within thirty days of the decision in London to seek a peace to maintain the military status quo, Nicholls had his orders to prepare for an invasion of Louisiana and Lockyer was on his way to Grande Terre. New Orleans would become a prize to be won, one that would add to the glory of England.[3]

Once it was evident invasion was imminent, the French-speaking inhabitants of the state were ready to fight. Jackson's dramatic arrival in the city stirred most to a determination to resist. No one could be of French heritage without detesting the thought of a military domination of the territory by the English.[4]

64

After the battle, a British officer reported his troops had been led to believe the inhabitants of Louisiana "would receive us with open arms" or at least remain neutral. He and his men were surprised to discover that the French were "the greater part of the Force opposed to us."[5]

Although Laffite's warnings of an attack had been taken with little seriousness, as the certainty of invasion became apparent, his credibility was enhanced. The fact he had offered his services to Jackson was widely known. This was an element that helped galvanize local willingness to resist. Blanque and Livingston were members of the Committee for the Defense of New Orleans. Both knew Jean Laffite. In addition, they were aware of his rejection of the British offer. They used this information to rally members of the French-speaking community around the American standard.

Even before Jackson had arrived in New Orleans, the vanguard of a British armada had sailed from Jamaica. Nearly 6,000 troops, sufficient seamen to man the fifty-ship fleet, and 1,500 marines were moving westward along the northern shores of the Gulf toward New Orleans.[6]

Jackson was aware of the strength of the attack force. His immediate concern was how best to concentrate his limited defenses. At least half a dozen routes were open to the British ranging from Barataria Bay west of the delta to Lake Borgne east of the city.[7]

Jackson sought the advice of men like Lacarriere Latour. Once he was convinced of Laffite's reliability, he included him among his advisors.[8] His knowledge of the lands south of New Orleans would be valuable to Jackson and his lieutenants.

By mid-December, there was no longer any uncertainty as to the direction from which the attack would come. Intelligence reached Jackson on December 12 that the British were en route toward Lake Borgne.[9] Under the command of Vice-Admiral Alexander Cochrane, the English armada began its passage into the lake on December 10. The fleet cautiously maneuvered around Cat Island. Some may have remembered that at this point Baratarian privateers had successfully challenged a British reconnoitering expedition. Once on Lake Borgne, Cochrane had control of the coastal waterways of southeastern Louisiana.[10]

The troops on board were an impressive array of fighting

men. Some had participated in earlier North American campaigns including the burning of Washington. Others were seasoned veterans of European battles under Wellington. Two West Indian regiments and the famed Ninety-third Scottish Highlanders were among those assigned the task of taking New Orleans.[11]

On the same day Cochrane's fleet entered the lake, *Niles' Weekly Register* published a report on the progress toward peace. American ministers were in Belgium negotiating with the British. Niles reported that the United States was determined not to give up "the purchase of Louisiana from France."[12]

On December 11, Patterson's gunboat fleet, commanded by Thomas A. C. Jones, sighted the invasion armada. Jones sent a message to his commodore: The enemy was "increasing to an alarming force . . . too strong for us to make any stand against him east of the Malheureux islands."[13]

The five gunboats could only delay the British. When the fleet passed the middle of the lake, Jones made an effort to lure the heavily armed warships into shallow water. Cochrane sensed his strategy and took no chances. Lockyer was sent in pursuit with a fleet of shallow draft boats that could be rowed into the isolated portions of the lake. On December 14, after a two-hour battle, the American effort to halt the attack was quelled. Jones and his surviving crews were taken captive.[14]

The Royal Navy was in complete control of Louisiana's inland waterways.

Major C. R. Forrest, a British officer on board the armada, recorded the action in his journal: The "Enemy's Gun Boats, five in number, were attacked and captured by the Boats of the Fleet."[15]

The menace that had long lurked beyond the offshore mists had become reality.

CHAPTER 15

Desperate *Need*

By December 15, 1814, news of the battle on Lake Borgne and the capture of American gunboats reached New Orleans.

Patterson conferred with Claiborne. The commodore had demanded that the writ of habeas corpus be suspended so he could impress men into service. The Legislature heard his request but refused to act.

Patterson was in desperate need of seamen. He was willing to agree to any measure that would gain the services of the former residents of Grande Terre. On December 19, a bill reached the floor of the Legislature that would recommend "to the President of the United States . . . a full pardon to all such persons for any offence they may have committed against the laws of the United States."[1]

Judge Dominick Hall had suggested that the measure be presented to the Legislature. The bill passed unanimously.[2] This placed state authority behind the agreement between Jackson and Laffite. Impressing men into service would not be necessary. It would be left to Jean Laffite to rally sailors and cannoneers for a defense of the city.

The seriousness of the situation was emphasized by Jackson's martial law decree. Persons entering the city were required to carry passports subject to the scrutiny of military authorities. All street lamps were to be "extinguished at nine . . . and every person . . . found abroad without permission in writing, was to be apprehended as a spy."[3]

Jackson renewed his call for reinforcements. Gen. John Coffee was en route to New Orleans. By December 16, he and his troops were camped north of Baton Rouge. Jackson learned of his position and sent an order that he was to move his command "day and night to this place."[4]

By December 21, Coffee's force of 800 men set up camp near the city, and on the next day Gen. William Carroll arrived with a troop of Tennessee volunteers who were later joined by a company of Mississippi dragoons.[5]

But Jackson needed more than poorly armed militiamen. If he was to withstand the well-equipped veterans who would soon be thrown against him, he needed munitions, expert cannoneers, and experienced seamen.

Years later, Jackson would be quoted as having complained before the British landed, "We have no arms here." Both James Monroe, then secretary of war, and James Madison reacted angrily to this statement. "Arms [were] in the arsenal of New Orleans at the arrival of General Jackson," Madison stated in his correspondence with Monroe.[6]

The former war secretary declared in a letter to an associate written in 1827 "nothing was omitted on my part, that was necessary for the defense of that city." He angrily declared that the charge of neglect was unjust.[7]

But it was not a matter of neglect. There were simply far too few military supplies to withstand a massive invasion of Louisiana. Jackson needed both men and weapons.

Once the Legislature had legalized the agreement between Laffite and Jackson, the privateer chieftain left the security of his plantation retreat and went to work. He knew the territory and was able to furnish information for the recently arrived defenders of the city. Jackson sent a communication to Maj. Michael Reynolds who was assigned responsibility for defending the bayous west of New Orleans. He was instructed to gain assistance from Laffite and, in return, provide him with "necessary protection from injury and insult." When he had done so, he was to "furnish him with your passport for his return dismissing him as soon as possible as I shall want him here."[8]

According to one account, Laffite supplied a troop of carabiniers with much-needed gun flints. The company, under command of J. P. Plauche, was mustered near the levee. Laffite boarded one of the schooners seized by Patterson, and "with assistance rolled up a large keg of choice flints." Once the keg was broken open, "he passed along Plauche's line, and, with his own hands, distributed them to the men." The tale concluded with the claim that "Laffite's flints saved the city."[9]

Although this record, written sixty years after the event, has about it the aura of legend, it is possible that Laffite did procure munitions from sources known only to members of the Grande Terre community.[10]

Whether or not he provided material assistance to the city's defenders, it is clear that he did encourage his former associates to join in the city's defense. Possibly this was his most significant contribution to the American cause.

Soon after the action of the Legislature and Laffite's conference with Jackson, Lt. Charles Thompson signed a crew of 170 experienced seamen for his ship, the *Louisiana*, and Master Commandant John Henley found all the replacements he needed for the *Carolina*. Renato Beluche, Dominique Youx, and three full artillery companies joined the defenders at Fort St. John.[11]

The British continued to move closer to the city.

Rather than take the less difficult route through Lake Pontchartrain and attack New Orleans from the north, the invasion force bypassed Fort St. John and moved directly westward toward the banks of the Mississippi. Taking full advantage of the extended period of darkness on one of the shortest days of the year, the advance units reached the river early on the morning of December 23.[12]

Making use of the Villere Canal, Cochrane's ferrymen brought up additional troops. At midday Jackson received a report that the enemy was entrenched dangerously close to New Orleans. A company of dragoons under Thomas Hinds was dispatched to ascertain the exact position of the invaders. Shots were exchanged, and Hinds withdrew his horsemen.

Major Forrest, who recorded the action from behind the British lines, was confident of success. He declared that when "the Enemy's Cavalry" appeared, upon "being fired at, and two of their Horses killed, they quickly retired."[13]

At seven o'clock, Jackson arrived at the hastily established front line. An hour later, the *Carolina* opened fire from a position opposite the British position.[14]

Forrest expressed surprise. While he and his men were cooking provisions, "a Schooner of the Enemy mounting about 14 Guns, and two Gun Boats . . . anchored off our Bivouac . . . immediately opened a heavy fire of round and Grape [shot] upon our Troops."[15]

Jackson ordered an assault hoping to dislodge the advance guard before they were reinforced. Mississippi mists and early December darkness made visibility impossible. An eyewitness later recalled that by ten o'clock the fog had "rendered it necessary in the opinion of our general to desist."[16]

Forrest's journal continued to express confidence: in spite of the American attack, our "troops remained thus posted through the night immolested *[sic]*."[17]

The next day, a sullen haze hung over the battlefield. Rowboat ferries from the armada on Lake Borgne were steadily increasing the size of the attack force. Jackson ordered his volunteers to fall back and regroup. For the moment, the seventeen-day contest reached a stalemate. The position of the *Carolina* prevented the British from advancing, but Jackson was aware his citizen troops were no match for the seasoned veterans entrenched on the river bank.[18]

On Christmas Day, a salvo of artillery startled the defenders of New Orleans who braced themselves for an assault. This was a welcoming volley for a new commander. Maj. Gen. Sir Edward Pakenham, brother-in-law of the duke of Wellington, had arrived in camp to take charge of the final attack.

Pakenham was not pleased with the position in which he found his forces, but Cochrane assured him that it would be unwise to attempt another landing. The defenses were weak and were manned by inexperienced and poorly armed militiamen.

On the American side, one of Jackson's aides noted a deficiency in the deployment of troops: The line of defense was too short and should be carried to the impassable swamp to avoid encirclement. He mentioned this to Livingston, who conveyed the suggestion to Jackson in a communique that gave Laffite credit for the observation. The extension was immediately ordered.[19]

The British noticed the alteration in the American defenses. Forrest recorded "that the Enemy had a force (said to be 1,500 Men) in the Neighborhood of Detour des Angalais . . . the position of the Line was changed."[20]

Pakenham was confident of early victory. The day before he arrived in camp, United States and British commissioners signed a treaty of peace in Ghent, Belgium. He knew a conclusion of hostilities could take place during the battle, but he had been instructed that whatever the terms of the treaty, it would not apply to Louisiana. The invasion force would hold its position until Pakenham received direct orders from the Crown.[21]

On December 26, the two-ship American navy, manned partly by Baratarians, moved downriver opposite the enemy camp. According to an eyewitness, both "opened a brisk, destructive fire."[22]

Pakenham had anticipated this. A furnace was erected in the river camp capable of heating mortar shot to the level of fiery missiles. By the next morning, his gunners answered the cannon fire from the river by directing burning shot toward the wooden ships. The *Louisiana*, a floating munitions depository, was maneuvered beyond the reach of destructive projectiles, but the *Carolina* was becalmed and set ablaze. Fire swept toward the ship's magazine. The crew scrambled over her side moments before the vessel blew up.[23]

By December 28, the British had positioned sufficient artillery to begin harassing the American entrenchments. The destruction of the *Carolina* encouraged the invaders. According to one of Jackson's men, the enemy began "a cannonade and bombardment of our lines," that was met with "great spirit and vivacity by our batteries." The British retired "with disappointment and mortification to their camp."[24]

The assault had been halted by cannon fire directed by Laffite's former lieutenants. Jackson had ordered Renato Beluche and Dominique Youx to abandon their assigned posts at Fort St. John and man a twenty-four-pounder battery opposite the British camp.[25] Two gun crews were formed from the Baratarians, some of whom had escaped from the destruction of the *Carolina*.[26] Gun emplacements were erected capable of destroy-

71

ing protective buildings. When the attack began, a command was given to fire. Sheltering structures exploded, and the British took cover.[27]

Pakenham's troops made use of a weapon unfamiliar to Jackson's volunteers, the Congreve Rocket, a pyrotechnic device designed to bring terror to inexperienced troops.[28] At first, the militiamen wavered, but the battle-seasoned Baratarians were undaunted. As cannoneers blasted the assault from land, Patterson brought the *Louisiana* into range once more. The ship's guns were able to provide flanking fire from the river under cover from land batteries.[29]

Even Patterson was ecstatic about his gunners. He later reported that most of the enemy projectiles burst harmlessly over the decks of the *Louisiana,* while the former privateers, manning the ship's guns, delivered 800 rounds into the British positions. "The crew is composed of men of all nations, (English excepted) taken from the streets of New Orleans . . . yet I never knew guns better served, or a more animated fire than was supported from her."[30]

According to another eyewitness, the attack was thwarted by cannon fire. Our artillery "kept them at a respectable distance."[31]

This action brought renewed confidence in the city's defenders. Several of New Orleans' leaders had discussed the advisability of surrendering, fearing total destruction. On the evening before the failed attack, Magloire Guichard, Speaker of the Lower House of the Legislature, had talked with close associates about the possibility of making terms with the enemy to save the town from bombardment.

Once the British advance had been halted, there was no more talk of a truce.[32]

CHAPTER 16

Hardships and Fatigues

*F*or the moment, the cannon were silent.

The men in the trenches knew another attack would come. The artillerists had done no more than temporarily halt the British.

Frantic activity followed the battle of December 28, 1814. Houses in the city were searched for usable weapons. Cotton bales were sunk into muddy soil. Platforms were built upon them. Extra bales were set in place to protect gun crews.[1]

Both sides sought additional artillery.

On December 29, a twenty-four-pounder from one of the Baratarian ships was installed on the west bank of the river. Pakenham's invasion force brought up guns from the ships anchored on Lake Borgne.[2]

On December 30, the British threw up a redoubt on their right. The American line responded. Two additional cannon were positioned and directed toward the enemy. One was manned by a crew led by Dominique Youx.

"Notwithstanding the distance," according to one account, most of the balls from Youx's gun "struck the parapet, demolishing the works and killing or wounding many men."[3]

The battle had become an artillery duel. The British command had not anticipated that. On the night of December 31, seventeen additional pieces of ordnance were brought to the front.

Time and rations were running out. Pakenham had to act.[4]

At dawn on January 1, 1815, Pakenham's artillery opened fire. Shells aimed by Royal Navy veterans shattered the house where Jackson had established his headquarters. He had vacated the building only minutes before. Gun emplacements on the American line were hit. Cotton bales were set on fire, a gun carriage demolished. But before British infantry could attack, Jackson's cannoneers had their guns back in service.[5]

Forrest lamented the fact that "Our Batteries made no impression on the enemy's parapet."[6]

The assault began. Once more it stalled in the face of cannon fire. Some of those who survived were picked off by the marksmanship of General Coffee's Tennessee riflemen.[7]

An American officer later recalled that the British advanced within "six hundred yards of our works . . . The steady and skillful fire of our batteries soon arrested their progress and put them to flight."[8]

By three o'clock, the exchange of artillery fire ended. The British had used hogsheads full of sugar to protect their gun emplacements. Rain dissolved the contents of the casks that lay broken in the river mud. Pakenham's troops were forced to drag their silenced weapons back to a secure position.[9]

Jackson's cannoneers gave him an advantage. The guns of the *Louisiana* were removed and placed in position across the river from the British camp. Taking a cue from his opponent, Jackson had a furnace erected capable of producing red hot missiles similar to those that destroyed the *Carolina*. Houses that had provided shelter for the invader were set ablaze.[10]

On January 4, reinforcements arrived.

Over 2,000 militiamen from Kentucky entered the city bringing encouragement, but little else. The new arrivals were almost completely unarmed. Homes and shops were ransacked for any type of weaponry.[11]

Jackson continued to strengthen the defenses on both sides of the Mississippi. Breastworks were built on the river's east bank to protect the cannon Patterson had mounted.[12]

On January 6, Jackson detected signs of a major assault. Through his telescope, he saw boats and barges dragged from Borgne to the river. On the next day, body shields were fashioned from cane stalks. Scaling ladders were under construction.[13]

The attack was imminent.

American troops braced for the inevitable. Even before dawn on January 8, an eyewitness later recalled "an uncommon stir was prevailing in [the British] camp."[14]

The night before, Pakenham had briefed his officers on the battle plan. There would be a frontal assault in multiple columns concentrating on the weaker portions of Jackson's line. Other troops would be ferried across the river to silence Patterson's guns. Taking full advantage of the dense night mists, barges moved to the bank ready to carry men across the river. During the final hours of darkness, infantry units maneuvered into position.[15]

Men in trenches on both sides waited in the shadow of death.

Behind the American lines, Kentucky militiamen and Tennessee volunteers crouched in predawn chill. Cannoneers checked their shot and powder.

Jackson moved among the defenders.

According to one legend, the American general came upon a circle of men huddled about a mound of red embers dripping coffee in the Creole way. "That smells like better coffee than we can get," he remarked. And then turning to Dominique Youx, he asked: "Smuggle it?" Laffite's former lieutenant did not deny the possibility as he handed Jackson a cup. The general commented: "I wish I had five hundred such devils in the butts."[16]

But in all likelihood neither Dominique Youx nor Andrew Jackson had time to prepare or savor Creole coffee on the morning of January 8.

As the fog hung above the Mississippi, a signal rocket arched into the murky darkness. The British barrage began. Two columns advanced toward the American lines carrying equipment necessary for scaling the parapets.[17]

Jackson had stationed his sharpshooters in position to rake the attackers.[18] One of the defenders recalled that the cannonade was "immediately returned by the artillery on our works . . . under skillful officers who tore their columns, as they approached, with a frightful carnage."[19]

On the British came.

75

Pakenham's horse was hit. He mounted another.

The Scottish Highlanders responded to the command to left oblique march across the field to aid a unit that had hesitated in the attack exposing their flank. Pakenham called up the reserves. This was his last order. Realizing his men were faltering, he galloped to rally his troops. He was hit by American grapeshot and died 300 yards from the defensive line.[20]

The reserves came as close as 250 yards before they bolted and ran. The Scots advanced even further to leave their broken bodies within 150 yards of the American ramparts. By 8:30 A.M., there were no longer any standing targets. The cannoneers continued to blast away at the British encampment until well past midday.

At two o'clock, the British asked for a cease-fire to bury their dead.[21] Jackson watched in amazement as 500 Britons who had lain motionless on the field all morning emerged from among the bodies of their fallen comrades.[22]

On the other side of the river, American arms were less successful. The British troops ferried across the Mississippi outflanked the poorly armed militiamen. Patterson was forced to spike his cannon and retreat.[23]

British success on the river's east side was of no consequence. The decisiveness of Jackson's victory on the west bank forced the invaders to withdraw. After an unsuccessful attempt to take Fort St. Philip on January 9, the invasion force abandoned an effort to bring ships upriver. On January 18, there was a request for an exchange of prisoners.[24]

The casualty figures for January 8 indicate the totality of the American victory: the British suffered 2,037 losses, 291 killed, 1,262 wounded, and 484 captured; Jackson's troops counted only six killed and seven wounded. During the seventeen-day contest, a total of fifty-five deaths were recorded for the defenders with 185 wounded and 93 missing. Of the various units Pakenham had sent into battle, the Scottish Ninety-third Highlanders experienced the heaviest casualties, losing fifty percent of their total strength.[25]

On January 20, Jackson issued a communique declaring "The enemy have abandoned their enterprise against New Orleans and have embarked their forces after a complete defeat."[26]

He followed this with a message to Secretary Monroe stating

that the British have "decamped," but that an effectual defense should be maintained "should the enemy meditate a renewal of his attempts."[27]

On January 21, Jackson issued a statement that was to be read to each corps.[28] He praised his troops for their "undaunted courage . . . patriotism and patience under hardships and fatigues."[29] This was followed by General Orders under the same date in which he gave credit to those units that played an important role in the victory. The cannoneers received the highest commendation: "Captains Dominique and Beluche, lately commanding privateers of Barataria with part of their former crews and many brave citizens of New Orleans, were stationed at Nos. 3 and 4." He gave them "warm approbation" for their gallantry.

The future president singled out two other persons for having "exhibited the same courage and fidelity . . . the government shall be duly appraised of their conduct."[30]

Those two were the brothers Laffite.

CHAPTER 17

The Celebration

There was cause for rejoicing.

In spite of the general's prediction that the enemy would return, by mid-January, the citizens of New Orleans believed the crisis was over.

They were ready for a festive event. Jackson was aware it would be wise to celebrate.

On January 19, he personally inspected the deserted British camp. Even before he prepared his address and General Orders, he dictated a note to the Reverend Abbé Dubourg suggesting that the departure of the enemy called for an act of religious observance. "Permit me therefore, to entreat that you will cause a service of public thanksgiving to be performed in the Cathedral in token at once of the great assistance we have received from the Ruler of all Events." [1]

Father Dubourg acted quickly. A service would be held in St. Louis sanctuary, the centerpiece edifice of the city. But, perhaps, as Jackson had suspected, the people of New Orleans anticipated more than a religious ceremony. There would be celebration outside the somber church, one in which the entire populace could participate. The city would show the austere American general they knew how to honor heroes and commemorate a victory.

An arch was erected near the cathedral doors. Young girls, under the tutelage of one of the town's socialites, Madame Floriant, prepared for the occasion. Costumes were assembled. The female entourage would be dressed in white, with silver stars upon their heads.[2]

Niles' Weekly Register later reported that "the ceremony sprung from female gratitude and was arranged entirely by the ladies."[3]

Early in the day, crowds began to assemble on the Place d'Armes.[4] The square was soon crowded. An eyewitness recalled that "at least 1,000 women, ladies and young girls" were waiting expectantly in front of the cathedral for the arrival of the general.[5]

Jackson's order requiring his men to maintain defensive positions was temporarily relaxed. Two weeks had elapsed since the battle, but the general feared another assault. Only a limited number of military units would be allowed to leave their posts. Plauche's volunteers were among those permitted to join the celebration. The uniformed battalion lined up smartly on the walk leading from the church to the river.[6]

Jackson arrived at midday. Followed by his staff officers, he entered the Place d'Armes by the river gate. He walked toward the cathedral to the music of a military band. *Niles'* account detailed the event. Wreaths of laurel covered an "elegant arch." Eighteen pillars were erected in the square, each festooned with greenery and graced by the presence of a young lady dressed in a flowing white gown. Each symbolized one of the states of the American union. One represented Louisiana. A silken banner fluttered across her bosom carrying the words "Glory and Safety."[7]

As the general marched across the square, flowers were thrown in his path.[8] Two of Madame Floriant's young women suspended a laurel wreath over Jackson's head as he passed under the arch.[9]

Father Dubourg, attended by fellow clergymen, met Jackson at the sanctuary entrance. Father Dubourg lauded his success and presented him with a laurel wreath. The future president made a proper response: "I receive with gratitude and pleasure the symbolical crown which piety has prepared. I receive it in the name of the brave men who . . . well deserve the laurels."[10]

Jackson was escorted to a chair near the altar. The cathedral choir sang the *Te Deum*.[11]

Jean Laffite was not included in his commander's entourage, but he was present for the ceremony, one of a small company of celebrators who found their way into the sanctuary.

Some accounts report that festivities continued into the evening hours and a victory ball took place later on the same day.[12] But Jackson's ban on socializing did not permit a nighttime gathering.[13] Once the military and religious rites were completed, Jackson ordered his troops back to their posts. For the moment, the city rejoiced in victory without a grand ball.

Jackson had reason to be concerned about the military situation. The British still controlled the inland waterways of the Gulf. Another landing was possible at some point from which the enemy might yet march upon the city. Even before the official celebration, reports had reached Jackson that Cochrane's armada was receiving reinforcements.[14]

Jackson demanded that all units remain on duty. He was adamant that there be no more festivities until it was certain the invaders were gone from American shores.

This was too much. The general's popularity began a rapid decline. The battle was over. New Orleans had been saved from bombardment. The enemy had been repelled.

As the city's residents grumbled about the extended period of austerity, Jackson took steps to conclude the state of hostilities. Edward Livingston and a committee representing the general were sent to negotiate with the British for an exchange of prisoners. Arriving on board the admiral's flagship as the Royal Navy was about to launch a new attack on Fort Bowyer, Livingston and his fellow arbitrators were detained. Two days later, a communication reached Cochrane that the treaty of peace had been signed at Ghent in the final days of the preceding year.[15] Jackson's representatives were allowed to return to New Orleans.

On February 20, Livingston relayed the information he had received from Cochrane to the general. Jackson refused to believe the report. This might be a British trick. He would not disband his army or relax control until he had confirmation of the signing of a treaty.[16]

Claiborne appealed to Jackson to give his men leave to return to their homes. The general refused. Many of the volunteer troops had already left their posts to join their wives and mistresses. In order to legitimize their departure, some registered with the French consul as citizens of France. The American commander retaliated by ordering all French nationals to leave Louisiana.[17]

Anger swept the city.

There were some who insisted Jackson was not the sole hero of the battle. Bernard Marigny, a member of the Committee of Defense, declared that "of the ten or twelve pieces of cannon on the Jackson line, six at least, were served by Creoles . . . or by Frenchmen." He listed the following among those who had done the most: "Beluche . . . Dominique Youx and the Lafittes."[18]

An anonymous letter was published accusing the general of abusing his authority. Jackson learned the identity of the author, a local resident named Louaillier. He was arrested and placed in prison for his impertinence. Louaillier applied to Judge Dominick Hall for a writ of habeas corpus. The judge granted the writ and ordered his release. Jackson was furious. He sent armed troops to arrest and imprison the judge. After his release, Hall resumed his position on the bench and cited Jackson for contempt of court. The general was ordered to appear before the judge. The future president did so, defending his actions as necessary for military security. Hall heard his defense, judged him guilty and assessed the hero of New Orleans a fine of $1,000 in lieu of a prison sentence.[19]

Jackson paid his fine, and according to one record, was carried in triumph from the courtroom by several of his strongest supporters. Among them was Laffite's former lieutenant, Dominique Youx.[20]

By this time, the conflict between the military and the judiciary was no longer important. Eleven days earlier, Jackson had received official notice of treaty ratification. Only then did the military commandant revoke martial law. His grip upon the city was relaxed, and his army given official leave to disband.[21]

Once more, there was celebration.

This time it would be a social event. The Louisiana militia gave a banquet for the officers of the Kentucky, Tennessee, and Mississippi militias. Father Dubourg made the major address of the evening. Andrew Jackson was not invited to speak. One of the Tennessee volunteers, an officer fluent in French, made a response to Father Dubourg in the language most of those present understood. He declared that the American Republic may have been born at Yorktown, but it had not been confirmed until January 8, 1815.[22]

Long before the Jackson-Hall incident, the general fulfilled his promise to Jean Laffite. He sent a formal request to Washington for clemency for the Laffites and the men of Grande Terre.

On February 6, President Madison declared that a "free and full pardon of all offenses committed in violation of any act or acts of congress of the said United States" be granted to Jean Laffite and all members of the Baratarian community who had aided in the defense of New Orleans. Any matter "touching on the revenue, trade and navigation . . . or touching the intercourse and commerce of the United States with foreign nations, at any time before the 8th day of January" was forgiven. Not only were all of the charges against the Baratarians dismissed, but "all suits, indictments, and prosecutions, for fines, penalties, and for forfeitures . . . be stayed, discontinued and released."[23]

Niles' Weekly Register printed an account of the pardon based on the fact that Laffite, whom Niles had denounced only weeks before as a ruthless pirate, had "manifested a sincere repentance . . . and exhibited, in the defence of New Orleans unequivocal traits of courage and fidelity."[24]

Jackson did more than recommend pardon for Laffite and his men. Before he left the city, he wrote Jean a personal letter: "I do an act of justice, and at the same time one very agreeable to my feelings to state the services you have rendered during the late invasion of your country." He made mention of Coffee's commendation of Laffite for bravery in action on December 23, and then declared:

> From that time to the end of the campaign, I have had frequent occasion to avail myself of your activities and zeal for the service which always was reported with the utmost cheerfulness . . . considering you, Sir as one of those to whom the country is most indebted on the late trying occasion, I feel great pleasure in giving this testimony of your worth, and to add the sincere assurance of my private friendship and high esteem. I am, Sir . . . your most Obed and humble servant.

The letter was signed with the vigorous scrawl of the future president of the United States.[25]

There were others who affirmed Laffite's steadfastness to the American cause. On April 22, 1815, Jean Blanque prepared a written statement about the packet sent him after the British had visited Grande Terre. Blanque declared he had "delivered these documents to Governor Claiborne." He reported "a few days later I received a second letter also signed Laffite . . . which gave some light on the situation of the English, as much as he could furnish." [26]

Blanque's declaration countered the accusation that charged Jean with having correspondence with the enemy. Blanque believed Laffite was sincere in his affirmation of American citizenship.

The Baratarian chief could accept life in the river city and use his skills in legitimate merchandising. There was no pursuit in which he could not have achieved success.

For him, this should have been a cause for celebration.

CHAPTER 18

A Restless Yearning

Some would return to the sea.

Not all of the pardoned would accept forgiveness. Madison's decree had included all Baratarians who had joined in the defense of New Orleans. But there were some who had no intention of becoming law-abiding citizens.

Vincent Gambi was one of the first to spurn clemency. Claiming he was acting in behalf of Jackson, he mounted cannon on one of the impounded ships. He gathered a crew from men who had been a part of Laffite's colony and set sail as a sea raider. He captured a vessel with a cargo of livestock, staples, and specie off the coast of Tampico. Mexican revolutionists purchased the ship and its supplies, and he returned to the Gulf to take more prizes. In April 1815, he and his crew were captured by United States gunboats. On May 6, a federal grand jury indicted him for piracy. But the people of New Orleans would not condemn a sea raider who claimed to be a privateer and had fought against the British. A jury made up of citizens of the river city found Gambi not guilty. He continued his career of piracy on the waters of the Gulf.[1]

Another of Laffite's associates returned to the sea — Renato Beluche. His biographer noted that even before Jackson lauded his patriotism he was on his way to "wherever it was he had anchored" his ship, *La Popa*. By the time New Orleans was celebrating victory, he had captured a Spanish merchant vessel, *La Caridad*, off the coast of Cuba.[2]

Beluche, unlike Gambi, would remain on the legitimate side of the thin line that separated nineteenth century privateering from outright piracy. His American letter of marque was no longer valid, but, acting within the terms of his Cartagenan commission, he placed a prizemaster and crew on board *La Caridad* and sent the ship to Cartagena for judication.

Before the prize reached port, an American navy patrol overtook *La Caridad*, and forced the ship into harbor at Wilmington, North Carolina. Using the name Brugman, Beluche filed a cross claim for the prize. He won his case and claimed the value of the captured goods.[3] Sea raiding was still an acceptable profession even when practiced under the guise of a questionable letter of marque.

Beluche continued his raids against Spanish shipping. In July, he captured the *Cleopatra* off the coast of Cuba. He later claimed he had instructed the crew to sail the prize into the port where he held his commission. But, before the prizemaster found it convenient to complete the voyage to Cartagena, the ship was overtaken by another sea raider. A United States schooner, *Firebrand*, forced both vessels into Beluche's home port. A New Orleans court sought to untangle the question of who had a reasonable claim to the cargoes of the captured ships. Renato was saved embarrassment in the city of his birth only because his seamen testified they did not know their captain's name. The cargo of one of the vessels under judication included casks of vintage wine. Considerably less wine was inventoried at dockside than had been on board at the time of capture.[4]

Beluche was one of the few sea raiders of the period who took seriously his relationship to the country that had issued him a commission. In May 1813, he joined an attack on Spanish royalists. By this act, he cast his lot with Simon Bolivar's revolution. He had every reason for supporting the insurgents, for if Spain had been successful in suppressing the revolutionary movement, Beluche's papers would have been worthless. His cannoneers provided protection for the insurgent squadron, an action that earned him rank as an officer in Cartagena's fledgling navy.

Beluche participated in other expeditions in support of Bolivar, intertwining the roles of revolutionist and sea raider.[5]

In December 1815, Simon Bolivar was on board Beluche's ship, *La Popa*, where he narrowly escaped death at the hands of a paid assassin. Beluche safely delivered the liberator to his destination at Aux Cayes.[6]

From time to time, Beluche appeared in New Orleans. He was in the city during the trial of Andrew Jackson in 1815. Two years later, he purchased two lots in the first suburb to be developed below the old town and remained in the area during the fall of 1817.[7] Prior to this, Beluche owned property in the Vieux Carre at the corner of Royal and Dumaine.[8]

In 1818, the British charged him with piracy. While refitting his ship in Kingston harbor, he was arrested and imprisoned. When placed on trial, the Crown could prove no charge against him other than that of having taken on board his vessel a small boat, worth less than $50. Once again, he was able to convince a jury he was an honest privateer. The Jamaican court judged him not guilty.[9]

Beluche was one of the few of Laffite's associates who would live long enough to die as a respected member of society. Having accepted a commission as an officer in the navy of the Venezuelan republic, he eventually rose to the rank of commodore. Death came to him in 1860 at the age of seventy-nine, and he was buried in his adopted country.[10] A century later, his bones were removed from the original grave on order from the Senate of Venezuela and reinterred in the Pantheon Nacional, an honor bestowed only upon the nation's greatest heroes.[11]

Some of Laffite's Baratarians accepted presidential pardon. Dominique Youx was one who did.[12] Basking in his fame as a cannoneer during the battle, he spent his remaining years in a residence in New Orleans at the corner of Love and Mandeville Streets. He became a familiar figure in the city's coffeehouses and cafes.

Because of the legends that evolved around him, his name became associated with the plot to rescue Napoleon from exile on St. Helena and bring him to Louisiana.[13] The scheme was never more than talk across absinthe glasses in the town's drinking establishments, but there were many who believed if anyone could have accomplished such a feat, Dominique could. After the death of the French emperor in 1821, conversations at the social gatherings of New Orleans turned to other subjects: Dominique would have told of the battle that saved the city, of Andrew Jackson, and on occasion of Barataria in its days of glory.

At times, he spoke of Jean Laffite.

Death came peacefully to the old cannoneer in 1830. A New Orleans French language newspaper invited the public to attend the funeral of "Le Capitaine Dominique," that was to be held on November 15. Flags in the city were lowered to half-staff. The elite Louisiana legion donned parade uniforms to give him a fitting funeral.[14] An oration lauded him for his "services rendered . . . in the engagements of the 23rd of December 1814, and 8th of January, 1815."[15]

He was buried in the cemetery beyond the ramparts. His tomb can still be seen in a burial ground designated as St. Louis Cemetery Number Two. Words inscribed on the grave described him as "a warrior bold" who "in hundred battles proved his bravery."[16]

Others settled peaceably in southern Louisiana. An Italian named Chighizola, known as "Nez Coupe" because he had lost most of his nose in a sea battle, took up residence on Grande Isle where he lived for his remaining days.[17]

Pierre Laffite claimed pardon. Charles Gayarre noted that after the Battle of New Orleans, he "seems to have suddenly disappeared from public notice."[18] Recent research indicates that he continued to aid his younger brother in his more daring enterprises operating from within the bounds of the city of New Orleans while maintaining an aura of orderly respectability.[19]

Pierre acted as a second in "an affair of honor" in the year 1815 along with St. Geme who "had no superior in New Orleans as to social position." Gayarre cited this as proof he was accepted in the highest levels of the city's society.[20]

A Pierre Laffite filed suit in 1816 for control of the Attakopas Canal that connected New Orleans to the Teche country and Texas.[21] Although there were other Pierre Laffites in the area at the time, it is possible that this was the brother of Jean. In any case, the pardoned smuggler established himself as a respected member of Louisiana's planter caste.

Many of the ships captured by Patterson at Grande Terre still languished at dockside. After the battle, the Laffites attempted to process their claims by joining the shipowners in a suit for recompense.[22] Court proceedings had been initiated late in 1814 establishing the right of confiscation.[23] The November sale ordered by the district court included only a small portion of the property captured in Patterson's raid.[24]

Efforts to reopen the case in 1815 were futile. Only one of the investors, Sauvinet, recovered any part of his loss through repurchase of one of the judicated ships at public auction.[25]

The presidential pardon did not provide a means for restoring property the Laffites claimed. Perhaps it would prove to be of practical value in Washington. According to one account, Pierre visited the nation's capital on the Potomac in late 1815.[26] Stanley Faye, in his study of the Laffites, concluded that it was Jean who made the trip to Washington. Possibly, the younger brother believed he might be able to intervene personally with the American president.[27] Jean would have relished a visit to the national seat of government. After a voyage to the eastern coast of the United States, he visited the capital and other nearby cities.[28]

His petition to the president was filed on December 27, 1815. He declared that no resistance had been made to the seizure of ships and property because he "had not the least apprehension of the equity of the United States once they would be convinced of the cinserity *(sic)* of my conduct." He made reference to the fact he had joined "the army which was organizing for the defence of the country. I claim no merit for having, like all the inhabitants of the State, co-operated in this welfare. I claim the equity of the Government of the United States . . . for the restitution of at least that portion of my property which will not deprive the treasury of the United States of any of its own funds."[29]

Whether the document was taken to Washington by Pierre or Jean, the claim was presented in behalf of both Laffites. The bearer of the petition returned to New Orleans during early 1816 without success.

For a time, Jean appeared willing to settle quietly within the city, continue his sexual activities, and on occasion join his former comrades in recalling days on a seaward island.

But he was not one who, like Youx, could be content to live within the bounds of the security that his pardon had purchased.

He yearned for more, much more.

And his was an unbounded, restless yearning.

CHAPTER 19

Mistresses and Espionage

It was a time of sexual gratification.

Jean made frequent trips to the dwelling near the ramparts. There were other encounters with women.

Both Laffite brothers were in New Orleans during the final months of 1816. By then, it was clear there would be no help from Washington in reclaiming the confiscated property. The two appeared content to enjoy the amenities of southern Louisiana.

During the year Pierre's mistress, Marie Villars, gave birth to a son. He named his offspring for Jean.

A baptismal record provides evidence of Jean's activities. Signed by Father Antonio de Sedella, the document attested that the quadroon girl, Catherine Villars, then scarcely sixteen years of age, described as a "free woman of color," gave birth to the "illegitimate son of Jean Lafitte." Jean named the child for his brother, Pierre.[1]

There are other records of Jean's ability to charm and seduce. One account referred to a "wife" of Laffite named Madeline Rigaud.[2] There were a vast host of other victims of his wiles of whom there are no records.

Jean was not capable of remaining for any length of time

enjoying a self-indulgent lifestyle. Whenever ships docked at the river quay, there were seamen who frequented the town's cafes and rum shops. They spoke of sea rovers who had gained great wealth and of new nations being born from the crumbling ruins of Spain's colonialism. Some had seen sun-drenched islands with glistening white beaches yet unclaimed. The more the grog flowed, the more they talked.

Laffite listened.

For a time he would wait. But he was not one who could wait for long. He had commanded a ship upon the Gulf. He had seen battle and heard the cannon roar. He had experienced the exhilaration of leading and controlling men, of dealing with persons of influence and power. His nature was such that he could not long remain idle.

It was during this period the two brothers entered into a strange alliance, one with officials of Spain, the nation upon whose vessels the Baratarians had preyed. On November 17, 1815, Pierre contracted to serve the Spanish Crown as an informer. It was soon after this, probably immediately following his return from Washington, that Jean agreed to participate in espionage. Juan Mariano Picornell acted as intermediary between Pierre and the representatives of the Crown. Father Antonio de Sedella gave encouragement to the pact.[3]

The older Laffite was the first to realize there would be no redress by the government for their claimed losses. Jean, after the unsuccessful effort to petition the American president, consented to the project.

The Laffites were assigned a code name: "Number thirteen." Pierre would remain in New Orleans and convey to the resident consul what information he could gain, while Jean was to visit Galveston Island, the base of a sea raider, Louis-Michel Aury, who claimed to be a Mexican revolutionary.[4]

Aury had operated out of Cartagena as a privateer in 1815.[5] In the summer of 1816, he took possession of the coastal island known as Campeche or Galveston.[6] Declaring his establishment a part of the Republic of Mexico, he proclaimed himself a contender *"por la libertad."*[7] Aury proceeded to issue letters of marque under the questionable authority of a Mexican named Mañuel de Herrera, a self-proclaimed minister plenipotentiary of Mexico. Commissions were granted to privateers who agreed to return their cargoes to Galveston to be appraised by Aury's "Court of Admiralty." The ships were manned by crews described as "vagabonds [and] Baratarian refugees, the remnant of Lafitte's pirate band."[8]

In November, an eight-ship fleet commanded by Francisco Xavier Miña docked at Galveston. Taking Aury's revolutionary claims seriously, he enlisted his support in freeing Mexico from Spanish domination. A few months later, a small band of Americans led by Col. Henry Perry joined the schemers. During the early months of 1817, the three conferred on plans for a campaign against Spanish authority.[9]

Beverly Chew, collector for the district of Mississippi, reported to Washington that Mexican armed vessels based at Galveston had visited the port of New Orleans.[10] Spain was even more concerned than Washington and was willing to pay for intelligence of potential insurgents. With only one armed vessel in the Havana naval station, Cuban authorities had little choice but to rely on any source of information, even one as questionable as the brothers Laffite.[11]

Early in 1817, a "John Williams" made the voyage to Havana. This was the code name that appears in the transcripts of Spanish documents for Lacarriere Latour.[12] Williams was received by Captain General Cienfuegos and the intendant, Alexandro Ramírez, and then introduced to Felipe Fatio, who would supervise the data-gathering service. Fatio left Havana on April 16 and on May 7 assumed control of the New Orleans consulate.[13]

By this time, Jean Laffite had completed his first assignment at espionage. On the night of May 9, he and his brother met with Fatio and presented a report of Jean's voyage to Galveston in March. This was one of two documents the brothers brought to the meeting. On May 24, Fatio forwarded an account of his contact with the Laffites to the Captain General in Cuba. Initially, Fatio was suspicious of the Laffites, but after interviewing them, he was confident they would be useful to the Spanish cause.[14]

The priest, Antonio de Sedella, vouched for the Laffites and assured the consul that he "knows them thoroughly, is convinced of the sincerity of their promises."[15]

Fatio reported to Cuba that "all the information that I have gathered concerning their moral and public conduct . . . eulogies of their humanity and generous character." Although the Laffites

91

had been involved in sea raiding, they had been charitable "not only toward the Spaniards taken as prisoners by their boats," but also other captives. Therefore, the consul declared, he was "assured of the good faith of the indicated persons No. 13 . . . they have worked constantly since their offer was made."[16]

In addition to the record of Jean's trip to Galveston, the Laffites had brought a proposal for a "Plan of Operations" that would "make a decisive stroke, not only seizing the port of Galveston," but preventing the gathering of the forces led by Miña, Perry, and Aury.[17]

Jean Laffite had sailed for the Texas coast on March 20 aboard the brig *Devorador*[18] and had arrived on March 23 "off the port of Galveston." There were vessels in the harbor. One was a "privateer that Aury commanded with 40 men in the crew, 20 officers as passengers and a few soldiers." Another was the *Cleopatra* "in which Miña had travelled from New Orleans . . . having on board a few officers and soldiers." He sighted two prize brigs and two captured schooners. The only other ships of war were "a sloop belonging to Aury . . . armed with four carronades and about 30 men in the crew," and "a privateer from New Orleans . . . armed with 10 guns and 70 men."[19]

On March 30, Laffite met with Miña and learned he planned to land troops at Soto de la Marina. He later talked to Aury and found that the two insurgent leaders were at odds. But by April 7, the two agreed upon a plan of action and left the island.[20]

The following day, "seeing that the port was left abandoned by Aury," Laffite took command of Galveston, appointed officers, and "established the administration under his direction." He concluded his account by declaring that on April 18 he "set sail for New Orleans."[21]

During his brief stay on the island, he made note of the base's financial undergirding: the confiscation of ships carrying slaves. He reported two schooners, "laden with negroes . . . captured by an American privateer with the flag of Buenos Ayres," arrived in the harbor.[22]

Jean Laffite had found an island.

There would yet be another Barataria.

CHAPTER 20

Immune from Attack

In 1817, Galveston resembled Grande Terre.

A seaward island on the Gulf, it could be accessed from areas where there was demand for duty-free goods. At the time, Galveston possessed one significant advantage: It was beyond the reach of American gunboats in a country in political turmoil.

The two islands had at least three significant similarities.

Both were seaward islands and shared the same approximate latitude.

Both served as protective barriers for large inland bays that in the early nineteenth century could provide secure harborage for seagoing vessels.

Both could be readily accessed from the sea and were conducive to the craft of the smuggler.

Galveston was larger than its Louisiana counterpart, stretching nearly twenty-eight miles along the Texas coast. The island was inhabited much of the year by Karankawa Indians who sought security further inland during the hurricane season and returned at regular intervals to claim sea life off its shores.[1]

Aury had arrived in Galveston on September 1, 1816,[2] where he was later joined by Miña and Perry. While the schemers planned their conquest of Mexico, the colony was supported through sea raiding.

Although Aury had only a limited outlet for the merchandising of captured goods, he had discovered one form of trade that brought immediate profits: catering to the demands of Louisiana planters who were willing to pay high prices for smuggled black laborers.[3]

Laffite managed to be conveniently available when Miña's invasion force left Galveston. He had gained Aury's confidence promising to maintain order on the island until his return.

But this was not the report he gave the Spanish consul in New Orleans. Once Aury and Miña had cleared the island, Laffite hurried back to Louisiana to convince both Father Sedella and Fatio that he was acting in the best interests of Spain.

In the operations proposal the two brothers presented to their Spanish employers in May, Jean promised to return "to Galveston to inform himself concerning the privateers and prizes that will be there up to the end of June." He assured Fatio of his continued efforts at espionage: he would be "making weekly reports of whatever happens, and a schooner will also be sent to Soto de la Marina to gather likewise all news of Miña's landing."[4]

A few days after the meeting, Jean Laffite returned to Galveston. This time, he took control. He had surmised that the Miña-Aury invasion would end in failure and that there was little chance any of the insurgents would return to the coast. He was only partially correct. Aury would return, but his military associates would not.

Col. Henry Perry led his followers into south Texas where they were overtaken and surrounded by Royalist troops. Rather than face death before a firing squad, he took his own life.

Miña was only slightly more successful. He managed to capture Soto de la Marina, but was quickly overwhelmed by Spanish forces and executed.[5]

But before either of the insurgent military commanders had met their fate, Laffite was master of Galveston. Among the remnants of Aury's followers who had chosen not to join the ill-fated invasion, there were some who once had been on Grande Terre.[6]

There were others who had come to the island with Aury. One of these was James Campbell, a naval veteran who had seen duty on both the American warships *Constitution* and *Constellation* and had served as a sailor in the War of 1812 under Commodore Perry. Claiming an honorable discharge from the United States Navy, he became a privateer "in the Columbian service."[7]

In New Orleans, he met both Aury and Miña and "agreed to sail with them . . . for Galveston" where he became "attached to Lafitte and Lafitte with him." On his first cruise under the island's new commander, Campbell took five prizes valued at $100,000 "in cask and the same amount in dry goods." An effective raider, he brought into the harbor "dry goods – plate, silver and gold watches." A staunch supporter of Laffite, he assisted him in disciplining a potential rebel named Marott.[8]

By April, immediately after Aury's departure, Laffite had gained complete control of Galveston. He accomplished this by enlisting subordinates who were loyal only to him.[9] These trusted lieutenants maintained order during his trip back to New Orleans.[10]

Upon his return in May, Laffite perfected his organization of the island. At no point in his career was his managerial ability more apparent.

Privateering vessels continued to dock. Among them there was a prize schooner and a ship sent to Galveston by Renato Beluche. Others entered the harbor: a sloop "consigned to Mr. Champlin" and a privateer commanded by Captain Baptista.[11]

The rude huts that had been abandoned by the followers of Miña and Perry were replaced with stable, one-story buildings constructed by sinking posts into the island's shifting sands. Later, as refugees from other freebooter communities came to Galveston, boarding houses were built. An early nineteenth century account declared that under Laffite's management, "a village sprang up – more than 200 houses – stores, hotels, billiard-tables – and all in perfect order and subordination."[12]

The island became an efficient sea-raiding community. When ships that had sailed from Galveston under Aury's commissions returned to the port, the former Baratarian chief perfunctorily appraised their cargoes and sent them to their destinations under his personal authority.[13]

Laffite reported to New Orleans soon after his return that he had "the intention of reestablishing a new government in Galveston." This administrative task was consuming all of his time: "Mo-

95

ments are precious," he wrote, "and there is no time to lose. What we might be able to finish in two or three months might perhaps cost us six."[14]

Although Laffite still claimed that his control of the base was but a temporary measure, it soon became apparent he was building a long-term operation. In July 1817, Jean wrote Pierre: "Up to now I have had all the success I could wish for in relation to our enterprise, which I promise you not to abandon until it is quite finished . . . I will keep it even though I lose my life."[15]

Three months after Laffite became the master of Galveston, Beverly Chew wrote William Crawford, United States secretary of the treasury, that the raiders at "Galveztown were getting stronger all the time . . . a motley mixture of freebooters and smugglers . . . under the Mexican flag [which was] a reestablishment of the Barataria band." He bemoaned the fact that they were "removed somewhat more out of the reach of justice."[16]

Even the merchants of New Orleans were suspicious of the new Barataria. Too far away to benefit them with a wholesale infusion of duty-free goods, and fearful that continued sea raiding on the Gulf could adversely affect the flow of basic supplies into the city, a protest was made on July 28, 1817, to Laffite's old nemesis, Commodore Patterson: "Vessels carrying the flags of the several new republicks," the document stated, "pretending to have commissions from the constituted authorities there," were infesting the Gulf manned with "renegado crews of all nations."[17]

In spite of the protest, there was little the commodore could do. In the year 1817, Jean Laffite was beyond the reach of the American navy.

In the meantime, he continued his organizational task. Although raiders sailing from Galveston still flew the flag of Mexico, there was no longer a pretense that this was a center for revolutionary activity. Laffite had come to the island under the authority of the Spanish Crown and was determined to do as little as possible to antagonize the captain general in Cuba. He continued to play the Machiavellian role: He would seek to appease Spain and, at the same time, hope for immunity from the navy of the United States.

Aury made an effort to regain control.

During the summer of 1817, he returned to Galveston. By

96

then, Laffite had gained absolute mastery. Those who had remained after the departure of the invasion force were no revolutionaries. These were men who had but one interest, that of engaging in the ancient craft of sea raiding for profit. Aury realized there was no longer a place for him on the island. In July, he left to seek another base.[18]

On October 17, Beverly Chew reported that six armed vessels under Aury's command were in the port of New Orleans. He reiterated his complaints about "the numerous cruisers under the Mexican flag that infest our waters."[19]

But Aury's ships could not remain in the Mississippi port, nor would they return to Galveston. He sailed east, established a base on Amelia Island off the Atlantic coast of Florida, hoisted the Mexican flag, and proclaimed himself military chief. Responding to Chew's observations, the American government continued to monitor Aury's activities.[20]

By late fall 1817, the United States was ready to take action against Aury. A fleet commanded by Commodore J. D. Henley was dispatched to Amelia. On December 20, Henley ordered the raiders to leave. Aury's response was a haughty one. He asked that his words be "laid before the president" insisting that the island had never been a part of the United States.[21] When troops were landed on the beach, he capitulated, and declared that as "Commander-in-Chief" of the "Republick" he would "surrender the island of Amelia."[22]

On January 18, 1818, President Monroe reported to Congress he had expelled Aury's "adventurers from these posts."[23] Although he had destroyed one privateer base, he was not ready to send American forces into Texas, a province that was still claimed by Spain. Later in the month, his forbearance drew criticism in Washington as Congress debated the "suppression of piratical establishments."[24]

For a time, at least, Laffite's operation was immune to attack by the warships of the United States. The chief of Galveston was skillfully playing the declining power of Iberia against the emerging strength of the North American nation.

CHAPTER 21

Suspicion

*I*t was an impressive sight.

From the sea, it appeared even larger than it was: a red building that stood out dramatically against white beaches. As ships approached the harbor, a variety of smaller structures could be seen beyond the scarlet mansion.

By early 1818, contemporary accounts indicated Laffite's sea-raiding community was solidly established on Galveston. J. Randall Jones described the colony as one that consisted of "100 or 200 men . . . of all nations and some few women." He noticed "a number of boats of different sizes" in the harbor. One was "a large schooner . . . laded with Sugar, Cocoa, Coffee and Wines." He was impressed by Laffite: "Six feet in height, proportionally made . . . tolerable fair skin -- his hair dark, a little gray mixed and was a very handsome man." He commented that "I was well treated by him and all his people."[1]

The command headquarters was a substantial two-story building surrounded by a moat-like ditch. Four cannon protruded from within. According to an 1845 map, the structure was located on Galveston's Avenue A at some point between the modern city's Eleventh and Fifteenth streets.[2] This was a site on one of the narrower sections of the island. Landings were made on the bayside.[3] The mansion faced the inland harbor, but could be seen from the open sea.

Because the building was painted a blood red color, it was known as Maison Rouge. Explanations for its scarlet hue range from legends claiming a pact between Laffite and the Devil[4] to suggestions that the building was deliberately marked as a possible target for cannon fire.[5]

Probably the choice of color was made by Laffite. Painted in such a dramatic fashion, it appeared greater in size than it actually was. From the deck of a vessel approaching Galveston, it loomed large against the sandy expanses of the island. On shore, as the slanting rays of the sun fell upon it in late afternoon or caught its bright color in early morning, its very existence symbolized power. The building was well constructed for, according to one record, the unique edifice was still standing thirty years after the abandonment of the privateer base.[6]

Laffite did not live in the impressive red house. He had his own brig, *The Pride,* a captured vessel that seldom put to sea and generally remained anchored on the leeward side of the island.[7] The scarlet mansion was used on special occasions, but its purpose was more symbolic than pragmatic, a statement of authority to all comers, both on shore and upon the Gulf.

Maison Rouge was a significant part of the island chieftain's mystique.

Laffite managed the sea-raiding base from the security of his brig. He personally interviewed all newcomers, requiring each to take an oath of allegiance acknowledging him as supreme commander.[8] There would be no more Gambis to challenge his authority. Exercising his ability both to command and to manipulate, he established Galveston as an efficiently managed commercial enterprise.[9]

The Maison Rouge was used to entertain persons of importance and guests of Laffite. One of those who visited the island was a Dr. Felix Forment. A physician trained at the University of Turin who had once served under Napoleon, he was invited to Galveston to attend a young woman whom he was led to believe was Laffite's daughter. For several weeks, he stayed in the building where he "was treated as a king," receiving many tokens of gratitude. After his patient had recovered, he was assisted in reaching New Orleans where he later continued his career as a physician.[10]

Laffite brought unique leadership skills to the island base. Extant manuscripts give details of his operational procedures. One document was a printed form that originally included blank spaces for sea-raiding data. The blanks had been filled in by hand granting the holder, Juan Desfarges,[11] captain of *Le Brave,* authority to sail as a privateer.

This was further evidence of Laffite's executive acumen. One of the shipping papers included detailed instructions for reentry to the harbor. The ship was to "come in west of the pass, have at her mizzen mast a white flag without any other." Upon approaching the island, the privateer was to "fire one cannon shot to announce its arrival" and proceed only when there was an answer to the signal. Under no pretext was the master of a commissioned sea raider to "make for shore, or to put in, at any other port than that of Galveston."[12]

Thirteen articles were a part of the contractual agreement. One-half of all captured goods were to be given to the shipowner plus a commission of five percent on the gross amount. There would be a deduction of five percent on the net proceeds reverting to the crew. If another vessel should have been captured more suitable for raiding, the corsair could be abandoned, and that vessel would, under terms of the pact, become the full property of the shipowner including implements of war. Provisions were outlined for the crew: an "indemnity of eight hundred dollars" would be paid to a seaman for the loss of "any one of his members." The first seaman to board an enemy ship was to receive one part under the title of reward. Any man who deserted or took property that was not his, or who was guilty of bad conduct, would lose his parts of the prize. The one who first announced the sight of a ship that was declared a good prize and subsequently captured would receive one-half part as a reward. The captain was allotted four parts to be disposed of by him in favor of the officers and sailors who rendered effective service at sea.

The agreement included a listing of the portions of the prize each crew member was to receive in addition to the incentive bonuses. The captain could claim six parts of the booty and other officers would be adjudged lesser portions according to rank. The importance of the ship's cook was recognized. He was to receive one and a half parts of the results of conquest while "the rest of the men of the crew" were each to receive one. Each ship that sailed from Laffite's establishment was to have a contract "executed in duplicate and in good faith" between Laffite and the master of the vessel.[13]

The Galveston community could no longer claim to be a legitimate center for commerce. Throughout his days on Grande Terre, Laffite had insisted he operated within the bounds of the traditional privateer's code. Beluche, Youx, and others of the Baratarian captains held letters of marque from some established political entity. Laffite claimed to have a commission from Cartagena. Neither he, nor any of his captains, were charged with piracy during the days he operated on the Louisiana coast. The pardon granted the Baratarians was based on the assumption that only one criminal indictment, the charge of smuggling, could be leveled against them.

Once Laffite commandeered Galveston Island, he usurped total power and produced his own commissions in the name of a nonexistent nation. No questions were asked about the origin of a vessel brought in under a white flag if the prize contained a rich cargo. The ships of all nations were subject to seizure.

Pierre may have relieved Jean as commander of Galveston on one or more occasions. Stanley Faye concluded from his study of extant documents that the older brother went to the Texas island in June 1817 and, for a brief period, served as base commander,[14] but Pierre's primary contribution was that of maintaining supply lines from New Orleans. One communication from the older brother stated he would "send out another vessel in which we shall ship the cannons, muskets, powder, etc. . . . this shipment will be increased."[15] The lading of another dispatch included a box containing printed privateer commissions, an engraved seal, and a hand stamp.[16]

Although Pierre may have visited Galveston, it was his preference to remain within the bounds of the United States. Late in 1817, he made a trip to Washington. Perhaps he believed he could achieve results in the nation's capital where his younger brother had failed two years earlier. Possibly he could lessen the suspicion that the Galveston enterprise had generated among American officials. He arrived in the city on the Potomac in November and found lodging at an inn called Washington Hall.[17]

Col. Samuel Williams later recalled boarding in the same establishment "kept then by Mr. Butler from Connecticut" where he believed he had talked with the privateer chief. He referred to his fellow guest simply as "Lafitte" implying that it was Jean who had returned to the capital, and who, according to William's own account, "conversed freely . . . and vindicated himself against the charge of piracy." It was not Jean that the colonel encountered at the boarding house. The description of the Laffite Williams met in Washington, "one eye partially shut," would agree with other records of the appearance of the older brother.[18]

But Pierre had business in the nation's capital other than that of defending the Laffite name. While in Washington, he made contact with the Spanish legation. Soon after the Laffites had agreed to enter into the service of Spain, Pierre had received $4,000 from the funds of the "Comision reservada."[19] Fatio had paid Jean $500 for his participation in the espionage operation.[20] As late as November 1818, Don Luis de Onis endorsed a claim for expenses in behalf of the Laffites totaling $18,889.68.[21]

The bill was never paid.

Earlier in the year, Fatio had received orders from Alexandro Ramírez, the intendant in Havana, "to cease all expenditures on account of the secret commission" to the Laffites.[22]

A few months before the record of expenditures was forwarded to Ramírez, Jose Cienfuegos wrote this report regarding the brothers: "The persons . . . indicated by the symbols 13-1 and 13-2, are putting themselves under strong suspicion by their double dealing . . . [for] it is they who maintain the place called Galveston and its privateers."[23]

Pierre failed in his attempt to convince Spanish diplomats in Washington of the genuineness of his allegiance to Spain. By this time, the older brother had received a new code name, Number 19.[24] But in spite of the facade, the Iberian representatives broke off relations with the brothers, and no further funds were advanced for their services.[25]

In the meantime, the younger Laffite was master of Galveston.

While Pierre conversed with Washington officials and Spanish emissaries, Jean ruled a twenty-eight-mile strip of land off the Texas coast.

CHAPTER 22

Blatant Misrepresentation

The Laffites no longer needed the funds sporadically paid by the Spanish Crown.

They had another source of income, one with far greater potential.

By the year 1818, Galveston was a lucrative base for sea raiders. Both brothers profited from the enterprise. The older brother acted not only as his brother's agent, but as his spokesman and defender. On February 6, 1818, an article appeared in print in New Orleans over the name of "Prre Laffite" addressed to the New Orleans Collector of Customs Beverly Chew, who had accused the Laffites of being among those who "most openly violate the laws of this country." The writer commented, "It was not without surprise that I saw my name appear in your letter" that was nothing more than a "foolish and tiresome heap of idle words."[1]

In spite of the customs officer's criticism, Washington would inadvertently aid the Laffites. On April 20, Congress passed a bill entitled "An act in addition to 'an act to prohibit the introduction of slaves into any port or place within the jurisdiction of the United States.'"

One critic of the 1818 law declared that it should have been entitled "An act to promote treachery among smugglers."[2]

The statute included the stipulation that "every ... ship" engaged in the slave trade "shall be forfeited to the United States," and when there was a "forfeiture ... one half thereof [would be claimed by] the United States, and the other half to him or them who shall prosecute the same to effect."[3]

The initial result of this legislation was a reversal of roles. Sea raiding was no longer a criminal act. Any vessel that successfully captured a ship with blacks on board could claim one-half of the market value of the human cargo in the hold of the commandeered vessel. The law's forfeiture clause applied even when slaves were brought in chains to a customs official.

Although some modifications were made to the 1818 law in the years that followed,[4] Laffite's corsairs had a license to prey upon any vessel suspected of engaging in the slave trade.

As the demand for black labor on Louisiana plantations grew, an increasing number of prizes arrived at the makeshift Galveston port. Once it was known that laborers were available for purchase, planters like J. Randall Jones made their way to Laffite's base.[5] Slaves could be purchased in small numbers by individual plantation owners and then transported as personal property to the sites where they would be put to work.

But Laffite's raiders brought more slaves to the island than could be sold to the planters who chose to visit Galveston. Laffite met the problem by inviting enterprising persons to purchase slaves wholesale at a fraction of the eventual retail price in Louisiana or Mississippi. This was entrepreneurship carried to an extreme, of profitability above all else.

By boat, the chained laborers were transported across Galveston Bay to the Bolivar Peninsular where they were marched eastward sixty-five miles overland to Lake Sabine and then ferried into the United States. Once more there was a long trek. On the final leg of the journey, the captives were forced to walk through swamp lands to a point where customs officials could conveniently intercept them.[6]

The slave runners then took advantage of the law. They denounced their charges to a United States marshal or one of his deputies, and then claimed a reward of one-half of the market value of the illicitly imported laborers. The captured blacks would be placed on auction where a representative of the smuggler company, knowing the site and the date of the sale, would purchase the slaves. The slavers could then transport the persons who had become legal property to the plantation that would pay the highest price.

It was a lucrative business. Not only did the smuggler receive a reward for his deceptive services, but often he made a final sale of a male black for as much as $800 to $1,000. The profit was sometimes in excess of ten times the amount of the initial investment.[7]

In addition, this was a system based on blatant misrepresentation, a procedure that demonstrated total disregard for human worth. Blacks experienced severe suffering during the several stages of transport. Many died en route. Only those who survived the vicious circumstances of sea transport and coastal treks reached the plantations of Louisiana.

A contemporary account reported that on one occasion "a motley mixture of freebooters," believed to have been based at Galveston, captured a ship with 300 slaves on board. When it was discovered there was a contagious fever among them, the vessel was cut adrift allowing the imprisoned blacks on board to die lingering deaths.[8]

One of Laffite's slave runners was the fabled James Bowie. Born shortly before the turn of the century in the southern United States,[9] James and his older brother, Resin, were raised in Catahoula Parish and later moved to Rapides in central Louisiana.[10] Resin served three terms in the State Legislature,[11] but James was noted for less peaceful pursuits. He claimed he could mount and ride any creature alive ranging from a wild horse to an alligator. Noted for an unmanageable temper,[12] he was a man of violence who, according to one account, had beheaded and disemboweled three men in a single contest making use of the large knife that he was credited with designing.[13] On another occasion, he was reported to have used his prowess in the legendary battle at Vidalia Sandbar on the Mississippi River as spectators from Natchez watched from nearby steamers.[14]

In 1831, Bowie married the aristocratic Ursula Beramendi, the daughter of a prominent San Antonio family. In order to do so, he promised a dowry to his prospective father-in-law based on land holdings in Arkansas. He had gained his claim to property through funds he had accumulated as a slave runner for Laffite.[15]

105

His death in 1836 as a defender of the Alamo later established him as a revered hero of Texas independence.[16]

But years before he was destined for unmerited immortality, he joined his brother in organizing the transport of slaves from Laffite's base to Louisiana.[17] Contemporary accounts claim that James Bowie and Jean Laffite were often seen together on the island and that the two bore a marked physical resemblance to each other.[18]

Between 1818 and 1820, James and Resin forced hundreds of blacks to take the long trek up Bolivar Peninsular to waiting ferries that carried them into the death-infested swamps of Louisiana. The Bowies then denounced the surviving slaves to the authorities, accepted the reward for having turned them in, bought them back at auction, and proceeded to sell to planters. During one brief period of a few months, Bowie's slave company claimed a profit of $65,000.[19] James Bowie later boasted about his participation in the smuggling enterprise, declaring he had surrendered "imported slaves" to customs officials and finally resold his human merchandise to plantation owners.[20]

La Courrier de la Louisiane, dated May 22, 1818, published an account of a visit to the privateer base. A letter, written a month earlier from Natchitoches by Dr. John Sibley, appeared in the journal: "Lafite, the younger was on the island, with near 100 persons . . . about 10 sail; he had burnt the ship Campeachy and some smaller prizes." The correspondent had been impressed with the merchandise he had observed during his visit: "A brig was brought in, a prize . . . with a valuable cargo . . . of wine, rum, velvet, soldier's clothing." Sibley had gone to Galveston to purchase slaves. He commented that "one of the privateers had taken a ship with 300 negroes."[21]

Some of the saleable goods were destined for markets much further inland than New Orleans. One ship left Galveston with a cargo assigned to St. Louis, Missouri. The vessel's inventory listed the following: "Twenty slaves, mulattoes, as follows: Ten of age mature have good teeth: males speak French. Ten young adults with teeth: women speak French. Plus five nurslings." Other items on board included "two hundred butcher knives . . . silk ropes . . . steel and flints . . . three hundred muskets, three hundred pounds powder, five hundred blankets . . . molds for casting balls, four casks wine . . . two hundred pounds tobacco, three hundred shirts, five hundred pounds dry sugar." [22]

The sandy beaches of Galveston Island had become a commercial center that supplied both labor and merchandise for the southern United States. But in spite of increasing economic success, Laffite's emporium of the Gulf faced serious problems.

Sibley's account made reference to the fact that settlers in Texas along the coast were "greatly distressed by the Indians." [23]

Initially Laffite maintained friendly contacts with the Karankawa tribesmen who fished along the island's shores. Another record noted that the "red men loitered about the Corsair" community,[24] and that the privateer chieftain allowed them free access to his headquarters. He would "often twit the tribesmen . . . who haunted the Maison Rouge." [25]

Good relations between privateer and native ended when an Indian woman was kidnapped. The Karankawas retaliated by attacking the base and killing five members of the colony. In the battle that followed, artillery was trained upon the angry braves.[26] The Indians fought stubbornly against superior weaponry, but Laffite's cannoneers gunned down most of the male members of the tribe.[27]

There is no record of how many women became sexual hostages of the raucous members of the colony following the slaughter of their men.

Having decimated the Karankawas, Laffite found himself faced with another threat, a force that could not be contained by artillery. The hurricane season of 1818 produced a gale that swept in from the Gulf to reek havoc on Galveston's unprotected harbor and beaches.

A contemporary recorded the event: "The storm was from the eastward . . . [and] occurred about the middle of September . . . Galveston Island . . . was all covered by water except about one acre where Lafitte's fort was on the Bay." [28]

Four vessels anchored in the harbor were wrecked and most of the buildings of the community were damaged.[29] The upper floor of the Maison Rouge collapsed under the weight of the cannon positioned within the structure, causing death and injury to several of the women who had taken refuge from the hurricane.[30] Only a half dozen dwellings remained habitable.[31]

Laffite maintained control, managed rescue efforts, and su-

107

pervised repairs.[32] His ability to act decisively in a crisis resulted in a temporary restoration of his pirate kingdom.[33]

But the winds of the Gulf and the threat of native invasion were not the only forces that threatened the colony. By 1818, the United States navy was warily cruising off the Texas coast. In August, George Graham arrived at the island harbor representing the government in Washington.[34] His mission was that of inquiring "by which authority" Galveston had been occupied.

Laffite received Graham, entertained him, and insisted that he had permission from Mexico to be on the island. He reiterated this statement in a letter dated August 28 and another document that he forwarded to the American envoy a month later.[35]

Graham later described his interview with Laffite to his superior, the secretary of state. He reported the Galveston commander's claim: that "he had commissions for his privateers from the Mexican Congress." It was Graham's belief that "they were like Aury's commissions." Both he and Secretary Adams were of the opinion the United States should take "immediate possession of Galveston."[36]

As the Washington officials suspected, Laffite's defense of his claim was a flimsy one. He knew this. He also knew American ships would return, and there would be further inquiries as to his right to occupy the island.

In the meantime, he would conduct business as usual.

Vessels continued to enter the harbor bringing with them cargoes of saleable merchandise as Laffite's sea raiders prowled the Gulf. Once at sea, a corsair captain sailing from Galveston would have few scruples about capturing any ship that carried within its hold any object or any person that could be sold for a profit.

In spite of storm and threats, the harbor on the coast of Texas had become one of the most efficient sea-raiding organizations since the zenith of the pirate nation of Madagascar.[37] It was a center for piracy, and Jean Laffite was its chief executive officer.

One of the women who lived on the island later penned her recollections. Her husband, James Campbell, had brought her to Galveston in 1817 where she lived for nearly three years.[38] She felt secure in the colony, for Laffite had declared that anyone who molested a married woman would be hanged.[39] She described the camp as one that consisted of 100 houses with a mixed population of different nationalities. She was impressed by the man who headed the sea-raiding base, describing him as "about 40 years old, dark complexioned, handsome, over six feet tall . . . strongly built, black hair, side-whiskers, hazel eyes." But it was not his physical appearance that made the greatest impact upon her, but rather his ability to maintain control. She marveled at the fact he "never wore a uniform nor weapons except once when he expected an attack by a rebellious officer."[40]

By the end of the year 1818, Laffite had reached the peak of a career based on deception. He had used his unique talents to manipulate the powerful and take advantage of the powerless.

A pirate kingdom stood upon the shifting sands of a seaward island. This he had maintained against hostile attack, the violence of a hurricane, and the threats of a powerful nation.

CHAPTER 23

A Balancing Act

L ight lingered in the western sky.

Before darkness fell, a two-masted vessel's sails were sighted to the southeast of Galveston. At sunrise, watchers on the island could make out the square rigging of a United States brig-of-war.

A boat was prepared to investigate the intruder. The vessel was the USS *Enterprise* commanded by Lt. Larry Kearny. One of the members of the crew, a young officer serving under Kearny, would later recall the events of that day.[1]

Kearny was under orders from Commodore Patterson to seek out Jean Laffite and confer with him in behalf of the government of the United States. Having arrived late one evening in the "latitude of Galveston bay," the brig's lookout sighted the "low lands of Galveston." The vessel anchored overnight.[2]

On the following morning, the crew made ready the captain's gig. Kearny and his aides boarded the boat. Upon nearing shore, they saw "a barge full of men rowing toward us" who were "well armed." It was expedient to declare the purpose of the visit. Asking for Laffite, Kearny's men were directed toward a brig, a vessel of 200 tons with sixteen guns, "ready for sea." When the landing party hailed the ship, they were told to proceed to a schooner nearby.[3]

At last, the seamen came face to face with the chief of Galveston. This was a meeting the young officer would not forget. He was surprised to find Laffite a "rather gentlemanly personage . . . dressed simply . . . [yet] rather impressive . . . exceedingly courteous." Inviting his guests below deck, he proceeded to lavish on them "all the luxuries of life — real chateau, burgundy, West India preserves and real havanas . . . the spoils of all nations."[4]

Later, the visitors enjoyed a meal of "good stew, dried fish, and wild turkey,"[5] followed by "Caffe," served properly by the ship's steward. This was but a prelude to an evening of congeniality and stimulating conservation.[6]

One person on board made an indelible impression on Kearny's aide: a quadroon beauty he described as a "lady — one of the most glorious specimens of the brunette ever dreamed of. A full and voluptuous form of faultless outline — beautiful features, and sleepy black eyes." At one point the woman, obviously a mistress of Jean Laffite, was "flirting dreadfully with our Mid." She left suddenly after the island chieftain dispatched her with "one single look of that black eye directed toward her."[7]

Their host was one who had "a talent for conversation,"[8] and who assured the representatives of the American navy he was not a pirate.[9] The evening ended on a congenial note. The visitors made their "adieu to the gallant rover" in order to return to the *Enterprise.*[10]

Although the flamboyant style of the account would bring into question some of the details, it is a firsthand record. But Kearny's landing on Galveston had a much more serious purpose than that of repartee with an able conversationalist. He had been instructed to make it clear the United States government wanted Laffite and his slave runners off the island. The author of the account recalled that Laffite promised to quit the Texas coast. "I am ready to leave," he told Kearny. "I am friendly with your country, Captain. I know New Orleans well."[11]

But Laffite gave no precise date for his departure. It would take more than a gentlemanly dinner party to send him away from the Texas coast as long as the Galveston base remained lucrative.

There were others who visited the island.

In early 1818, a group of Frenchmen landed at Laffite's port using the harbor as a point of entry for settlement. Moving northward along the Trinity River, 120 settlers established a base at Atascosito near the present-day town of Liberty, Texas.[12] The leader of the colony, Charles Lallemand, an expatriate of France who had fled his homeland after Napoleon's exile, sought Laffite's assistance believing him to be a fellow native of France. Both the United States[13] and Spain objected, fearing that the colony could be used for the extension of French colonialism.[14]

On February 17, Pierre had written to Jean that Lallemand intended to found a colony "this summer on the Trinity River. His intentions and those of his compatriots are to seize the province of Texas and . . . as soon as he has got enough men he will extend his frontiers farther." In spite of his suspicions, Pierre advised Jean to offer Lallemand his services and "be useful to him in every possible way." This communication, along with other papers including a sealed box of documents, would be carried to Galveston on board the brig, *New Enterprise.*[15]

When Lallemand's settlers did arrive, they were an embarrassment to Laffite. Although a colony of 1,500 had been projected, no more than 400 reached Texas. But those who did pass through the Galveston port were doomed from the outset. Laffite reported Lallemand's plans to Spanish authorities even before the first contingent of colonists arrived.[16] The two brothers still sought to maintain the facade of intelligence-gatherers for Spain, fearing that support of any new European colony would jeopardize the Galveston base.

Once aware of the French invasion, the Spanish governor of Mexico sent troops toward the Trinity River. Some of Lallemand's settlers had already perished from disease or conflict with natives. A remnant fled to Galveston, where the survivors found temporary refuge in the sea-raiding colony.[17]

Pierre's February 17 communication mentioned that General Humbert would be on board the dispatch ship. The brothers had known Humbert in New Orleans. He went to Galveston under the illusion he could succeed where Miña and Perry had failed. The letter repeated Lallemand's evaluation of Humbert: one possessed of "a mad and deranged mind." Pierre tempered this statement by declaring: "I know well enough that sometimes he has spells . . . set him at work at whatever turns up."[18] Humbert reached Galveston, but he posed no threat to either Spanish or American interests.

Others sought land between the Sabine River and the Rio Grande.

In the spring of 1819, an invasion of Texas was organized under the leadership of James Long. Seven years earlier, Augustus W. Magee led a band of adventurers beyond the Sabine in an effort to claim northern Mexico for Anglo-America. Magee's "Republican Army" formed at Natchitoches, Louisiana, marched into Texas, and established a base at Nacogdoches before moving into South Texas. His death and the superior forces that the Spanish amassed against his volunteer army ended the invasion in mid-1813.[19]

Long attempted to accomplish what Magee had failed to do: establish an independent nation west of the Sabine. Having served as a surgeon under Andrew Jackson during the war with Britain, he became the elected leader of a band of would-be settlers.[20] Resenting the fact that President Adams had signed an agreement with Spain in which the United States had withdrawn all claims to Texas, Long sought to grasp the territory by force.[21]

On June 6, 1819, Long followed Magee's footsteps to Nacogdoches. There he proclaimed the establishment of an independent government.[22] Like Magee, he had expected to gain the support of Mexican revolutionaries.[23] When it became apparent there would be no assistance from this source, he asked for help from the one person who might provide him with arms and munitions: Jean Laffite.

Long had reason to believe Laffite would aid his cause. A letter dated July 7, Galveston, to the insurgent leader, acknowledged receipt of a communication from Nacogdoches, and declared: "I never intend to abandon . . . the emancipation of the Mexican provinces."[24]

Although he offered abstract encouragement, Laffite would converse with Long only if the insurgent came to Galveston. Long accepted this reply as an invitation.[25]

The two men met and spoke of mutual support.

Laffite once again played the Machiavellian role. He assured Long of his friendship and addressed him as "General" and "President of the supreme council and commander in chief."[26] He entertained him as though he were an honored head of state.

In turn, Laffite accepted a commission from Long wherein the island chieftain was acknowledged as governor of Galveston.[27] On October 9, Laffite declared his colony a part of the "Republic of Texas" and "a port of entry."[28]

In this, he outdid himself in duplicity. Even as Laffite was exchanging courtesies with Long, he was in correspondence with Spanish authorities. He wrote the governor of Cuba that "he who called himself General Long had found refuge at Galveston with a certain number of Americans." He recommended that "it would be well to dispose of those Gentlemen in one way or another." Laffite later claimed he sent Spain notice of Long's plans as early as October 7 while he was entertaining Long in the Maison Rouge.[29]

While Long enjoyed Laffite's hospitality, Royalist troops were on the march.[30] On October 28, Col. Igñacio Perez entered Nacogdoches. By this time, most of Long's followers had fled to safety beyond the Sabine.[31] Long's wife, Jane, who had followed her husband into Texas, was among those who managed to escape.[32]

Laffite had reason to fear Spain. Only a few months later, Antonio Martínez, Spanish governor of Texas, conferred with his military commandant at La Bahia about reinforcements that might deal directly with "the pirate Lafitte."[33]

The betrayal of Long was designed to buy time for the Galveston base. But neither Laffite nor the Spaniards were rid of either James Long or his intrepid spouse, Jane. In April of 1820, the Longs returned to Texas and took up residence across the bay from Laffite at Point Bolivar. *Niles' Weekly Register* reported the renewed efforts at insurgency in the fall of 1820, commenting that the Longs were in an area where "Carrion crow Indians . . . devour all their prisoners."[34]

Long now numbered among his following a small but determined band of revolutionaries: Ben Milam, Jose Felix Trespalacios, and Jose Bernardo Gutiérrez de Lara.[35] Warren D. C. Hall, who had participated in the Magee expedition and had supported Long's initial effort to capture Texas, was present at Bolivar. According to one account, when Laffite learned that Jane Long had accompanied her husband to the peninsular, he invited both to dinner on board his schooner. Long had come to distrust the island commander and refused to accept the invitation. Jane would not be deterred. Accompanied by Warren Hall,

114

she crossed the bay to Galveston to accept the hospitality of a man who was considered a wily pirate chieftain.[36]

In September 1821, Long sailed for the mainland in another attempt to grasp Texas from Spain. He captured La Bahia, but eventually was forced to surrender to Spanish troops. The success of the Mexican revolution saved him from execution, but before he could return to his wife in Texas, he met death in Mexico City under mysterious circumstances.[37]

Jane Long continued her residence on Point Bolivar even after the news of her husband's capture. The garrison Long had left at Point Bolivar deserted the fort. Jane refused to leave. She maintained herself on the isolated peninsular by shooting birds for food and fishing the waters of the bay. During this time, she gave birth to a child. In later years, she joined Austin's colony and operated a tavern in Brazoria, including among her guests the first two presidents of the Republic of Texas, Sam Houston and Mirabeau Lamar.[38]

Laffite was aware he could only maintain his island establishment by appeasing the powerful forces on either side of him.

This he had sought to do through duplicity, an intricate balancing act that he could not continue indefinitely.

CHAPTER 24

A Body Left Dangling

*I*n spite of his ability as a master manipulator, there were forces at work over which Laffite had little control. In late September 1819, an event occurred that would jeopardize his remaining mainland support.

A dozen or more men who had been cruising the Louisiana coast broke into the plantation home of John Lyons. He, his wife, and children were threatened with death. The house was ransacked and family possessions were looted, including linen and wearing apparel. The planter's slaves were herded away. A New Orleans newspaper reported the robbery and printed Lyons' offer of $500 for the return of his human property along with descriptions of the ten slaves.[1] It was believed that the leader of the raiders, a man named either George or William Brown,[2] was a member of Laffite's Galveston colony.

Once it was known there had been a raid against the plantation home of a citizen of the United States, sympathy for Laffite began to erode. There were requests for government intervention from those who had once been his most ardent supporters.

In early November, a cruiser of the American navy appeared off Galveston. At first Laffite was defiant. Insisting he was beyond the bounds of American authority,[3] he sent a communication to the master of the warship, declaring, "I am convinced that you are a cruiser of the navy ordered by your government . . . I have therefore deemed it proper to inquire into the cause of your lying before this port without communicating your intention."[4]

Remembering Patterson's successful attack on Grande Terre, Laffite acted quickly to stave off a landing by American forces on Galveston. He rounded up the men involved in the Lyons incident and took statements from all who would talk. The leader of the raid was led to a gallows erected on the beach at a point visible from the sea. There he was put to death by hanging.

His body was left dangling from the impromptu scaffold for weeks, a symbol of the island commander's determination to deal harshly with any who would harm members of Louisiana's plantation caste.

This action satisfied the commander of the American naval vessel, J. R. Madison of the USS *Lynx*. On November 8, he wrote Laffite: "Your note of yesterday has been received, stating the execution of William Brown." He then added that he was convinced all would be brought to justice who had "committed direct acts of piracy on the citizens of the United States."[5]

Obviously Madison was relieved Laffite had responded with an apparent show of cooperation. The *Lynx*, a six-gun schooner, was no match for any one of the several heavily armed brigs that frequented the island harbor.[6]

But the cruiser's task was not complete. Madison would need some proof of the success of his mission other than the report of the execution. A detail of men went ashore to bring back for trial any others implicated in the raid.[7]

Madison had been invited to visit Galveston, but he sent a ship's officer in his place thanking Laffite for "your kind and polite invitation." He excused himself because "the weather will not permit my leaving the vessels at sea."[8]

The commandant's instructions were carried out. During the shore party's stay on the island, the American navy men reported treatment that was "most friendly, generous and hospitable."[9]

At this point, Laffite acted as the gracious host as well as an enforcer of the law: "Every possible means [was] extended in making the situation of myself and crew agreeable and comfortable," Madison's representative later stated. "Every assistance [was given] in securing their prisoners which had been delivered to me during my stay."[10]

Once the landing party returned to the ship with prisoners, the *Lynx* sailed for New Orleans. On November 24, the *Louisiana Courier* announced: "Yesterday a boat of the United States Schr. Lynx arrived here with four of the men who were concerned in robbing the house of Mr. Lyon *[sic]* in Attakapas, in the month of September last. Part of the robbers" had made their way to Galveston where they had been arrested, "tried and all sentenced to death, by a Court and Jury appointed by Lafitte for that purpose." After the hanging of Brown, the captain of the *Lynx* had demanded that the remaining prisoners be turned over to him. "They were delivered . . . without difficulty."[11]

Niles' nationally read journal printed a similar report. After the execution of Brown, the "remaining pirates who robbed Mr. Lion *[sic]* were taken into custody . . . and are sent to New Orleans for trial."[12]

Laffite had successfully protected his Galveston base from annihilation. He had appeased those who were charged with scrutinizing his enterprise and had gained favorable press both in New Orleans and across the nation.

His artful handling of this situation might have gained renewed support had it not been for the sequence of events that followed.

Before the end of the year 1819, government authorities in New Orleans would have in their possession documentary evidence that Laffite had both sanctioned and encouraged piracy. Acts of violence continued to be reported, many of which were attributed to raiders based at Galveston. In mid-1819, Patterson had decried the increase of attacks on merchant vessels.[13] But there was no proof, certainly nothing other than circumstantial evidence, that Laffite was anything other than a master smuggler.

In December 1819, the proof necessary for prosecution in a court of law was provided by two of Laffite's own men. Jean Desfarges and Robert Johnson had been dispatched to New Orleans to purchase a new schooner. This they did, naming the ship, *Le Brave*. With a crew of sixteen men, less than the usual compliment for a raiding vessel, they were to bring the ship to the island harbor. Hardly had they cleared the Louisiana coast than they sighted a Spanish merchant ship that seemed easy prey. The temptation was too great. Although *Le Brave* was under-manned, Desfarges, acting as master of the ship, ordered an attack on the Spaniard. An American revenue cutter, the *Alabama*, appeared, and after a brief fight, Desfarges was forced to surrender. He and his crew were returned to New Orleans as prisoners charged with the crime of piracy. In addition to an error in timing, the raiders were guilty of another fatal mistake: They allowed the American authorities to capture a copy of the privateer commission issued to them by Jean Laffite.[14]

This was the evidence the courts needed to convict. Members of the crew of *Le Brave* were required to stand trial in the United States District Court of New Orleans. All were sentenced to death.[15] One report stated that Jean Laffite went in person to the river port in an effort to save his henchmen from hanging.[16] This he could not have done. He would have been recognized and imprisoned, for he was as deeply implicated as the men who were on trial. He had issued a commission for sea raiding that, under the laws of the United States, had no legal standing.[17]

There was still sympathy in New Orleans for the plight of the accused pirates. When the prisoners were condemned to death, only the militia could control a citizen protest outside the prison. Temporary reprieves were issued for the convicted sea raiders, and one of them, John Tucker, was pardoned. But by May 1820, all judicial appeals were exhausted. After public indignation had subsided, Desfarges and Johnson were hanged as pirates at the Place d' Armes.[18]

They had been executed for acts committed under the authority of the master of Galveston. The body that had been left dangling on a windswept Texas beach was no proof to the American nation that Jean Laffite was an adequate dispenser of justice.

CHAPTER 25

Sails in the Sunrise

When the taut ropes of hangman's nooses took life from Desfarges and Johnson, the reverberations would be felt all the way to Galveston Island. The final days of Laffite's establishment were near. The executions made it clear his commissions were not valid even in New Orleans.

Pierre found it necessary to distance himself from responsibility for the operation. While the convicted men were awaiting their fate in prison, heated discussion took place in New Orleans about the facts presented in court. Commodore Patterson was quoted as having publicly declared that the "nest of brigands and murderers at Galveston," should be broken up. Pierre Laffite responded to Patterson's statement: His family name had been unfairly "tarnished . . . without any foundation." In a letter dated January 3, 1820, written in New Orleans, he proposed to Patterson as the "Commanding Officer for the New Orleans station," to "offer myself to you willingly, and at my own risk and expense, to clear Galveston, and disband all those which are to be found there."[1]

The American press reflected the public's rejection of the craft of the privateer. In January 1820, *Niles' Weekly Register* declared that "between privateering and piracy . . . we have absolutely lost not less than fifteen or 20,000 seamen since the conclusion of the war with Great Britain."[2]

The privateer, the smuggler, the pirate were, by the year 1820, regarded as one. As Laffite sought to sustain his island domain, the news media continued to monitor his activities. *Niles' Weekly Register* reported in December 1819 that *The Jupiter,* a ship commissioned by Laffite, had returned to Galveston "with a valuable cargo, principally specie. She sailed again on the 1st inst."[3]

James Campbell was one of the captains who commanded corsairs based on the island during the early months of 1820.[4] He remained with Laffite through late spring when it became apparent American intervention could close the port. Campbell later recalled he left the island in midyear believing Laffite would follow. He had agreed "to meet at the Isle of Muger at a particular day."[5] Campbell claimed "instead of sailing direct to the Isle of Muger," he "cruised about Cuba, Vera Cruz, Trinidad, making a few insignificant reprisals." He never saw his commander again, believing rumors that Laffite died soon after the two separated.[6] He eventually gave up seafaring, "lived for a while on the Trinity [River], sold out, went to New Orleans, and from there came to his present residence" that, in 1855, was located on Galveston Bay.[7] After three years as commander of vessels sailing under Laffite's authority, he accepted the more mundane role of a respected citizen and recounter of tales of the sea.[8]

Charles Cronea was one of the men who admitted he had sailed with Campbell. Years later, he remembered Campbell as "Laffite's right hand man." Cronea denied that the crews sailing from Galveston could rightly call themselves privateers because the vessel on which he had sailed often attacked "Mexican shipping most of whom always surrendered quick." In 1820, when his "brig put into Mermenteau, I did run away from her."[9]

During the year, others would desert the colony.

In the spring of 1820, the USS *Enterprise,* under orders from Commodore Patterson, anchored off Galveston. The next morning, Lt. Larry Kearny went ashore with a detachment of men to extract from Laffite a promise to quit the island.[10]

On May 24, 1820, the Galveston commander prepared a letter addressed to the commodore. Jean reiterated the verbal statement he had made to Kearny. This document was carried by the master of the *Enterprise* to his commanding officer as proof he had accomplished his mission. It was like Laffite to treat even his most determined adversaries with the utmost courtesy. In his letter to Patterson, he cordially assured his nemesis that he "will leave" Galveston.[11]

But he used the future tense. He would abandon the island, but he would do so at his own convenience.

By the time Laffite conferred with Kearny, the strength and size of his operation had diminished substantially. The account of the conference, written by Kearny's aide, indicated surprise that the base was so poorly manned. The *Enterprise* captain was quoted as stating: "We supposed your flotilla was larger." Laffite turned the conversation to other matters, "not apparently noticing the remark."[12]

No longer were the Bowie brothers or any of the other trading companies operating from the island. There were no more huge profits to be gained from the capture of slaves. The law of 1818 had been twice revised by Congress tightening the ban on slaving and altering the clause that had made capture at sea profitable.[13] The American navy had increased its efforts at patrolling coastal waters. Both arrests and convictions of those who were guilty of the crime of "procurement" were being reported in the nation's news media.[14]

One account indicated that by the time Kearny visited Galveston, Laffite's colony had been reduced to securing food by hunting wild game and bartering for other essential supplies with settlers on the banks of the Trinity River.[15]

In May 1820, one of Laffite's vessels was captured after having overtaken a Spanish ship. All members of the crew were imprisoned, charged with piracy, and convicted by the United States District Court in New Orleans. The jury recommended mercy for only three of the men, Jacques Lacroix, Michel Lebrequet, and James Roeny, on the grounds "they were deceived in regard to the objects of the cruise." These three received presidential pardons while the others were condemned to death.[16] The news media continued to record arrests and indictments of pirates, some of whom, only a few years earlier, would have been considered legitimate privateers.[17]

Defections from the Galveston base continued. In September 1820, a crew of an armed brig that had sailed from the island mutinied, put their officers ashore, and brought their vessel in, delivering the commissioned ship to the customs officials at Balize.[18]

By the end of 1820, only a score of Laffite's most ardent followers remained with him. Among them were women who had followed him to the Texas coast.[19] The personnel of the once powerful colony of sea raiders had dwindled in numbers until none remained other than close associates and devoted admirers of Jean Laffite.[20]

The time had come to quit Galveston.

As soon as fair weather gave promise the gales that occasionally howled across wintery waters had ended, he would leave. Perhaps he could find another island. Or, if there were no more seaward isles, somewhere there would be a haven.

The final abandonment of Galveston was not the dramatic event some writers have described.[21] There were no longer hundreds of men who could put out to sea on board a large fleet.

One account declared that on the night before the final sailing of the pirate flotilla, there was a nostalgic dinner as men reminisced over a heroic past and then prepared to sail forth to a new adventure.[22] Another even more questionable source described the final departure as one in which "the sky brightened . . . [as] homes were put to the torch and blazed all along the shore . . . looking like a sunset."[23]

It should have been so.

It was not.

Long before the final abandonment of Galveston, the seafaring base had fallen into decay. Early in the year 1821, Jean Laffite was forced to keep his promise to Kearny and Patterson.

As the first taste of spring mingled with the salt air that came fresh from the sea, his schooner tacked beyond the sandy beaches of the island. A coastal breeze filled the sails of the mainmast. The vessel responded to the touch of the helmsman as the foresails pointed into the morning sun.

Charles Cronea returned to Galveston soon afterwards and reported that only a few structures were left on the island. He then added, somewhat pathetically, "Laffite had gone away."[24]

Stephen F. Austin described Texas in the year 1821 as "a howling wilderness."[25]

As the sails of Laffite's schooner disappeared beyond the ocean's rim, even the off-shore islands of Texas had become, once more, a desolate waste of windblown sand.

CHAPTER 26

An Isolated Cove

When Jean Laffite sailed from the Texas coast, he set a course for Cuba.

He could not return to New Orleans for fear of prosecution. No other port in the United States would be a safe haven. St. Dominique had become Haiti and was no longer a base for privateers. Mexico had ended its state of revolution. Cartagena had ceased to issue letters of marque to all comers. If he was to continue in the profession to which he had committed himself, he had but one choice: seeking a site on the island still controlled by Spain.

Contemporary accounts indicated that pirates were active in Cuban waters.[1] A history of seafaring, published in 1825, declared the island had become, by the year 1821, the center for the world's remaining buccaneers.[2]

Laffite had nurtured contacts with Spanish officials. Both he and his brother were in correspondence with authorities in Havana. He spoke the Spanish language. There was no place other than Cuba where there was any chance of establishing another Barataria. At some time during the spring of 1821, he made a landing on the island. Possibly he visited several isolated coves seeking a suitable location for a base.

124

In December 1821, *Niles' Weekly Register* reported the capture of "a piratical vessel." The crew was either killed or wounded "with the exception of the famous Lafitte and three others, who escaped in the boat at the moment of boarding."[3]

On June 1, 1822, *Niles' Weekly Register* reported a new rash of piracy in the West Indies that was attributed to the fact that privateering was "encouraged and protected by certain of the authorities in Cuba, especially by the governor of Holquin." The nationally read journal concluded: "It appears that the famous Lafitte is at the head of some of these parties . . . their business is increasing."[4]

Although it is unlikely that Laffite personally commanded raiding parties, he did, at least for a time, provide a base for those who did.[5]

During the year 1821, he made contact with persons of influence in Cuba, possibly the Spanish authority mentioned in the *Niles'* report. He convinced a Cuban official, it would be to his advantage to grant illicit authorization for the organization of the ex-privateers who had turned to piracy. In return, he could assure his benefactor of rich dividends from sea raiding, some of which could be conveniently added to the local overlord's personal wealth. In addition, Laffite guaranteed a measure of control of those who sailed from the cove. Certain Cuban vessels would not be subject to molestation.

For a brief time, a new Barataria came into being. This was no seaward island. On the Cuban coast, no exorbitant profits could be made from smuggling. But Laffite was once more in his element. He could make no claim, however, that this landlocked Galveston was a base for privateers. Not even quasi-legal letters of marque would be issued.

James Campbell believed his former commander operated during the early 1820s in both the Gulf and the Caribbean. Although his account made no mention of a base in Cuba, Campbell's descriptions of Laffite's activities after the two parted would suggest he maintained a harbor somewhere on the shores of the Spanish island of Cuba.[6]

American journalists continued to monitor the situation in the West Indies. The editor of *Niles' Weekly Register* reported in late June 1822 that an attack had occurred that he attributed to Laffite's leadership: "A schooner manned by seventy men [raided] off Sugar Key (Cuba)." The editor concluded his comments with these words: "The people of Cuba are very indifferent to these things . . . we were always opposed to the privateering system, and have only to wish that those who got it up were the sufferers by it."[7]

As marauders took advantage of the island's irregular coast, at first it appeared that sea raiding from Cuban shores could do little harm to Spanish shipping. Authorities continued a policy of leniency. By the early 1820s, Havana's sugar trade had been replaced with other forms of commerce, shipping that proved enticing to the sea raider. When this trade was threatened, Cuban officials could no longer ignore acts of piracy.[8]

A December 1819 issue of *Niles' Weekly Register* reported "rascally piracies [which] are still committed off the mouths of the Mississippi . . ." and called for "a floating force on the station sufficient to ferret out the villains and bring them to punishment with a strong arm."[9]

A May 1821 edition of *Niles' Weekly Register* denounced both privateering and piracy.[10] In the same month, the weekly journal reported the capture of the *Valiente Guaricuru* by American warships. This was a vessel sailing under a privateering commission. In June, *Niles' Weekly Register* declared that the captain was in prison charged with the crime of piracy.[11]

Throughout 1822 and during the following year, the *Niles' Weekly Register* printed regular reports of sea marauders and the details of the executions of those who had been caught and convicted.[12]

Accounts of violence on the sea lanes continued. In May 1822, the brig *Aurilla* was overtaken by pirates off the coast of Florida. The captain and crew were tortured until they revealed the location of hidden money.[13] Stories of raiding on the high seas came before the public with alarming frequency. One authority estimated that between the years 1815 and 1823, nearly 3,000 piratical attacks occurred in the West Indies.[14]

In August 1822, a merchant ship was seized and the captain and passengers, including several children, were threatened with being burned alive. A lurid account of piracy was published in 1824 by Aaron Smith, a member of the pirate crew responsible for the attack. Smith later escaped punishment by convincing a London jury that he was on board the pirate vessel under duress.

His testimony added momentum to the effort to abolish all privateering.[15] On recounting his adventures, he claimed authorities in Havana had regularly extended hospitality to pirate crews.[16]

By 1822, there were no more havens. Island officials who had once been lenient agreed to ban all forms of sea raiding. Laffite could no longer operate from Cuba.

In late fall, he left the inlet in which he had sought to organize a new Barataria and became a fugitive. A French language newspaper provided the only information on his activities during this period. On November 29, *La Courrier de La Louisiane* announced the wreck of a ship *"sur l'isle de Cube."* Laffite had been on board. He was taken into custody and transported to Port-au-Prince, where he was imprisoned. Laffite had not lost his ability to charm even his jailers. The Louisiana publication remonstrated that, unfortunately *"pour l'humanite,"* the pirate chieftain was allowed to escape from the Haitian prison due to *"personnes influentes de l'endroit."* [17]

The New Orleans-based account concluded with a denouncement of the man who had once been a hero in the city. He was described as *"le pirate, Lafitte, de scelérate reuommee,"* one who was to be wickedly remembered, *"le monstre,"* who had avoided for the hundredth time the sword of justice.[18]

Jean Laffite was a hunted man. After his escape, he may have returned to an isolated cove on the coast of Cuba. Perhaps it was one other than that in which he had sought to establish a pirate base. But Cuba was no longer a sanctuary. His only choice was that of seeking another island.

Charles Gayarre believed Laffite may have sailed as far as Buenos Aires in search of a secure haven.[19] One unreliable source claimed he took up residence in Charleston, South Carolina.[20] Another report from a contemporary who called himself a "Portuguese sailor," claimed he met Laffite in Charleston where the former pirate chieftain purchased a vessel in order to sail to the "Island of Mugeres *[sic]*." The seaman declared he followed Laffite to Yucatan.[21]

If Laffite was in Charleston in 1823, his stay would have been brief. He may have gone to the Atlantic port to purchase a schooner to make his escape possible. Gaining possession of a seaworthy vessel would have required all his remaining financial resources. At some time during 1823, Jean found sanctuary on the eastern coast of Yucatan.

War continued to be waged against piracy in the West Indies. Pirates were even blamed for the loss of ships destroyed by heavy storms at sea. When the daughter of Aaron Burr, Theodosa, was reported missing after a coasting vessel went down off Hatteras, many were convinced that she and the other passengers on board had died at the hands of sea marauders.[22]

Tales of violence continued to reach the United States. In 1824, the brig, *Betsey*, sailed from a New England port. The vessel ran into severe weather and began to flounder. The captain and the crew were able to gain the security of a small island and were soon picked up by a schooner. The rescue ship was overtaken by pirates and, according to the narrator, all on board were "tortured with knives across our throats." The master of the vessel was beheaded.[23]

In the same year, the schooner, *Mary*, was boarded by sea raiders. Only one survivor lived to tell of torture and death. According to the account published in 1825, one sailor was "strung up to the yard arm," the captain's arms were cut off, he was burned to death, and the other members of the crew were killed.[24]

Even before the garish details of the attacks upon the *Mary* and the crew of the *Betsey* were known to readers in the United States, the navy had resolved to put an end to sea raiding in the waters south of the nation's coasts. On January 16, 1823, Commodore Porter sailed from Baltimore commissioned to suppress "piracy on the coast of Cuba."[25] He commanded a powerful naval force. His flagship was the first steam war vessel to go into service. He soon had seventeen ships of the line in the West Indies along with twenty oared barges capable of following suspected pirates into shallow coastal waters.[26] Among his officers was a Lt. Larry Kearny, who was credited with the capture of "a piratical station in Cuba."[27]

The British supported the campaign. In February 1823, the admiralty reported the capture of ten pirates who were tried and executed in Kingston, Jamaica.[28]

In 1825, the United States frigate, *Constellation*, was ordered to join the task force commissioned to combat piracy. One of the most powerful ships of the day, the *Constellation* carried thirty-eight guns and boasted a broadside weight of 396 pounds with a crew of over 300 men. The warship's history was as illustrious as that of the sister ship, the *Constitution*, having defeated the heavily armed French ship, *L'Insurgente,* in 1799. Both later participated in the War with the Barbary States.[29]

In 1824, the editor of the *Niles' Weekly Register* reported that acts of piracy in the West Indian seas were rare, but noted that some did continue.[30] Late in 1825, the United States secretary of the navy declared that "the situation was well in hand."[31] Within a few months, piracy in the waters of the Gulf and the Caribbean was at an end. The *Constellation* returned to her home port after less than two years of service.[32] With the joint efforts of both British and American naval forces and the tacit cooperation of Spanish and Cuban officials, few places remained for Laffite's cohorts. One authority summed it up succinctly: "By 1825, the day of the buccaneer was over."[33]

An account that claimed to be based on a "faded clipping taken from a Baltimore newspaper printed in 1823" declared that Laffite had been killed in an engagement between a vessel under his command and a British sloop of war.[34] Charles Ellms' 1837 work enlarged upon this report and described in lurid detail how the pirate chieftain was "determined to sell his life as dearly as possible" fighting on "deep with blood and gore" even after he was disabled.[35] An engraving in Ellms' work showed Laffite after he had fallen to the deck of his ship. A black flag with skull and crossbones flew overhead, and even in the midst of cannon fire, raised weapons, and cocked pistols, a large-bosomed woman stood above the downed pirate with outstretched arms in an effort to protect him.[36]

Perhaps that was the way a legendary pirate commander should have died.

It was not.

By this time, Laffite had found another haven.[37]

CHAPTER 27

The Last Island

*J*ean Laffite's refuge was an island near the northeastern tip of the Yucatan peninsular. A seaward island facing the restlessness of open water, it sheltered a placid bay beyond which there was a tropical mainland.

The first Spanish explorers gave it the intriguing name of La Isla de las Mujeres. Legend claimed it was a site where mistresses of buccaneers were maintained. But, the Isle of the Women was named for a more prosaic reason: Early visitors found clay molded into shapes that resembled the human female form, objects that once had been part of Mayan religious rites.

In pre-conquest days, a small temple stood on the island. There the feminine deity, Ix Chel, was worshipped. Because the goddess was considered a provider of health, women sought her blessings as they prepared for childbirth. Her priests would mask themselves behind the pottery images to hear petitions.[1]

J. L. Stephens visited Mujeres in the fourth decade of the nineteenth century seeking information about Laffite's final days.[2] Another voyager described the island as it appeared at the time as a "little sand-covered outcrop of limestone . . . only about five miles long by one mile across . . . covered with dense low scrub."[3] He commented that he had observed the ruins of a Mayan center of worship on the island.[4]

When the devotees of the goddess no longer frequented the Isle, it was inhabited largely by fishermen, who in the late twentieth century were replaced by caterers to an extensive tourist industry. Today Mujeres is still touted for its beaches of fine sand and ideal climatic conditions. Even the sharks in its underwater grottoes are said to be lethargic and harmless.[5]

Laffite found sanctuary on the island. With powerful naval forces patrolling West Indian waters, he gave little thought to the reestablishment of a sea-raiding base.

The island's most important feature was that of easy access to the mainland. Once on shore, a fugitive could disappear into jungles dense enough for the ruins of lost civilizations to have gone undetected for centuries.

He and his associates survived on seafood supplemented by supplies from the nearby mainland. Stephens reported that Laffite lived among the island's inhabitants, one of whom commented, "whether it was true what people said of him, he never hurt the poor fishermen."[6]

But male companions were not his only associates during his final years. Laffite's "widow, a señora del Norte from Mobile," was still alive and was "living in great distress at Silan." Stephens made an effort to contact the former mistress but failed to do so.[7]

Probably she had lived for a time on the island. There were others who had succumbed to Laffite's charms, either on Mujeres or in the inland villages. Although the Isle of the Women was apparently named for the clay forms found by early explorers, possibly his ability to enthrall women lent some credence to the legend that the island's name had yet another origin.

There would be no reuniting of the two brothers. Once the Galveston base was abandoned, Pierre also became a fugitive. James Campbell had agreed to meet Jean on Mujeres. Very possibly the two brothers had decided upon the island as a safe haven.[8] There are other elusive accounts of Pierre's final days, one claiming he was in Louisiana in 1830.[9] An even more questionable source claimed he was a resident of St. Louis, Missouri, in 1837.[10] Quite possibly, Pierre attempted to join his brother on the Yucatan coast and died there in November 1821.[11] But there is no evidence that the reunion actually took place.

It was on Mujeres that Jean would live out his final days.[12]

At times, he kept an eye on the open sea, knowing that pursuit could come making it necessary for him to flee to the jungle.

Life on the island was simple. No more could he enjoy fine wines or gourmet dishes. He had few of the amenities of the life he had once enjoyed in New Orleans or the luxuries he had caused to be transported to Galveston.

Wind-driven sea spray, intermingled with warm sun upon white beaches, may have brought purging to his being. But he felt little need for atonement.

He had acted in keeping with a centuries-old heritage, one that accepted violence as a means of maintaining a narrowly defined cultural system. He had brought enjoyment and delight to the lady New Orleans in her time of difficulty. He had supplied her with goods and pleasantries. Twice he had been a hero: once as a smuggler providing wanted services; once as an aide to a man who was destined to gain the presidency of the United States.

He would not have counted himself a person prone to cruelty. He had killed and caused others to kill. He had encouraged vicious deeds and had profited from the evil of others, but he would have maintained a battlefield mentality, considering his actions necessary to his profession.

Certainly his greatest crimes were those that brought severe suffering to the persons he forced into slavery. Many died en route to the sites of abject servitude. If he thought at all about these acts, he would have rationalized his career as one that supported the economic system of which he was a part.

Perhaps, on some rare occasion, he thought of what might have been. His capabilities included a unique talent for leadership. He had within his complex personality the traits of both the statesman and the diplomat. If he had but chosen a different course, he could have risen to a position of respected honor. He had the potential of becoming a peer of those with whom he had associated: a Grymes, a Beluche, or even an Andrew Jackson.

Death came to Jean Laffite either in the year 1826 or 1827.[13]

He did not die alone. Both the testimony of the Portuguese sailor and the information gained by Stephens indicated that he died in the presence of companions.[14] Perhaps this in itself was some consolation, for, above all else, he was a social being.

Even before Stephens visited Yucatan, Mirabeau Lamar had sought information about the final days of Jean Laffite. S. Rhoads Fisher replied to an inquiry by Lamar in a letter dated February 26, 1838. During the previous summer, Fisher had been a passenger on an American schooner that stopped for water at the "'Island of Muger–' off the Coast of Yucatan." He had talked with a turtle fisherman named Gregorio who had known Laffite and who "spoke of him in high terms," and had helped bury the pirate chieftain after he had died of a fever. Fisher at first reported to Lamar only what he could recall from memory believing the burial site was "a small village on the main . . . Teljas." [15]

Fisher wrote Lamar on May 1 that, "in overhauling my papers, I find the following . . . Lafite died at Lasbocas 59 leagues from Campeche on the North Coast of Yucatan about eleven years since, and was buried at Salam [sic], two leagues from Lasbocas." [16]

Four years after Fisher sent Lamar his corrected information, Stephens visited Mujeres and made an effort to determine the location of Laffite's grave. Assuming that the death had taken place on the island, he sought the help of the local padre who could find no record of the burial. What Stephens learned about the woman who had lived in Silan would confirm the information given Lamar in Fisher's letter written in May 1838. [17]

The statements of the Portuguese sailor would lend additional credence to this account. He reported that Laffite died in "the Indian village of Celan [sic]," and that he recalled seeing the "remains of his beloved commander interred in the Campo Santo of Merida." [18]

Jean Laffite's body was buried in an unmarked grave. Those who attended him in his last moments had reason to fear that should the site be discovered either by his enemies or by curiosity seekers, it would be desecrated. The exact location of the interment will never be known.

When near death, Laffite sought assistance in reaching Silan. His burial took place at an unknown site either near the village or in the vicinity of the provincial capital of Merida.

He who had yearned for the sea and had profited from the restless waters of the ocean was forced to go inland to find refuge. His refuge would be death. His grave would carry no marker. His demise, like his birth, would remain shrouded in mystery.

It was as he would have wished it to be. Without the element of the mysterious, there would have been but little legend to accumulate around the name, Jean Laffite.

The Isle of the Women was his last island, but his mystique was destined to linger through the ages.

EPILOGUE

The Lure of the Sea

*T*here is a relentlessness about the river.

Gathering its strength from countless tributaries, the Mississippi rolls steadily toward the Gulf to the place where the lady New Orleans claims a portion of the soil that, centuries before, was drained from the continent's heartland. There the stream forms a croissant-shaped arch around her environs before it continues through its own delta into the waters of the ocean.

Like the river, there is a relentlessness about the legend that has formed around the name of Jean Laffite. Even in his own lifetime, the epos was already in place. There is reason to believe he willed this to be. His inconsistent statements concerning his own origin and the obscurity of many of his actions added impact to the legend.

He was one who came from nowhere and disappeared into nothingness. At least so it seemed to many of his contemporaries and to most of those who later attempted to record the enigma of his life.

He chose to be a person of mystery. Perhaps, in his final days, he took satisfaction in the knowledge that the tales that would be told about him would far outstrip his actual deeds.

135

There are many facets to the legend.

Grande Terre, Galveston Island, and the shores of both Texas and Louisiana have been fertile ground for the production of Laffite tales. Some stories are based on artifacts. Cannonballs have been preserved that were supposedly fired by, or at, his ships.[1] Claims have been made of the discovery of wrecks said to have been luxurious vessels once a part of his fleet.[2] Accounts of hidden passages, secret forts, and mysterious edifices[3] are interwoven into the legends.[4]

Many tales have no basis in fact. One claimed Laffite was kin to Napoleon Bonaparte and had once been one of the French emperor's lieutenants.[5] According to another tale, Laffite rescued Napoleon from exile on the island of St. Helena. The former ruler of France died at sea. His body was brought to American shores by a pirate armada where it lies buried in a grave south of New Orleans, in of course the logical site, the town of Lafitte.[6]

Even the descriptions of the man vary. Some accounts gave his height as five feet, ten inches,[7] others insisted that he was over six feet tall,[8] while yet another claimed he was "small of stature [and] reserved in his manner."[9] Almost all contemporary references described him as physically attractive and claimed he possessed a unique ability to charm women.[10]

The only picture of Laffite that could have been the work of a contemporary artist was a small painting by J. W. Jarvis depicting the two brothers and Dominique Youx sitting and drinking by firelight. Because of its size and style, the portrayal only adds to the uncertainty about the actual appearance of the alleged pirate.[11]

The Laffite legend includes tales of buried treasure. Most of the stories of pirate gold have as their locale the Gulf Coast. All are legends based on the assumption that large quantities of specie were deposited at isolated sites marked in ways known only to the sea rovers. They, or their specters, would some day return to claim this fabulous wealth.

Typical of the tales that have been woven into the fabric of the Laffite mystique is that of a treasure chest of gold buried beside the Lavaca River. A New Orleans bartender learned the location of the prize from an aging pirate who declared that the hoard was worth more than a million dollars. Before his death, he gave precise instructions to aid in recovery of the fortune. A

136

brass rod marked the site of the treasure. A field hand working near the river found the rod. Not knowing its importance, he removed it to show it to the property owner. Once told of its significance, he made an effort to relocate the spot. Even though the field was dug and re-dug, the fabled wealth was never found.[12]

Treasure tales abound in almost every area where Laffite was believed to have resided. Every foot of Grande Isle has been spaded for pirate gold. Search efforts have continued into the twentieth century.[13] During the preceding century, treasure hunters made frequent forays upon Galveston Island.[14] The banks of the Sabine River became the center of a search for a cache of silver.[15] J. Frank Dobie devoted an entire chapter of his account of lost treasures to tales about pirate booty hidden by Laffite.[16]

Along with the accounts of elusive wealth, there were stories of ghosts. In some cases, the spirits gave the would-be finders of opulence mysterious signs that could lead to treasure.[17] Others alluded to spectral presences that guarded a gold or silver cache. One insisted that Laffite supervised the burial of booty near Grand Lake, requiring his men to dig a deep hole. When the excavation was completed, he asked who of their number desired the treasure above all else. A recent recruit spoke up, admitted he wanted the wealth. The buccaneer chieftain obliged him. The novice pirate was beheaded, and both head and torso were buried with the gold.[18]

A book published in 1985 for a juvenile reading audience concluded with a chapter on the ghosts of Jean Laffite.[19] Sometimes it was claimed he killed men in order to create spirits to guard his wealth.[20] One account stated that the phantom of one of Laffite's mistresses guarded his treasure.[21] More often it was the ghost of the pirate commander who was a fearsome presence that presided over ill-gotten riches.[22]

Laffite, as generator of legendary lore, has been compared with both King Arthur and Robin Hood. One authority declared plaintively: "If there is a more romantic figure in American history than that of Jean Lafitte, I cannot identify it."[23]

Another writer, in commenting on the volume of dramatic material written about Laffite, stated: "More pamphlets, articles, stories and books have been written about him than any Gulf sea rover," but noted that "most of the accounts [were] inaccurate."[24]

The legend is many-faceted. His participation in the Battle

of New Orleans created the aura of the patriotically motivated hero. The fact that he was pardoned by a president of the United States has complicated the vision of what one writer called his "downright ruffianism."[25] Another considered him a person of dual natures calling him one who was both "ruthless and intrepid."[26]

Most of the early accounts of Laffite referred to him in similar terms. A volume published in 1828 that claimed to be "founded on facts" made him out to be gallant, and yet, at the same time, malevolent: He "killed a man . . . because he recognized him" on the streets of New Orleans.[27]

An 1837 work by Charles Ellms added credence to the belief that Laffite was a ruthless criminal. Using a few documentary sources, Ellms went far beyond the scant information he possessed. He portrayed the privateer chieftain as one who consistently committed dastardly deeds upon the high seas, describing imaginary acts of unmitigated cruelty in vivid detail. In order to enhance reader interest, he borrowed tales from the East Indian pirates of the late seventeenth century. Ellms' volume was embellished by the inclusion of imaginative drawings, a work that probably did more than any other to establish the one-time commander of Galveston Island as a vicious sea rover.[28]

In 1892, *Wild Heroes of the Sea* perpetuated the tradition. The author described Laffite as a reckless leader of a band of pirates who successfully attacked heavily armed merchantmen in the Bay of Bengal.[29] Other publications enlarged upon the theme of Laffite's violence by recounting fantasy-laden exploits on seas upon which he never could have sailed, describing him as a "bloodthirsty pirate."[30]

The stream of the Laffite legend reached its greatest magnitude in the hands of the fiction writer. Early in the nineteenth century, a sizeable literature developed around his name. Herbert Asbury compared his legend to that which accumulated around Robin Hood, whom Laffite "surpassed in audacity and success."[31]

Even in Laffite's own lifetime, the English poet Lord Byron composed *The Corsair,* an epic poem believed to have been based upon the life of the Baratarian chief.[32] Interestingly enough, although Byron wrote more than a decade before Laffite's death, his poem predicted at least one of the circumstances of the burial in Yucatan, noting that for *The Corsair,* "they raise not the record-

138

ing stone."[33] Byron's work reached unprecedented popularity selling over 10,000 copies the first day of publication and, within a few years, had spread the fame of the poet's pirate and his still-living counterpart throughout the English-speaking world.[34]

A novel with Laffite as the leading character appeared in 1827 and was popular enough to be reprinted the following year. Three later editions appeared in the 1830s.[35]

Joseph Holt Ingraham produced a fanciful account of Laffite that appeared in the same year as Ellms' work. Three years later, a London edition of Ingraham's novel was printed that quoted from Byron whose corsair's name, according to the poet, was "Link'd with one virtue and a thousand crimes."[36] Later printings followed: 1889, 1931, and as recently as 1970.[37]

Ingraham's writings have been described as "a treasure trove of cliches which mesmerized the devourer of the historical romance of the 1830's."[38] He did more than enthrall the romanticists of his day: He established firmly in the minds of nineteenth century readers a legendary Jean Laffite.

Two works in foreign languages appeared later in the century that included accounts of the island commander: Vincente Riva Palacio published a "novela historica" entitled *Los Pirates Del Golfo* in 1869; a Portuguese work entitled *Os Piratas Do Norte* by Henrique Lopez De Mendonca was printed in Lisbon in 1890.[39]

In 1883, Charles Gayarre published his *Historical Sketch of Pierre and Jean Lafitte, the Famous Smugglers of Louisiana*. A lawyer, · legislator, and historian, Gayarre attempted to correct some of the excesses to which previous accounts of Laffite had been prone and produced one of the first efforts to sort fact from fiction in describing the alleged pirate. He made a serious attempt to secure accurate information and was well aware of the complexities of producing an authentic biography. Born in New Orleans in 1805, he commented that he "might, in his youth, have informed himself thoroughly about the Lafittes; for he knew well several of their former companions, clients, and moneyed associates, who were men of veracity." At the time he initiated his research, he regretted to report, all of those who once could have provided factual information about Laffite "had descended into the tomb."[40]

After the turn of the century, there was a fresh spate of interest in the romanticized Laffite. In 1903, Mary Devereux's *Lafitte of Louisiana* was published. Again the alleged pirate broke the language barrier. He became a major character in Ludwig Jerrmann's *Claribelle Lafitte* published in Hamburg in 1913. Eleven years later, Elizabeth Wilkinson produced *Monsieur Lafitte, Pirate-Patriot.* Joseph Lewis French's *Great Pirate Stories*, which included the Baratarian chief, was published in 1922.[41] In 1926, Lawton Bryan Evans authored *The Pirate of Barataria.*

Romantic novels continued to appear during the late 1920s, among which were the following: George Gibbs, *The Shores of Romance*; Rupert Sargent Holland, *The Pirate of the Gulf*; and Lawton Bryan Evans, *The Pirate of Barataria.*[42] Alan Le May, a popular novelist of the time, produced a fanciful romance centering around Barataria in 1929.[43]

Lyle Saxon's *Lafitte the Pirate* was printed in 1930, a work that still stands as a major biographical portrayal of Jean Laffite. Written in a flowing literary style, the author made a valiant attempt to sort fact from fiction based on his own research. He faced the complexity of his task honestly, noting that although he took his information "from contemporary documents and letters . . . there are two versions of nearly every story."[44]

A biography of Laffite in the Spanish language by J. Ignacio Rubio Mañe was published in Mexico in 1938 entitled *Los Piratas Lafitte* that relied heavily on Saxon.[45]

Several works based on Laffite's life were produced during the 1930s among which were Mitchell Vaughn Charnley's, *Jean Lafitte, Gentleman Smuggler*; Sollie Lee Bell's, *Marcel Armand, A Romance of Old Louisiana,* and Reginald Wright Kauffman's *Pirate Jean.*

A 1933 novel by Hervey Allen again portrayed the Baratarian chief as a terror on the high seas.[46] Armstrong Sperry produced a piece of romantic fiction entitled *Black Falcon* in 1949, and six years later, Madeline Fabiola Kent authored *The Corsair.*

Jane De Grummond's scholarly volume entitled *The Baratarians and the Battle of New Orleans* was published in 1961 and reprinted in 1979. Two Laffite books in the French language have appeared in recent years: Raymond Borel, *Le Revolte De La Louisiana: Vie Mysterieuse de Jean Laffitte*, 1978, and George Blond, *Moi, Laffite Dernier Roi Des Flibusters*, 1985. In 1988, a novel by Tom Townsend, *Powderhorn Passage*, was published.

Even juvenile literature has been engulfed by the stream of

the Laffite legend. Children's books have generally been some-what kinder than their adult counterparts by developing plots related to the Battle of New Orleans. The following are represen-tative of this class of material: Robert Tallant, *The Pirate Laffite and the Battle of New Orleans*; Iris Vinton, *We Were There With Jean Lafitte at New Orleans;* Carl Carmer, *The Pirate Hero of New Or-leans*; Catherine Troxell Gonzales, *Lafitte, the Terror of the Gulf*; and Ariane Dewey, *Laffite the Pirate.*

The mystique of Laffite did not escape the notice of dra-matic scriptwriters. A nineteenth century melodrama entitled *Lafitte: A Play in Prologue and Four Acts* was printed in 1899. Eliza-beth Wilkinson's *Monsieur Lafitte: Jean Lafitte Pirate-Patriot, South Louisiana,* appeared in 1924.

Later in the century, the American Forces Radio and Televi-sion Services made a sound recording for overseas broadcast en-titled "The Pirate of New Orleans," and Cecil B. De Mille di-rected a film entitled *The Buccaneer.* The movie was remade in 1958 in color, the last film produced by De Mille. Both films were based on Lyle Saxon's biography and, in the final years of the twentieth century, have become popular items for VCR libraries and late night television.

The legend of Laffite continued to move like a relentless stream. A 1974 publication perpetuated the violent pirate theme by declaring that he "practiced wholesale murder,"[47] and a work printed in 1976 used twentieth century terminology by declaring him to be a "gangster."[48]

Philip Grosse called Laffite "one of the scum" who "dared attack the weak."[49] Others referred to him as "the terror of the Gulf,"[50] "the head of all corsairs,"[51] or as one who "terrorized the waters and ravaged the coasts of the Gulf of Mexico."[52]

Other sources described Laffite in very different terms. Gayarre noted that he "always objected to unnecessary violence." He cited the occasion upon which the transport of goods through the Bayou Lafourche was halted by revenue officers. Laffite "almost apologized for the blood he had shed [declaring] I am adverse to such strifes." His excuse for opposing force with force was "I prefer losing my life rather than my goods."[53]

Gayarre believed Laffite was a smuggler in a culture and a time that honored such a profession, and insisted he consistently avoided armed collisions with those who opposed him. This was a conclusion Gayarre reached "after as much investigation as I could bestow on the subject."[54] Based on his personal examination of court testimony, the Baratarian chief acted only as a privateer commander who insisted that his lieutenants take no prizes other than vessels sailing under the flag of Spain.[55]

Several authorities have accepted the legal privateer theory of Laffite's enterprises: Ray Miller,[56] Frank Lawrence Owsley, Jr.,[57] Hyatt A. Verrill,[58] and Gardner W. Allen.[59] One author evaluated Laffite simply as a shrewd businessman who took "a band of uneducated, unpolished and unorganized fishermen [and] turned [them into] smugglers."[60]

Lacarriere Latour, who knew the Laffites, declared they had committed no crime other than to have "infringed the revenue laws."[61] Another contemporary, Col. S. M. Williams, reported to Mirabeau Lamar that he had "conversed freely" with Laffite who had "vindicated himself against the charge of piracy."[62] Others called the two brothers "true gentlemen, men of honor . . . only slightly demoralized by an incurable antipathy . . . to revenue laws, restrictive tariffs and other impediments to free trade."[63]

Francis C. Sheridan, a member of the British diplomatic service, who visited Galveston Island in 1839 and 1840, believed Laffite had acted with honor in refusing the offer of Sheridan's own government.[64] His investigation of the activities of Laffite led the British diplomat to conclude that although the Galveston commander did engage in illegal activities, he remained "respected and beloved," noting that from all reports "his sailors adored him."[65] Both Jean and Pierre were almost universally lauded as patriots for their participation in the Battle of New Orleans.[66]

The river of Laffite tradition divides into two contrasting streams.

One branch of the flow of legend based on works such as those of Ellms and Ingraham described him as among the most vicious of all the villains of history, and declared that he committed acts that would outdo the cruelest deeds of a Blackbeard or a Calico Jack.[67]

The other branch of the stream of Laffite lore viewed him much more charitably, referring to him as a gentleman, a person of honor, and a loyal patriot. This evaluation was based on the writings of authors such as Latour and Gayarre, who assumed that no crime could be charged against Laffite other than that of organizing a smuggling ring at a time when the craft of the smuggler was essential to the well-being of southern Louisiana. Since privateering was legal under United States law until the middle of the nineteenth century,[68] Laffite was regarded as an entrepreneur who efficiently provided harbor, storage, and distribution for saleable goods brought to American shores.

Perhaps the two streams converge around a single question: Was Jean Laffite a pirate? Was he merely a master smuggler and entrepreneur, or was he a buccaneer chieftain deserving of execution by hanging?

The question could be put in more specific terms: If Lafitte had been brought before an impartial court of law, would he have been convicted for the crime of piracy and would that conviction have stood the test of time?

The exact nature of piracy has been debated since the beginnings of modern history. Roman emperors were forced to deal with sea rovers and generally considered any who used force to impede Rome's trade upon the Mediterranean as pirates.[69] After the decline of Rome, maritime robbery increased and continued unabated wherever there was a lack of governmental authority. With the emergence of the modern nations of western Europe, the question of what constituted piracy was complicated by the use of letters of marque issued by established governments.

Prior to and during the early nineteenth century, whether a sea raider was denounced as a pirate depended upon the interpretation a particular state chose to place upon his actions.[70] Deeds that were considered justifiable under the laws of one nation might be declared piratical by another. United States President Woodrow Wilson proclaimed the sinking of the *Lusitania* by a German submarine to be an act of piracy.[71] A committee of the League of Nations studied the issue in 1926 and conceded that no consistent code of law existed for determining which particular acts could properly be counted as piracy. The debate concluded with an agreement that the buccaneer was not punishable under international law, but that he was, nevertheless, "an enemy of the human race."[72]

In 1958, the United Nations Conference on the Law of the Sea once more attempted to define piracy. For the first time, an internationally acceptable definition was formulated declaring the pirate to be one who was guilty of "illegal acts of violence, detention or any act of depredation, committed for private ends." A person who engaged in "any act . . . of intentionally facilitating . . ." such activities was guilty of piracy.[73]

Whether or not Jean Laffite actually led a boarding party or personally commanded an attack on an unarmed merchant ship, he did facilitate piratical activities. He provided harbor for those who participated in the capture of goods at sea. He encouraged sea raiding by maintaining storage facilities and developing access to markets for booty gained from illicit sea raids. According to the mid-twentieth century understanding of the word, Laffite was a pirate. He did aid and abet sea raiders who, in his name, committed acts of violence.

Although he was not guilty of the crimes described by Charles Ellms and Joseph Ingraham, even in his own time there was reason to consider him a pirate. Some of his associates on Galveston Island were captured, charged with piracy, convicted, and condemned to death. This meant that had he been arrested and brought before an impartial tribunal, he would have suffered a similar fate. One of the primary pieces of evidence for the successful prosecution of the government's case against Jean Desfarges and Robert Johnson was the raiding commission issued under the authority of the commander of Galveston Island. An extant copy of this document bears the boldly inscribed name, "Jn Laffite."[74]

The chances of his capture and indictment increased dramatically after 1820. Laffite knew this. It was for this reason he left Galveston. His efforts to continue his activities and seek security in the isolated coves of Cuba were but a temporary expedient before he finally fled to the obscurity of Mujeres.

The two streams of Laffite lore flow beyond the shore.

By association they become one, for the river is captive to the sea.

But the mystery still remains. Why did Laffite allow himself to be swept to Galveston Island where he would operate an illegal pirate base? Why did he not accept the pardon offered him by a president of the United States?

He could have done so.

Others did, including one of his close associates, Dominique Youx. With his unique talents, Laffite could have become a merchant prince. Forgiven for his infractions of law prior to 1815, he could have resided comfortably in New Orleans, there to achieve material success. He had proven his expertise in merchandising. He had contacts with persons in high positions. He was a companion of legislators and generals. He had the makings of an astute politician.

He could charm almost anyone with whom he came in contact and could relate to individuals in all classes of society. If he had chosen to seek public office for a position dependent upon political support in French-speaking Louisiana, almost any position would have been open to him: the Legislature, Congress, or as a successor to William C. C. Claiborne as governor of the state.

Instead, he elected to appoint himself governor of what was no more than a desolate strip of land off the coast of Texas.

Jean Laffite had no apparent reason for leaving New Orleans.

Following the battle, he was a hero. Like others among his associates, he could have remained in the city as an honored and respected citizen.

What was his motivation?

Possessed by a restless psyche, he was not one who could continue in a restrictive society. He could no more have remained true to the lady New Orleans than he could have continued in the bonds of matrimony as a mate to any one woman.

Like the Mississippi, he was captive to a relentless course.

The great river provides the final clue to the mystery. Like the river, Jean Laffite was enslaved by the lure of the sea.

The romantic and pro-American Jean Laffite was already well entrenched in American minds when Cecil B. DeMille produced his first version of **The Buccaneer.** *Friedrich March played a clever Laffite who tried his hardest to win a home under the American flag.*

— Courtesy Institute of Texan Cultures

146

APPENDIX A

The Journal of Jean Laffite

One question must be answered in the search for Laffite data: whether or not a document purporting to be the personal memoirs of the pirate chieftain is authentic.

In 1980, a codex was placed in the Sam Houston Regional Library and Research Center in Liberty, Texas, that appears to be the journal of Laffite. Consisting of 258 pages, approximately 8° by 13° inches in size, the document is leather-bound and bears inscription dates beginning in the year 1845 and continuing until December 2, 1850.

The manuscript, written in French, begins with the statement that the writer proposes to prepare *un journal* in behalf of *mes descandants* that was not to be released until a century and seven years after the date of writing and would be based upon his own records to ensure that there was no exaggeration in what he wrote.

The preface, which consists of a little over a page, is signed on the second leaf in letters written much larger than the text, "Jn Laffite." Similar signatures, all of which contain flourishes beneath the cursive letters, appear throughout the manuscript. It is the repetition of the autograph that is one of the more noticeable features of the document.

Other materials that are a part of the holdings of the research center include two family Bibles in French that supposedly were maintained by the Laffite family. One, published in 1820, contains a Laffite genealogy that begins with the date 1742 and continues through 1932. The other, published in 1839, includes entries dated 1608 through 1912.

A complete set of copies of the journal were made available to the author. The library staff allowed viewing of the actual manuscript under glass and provided materials that argued both for and against the genuineness of the documents. The journal was impressive, a manuscript that possessed an aura of authenticity that tended to override the natural cynicism of the researcher.

The history of the collection is an interesting one. A retired railroader named John Andrechyne Laflin appeared in the office of

Charles van Ravenswaay, director of the Missouri Historical Society in St. Louis in 1948. He presented photostats of some of the materials now in the research center. At this point, he was anxious to establish that he was a descendant of Jean Laffite. Van Ravenswaay and his staff studied his documents, but could not authenticate his claim.[1]

Later Laflin proposed to collaborate with Ray and Sue Thompson of New Orleans in writing a biography based on the papers in his possession.[2] When the Thompsons indicated skepticism, Laflin approached another Louisiana author, Stanley Clisby Arthur, who produced a volume entitled *Jean Laffite: Gentleman Rover* that drew heavily upon Laflin's information.[3]

In 1958, the 258-page codex was published by Laflin under the title *The Journal of Jean Laffite*. Inferring that he was not able to translate the French document himself, he claimed he secured the services of several linguists in producing an English version. The result was a translation that was less than perfect, but followed the content of the original manuscript with a reasonable degree of accuracy.[4]

If Laflin had hoped to convince students of early nineteenth century Americana that the codex was the personal journal of Jean Laffite by publishing, his attempt was unsuccessful. The initial reaction to the printed work was anything but positive. A reviewer summed up scholarly response to the publication:

> This volume purports to be an English translation, the translator not identified, of a French manuscript, not located, alleged to have been written between 1845 and 1850. It is not likely to cause any historian to doubt that Jean Laffite disappeared from view and presumably died in the early 1820s.[5]

Laflin did not give up his effort to prove the authenticity of his documents. In 1962, he again requested the assistance of the Thompsons in writing a book based on the printed version of his manuscript. He had visited archives in Spain, Mexico, and Cuba and reported he had additional data to support his claims. Still, he refused to produce the actual codex and later declared that some of his supportive documents had been burned in a fire. The Thompsons, still suspicious of Laflin's claims, determined his home had burned and some of his papers had been destroyed.[6]

In 1969, only a short time before Laflin's death, his collection of Laffite materials was acquired by the William Simpson Galleries, Incorporated. Simpson, a professional documents dealer, believed the papers were genuine and that the memoirs were more than 130 years old.[7] His decision to acquire the documents was based upon evidence that the memoirs were of mid-nineteenth century origin. Both the paper and the ink had been analyzed. The paper of the codex was a heavy linen-based type used only up until about 1850. The ferrous ink had actually rusted causing the words to rise slightly above the page leaving an indelible imprint that would not wash out. Samples taken from the journal were certified authentic in age by the manuscripts division of the Library of Congress. An independent testing laboratory affirmed that both the paper and the writing fluid used to produce the document could be dated in the middle years of the nineteenth century.[8] In 1969, Richard Santos, archivist for Bexar County, San Antonio, Texas "pronounced the Jean Laffite collection authentic."[9]

In 1974, further efforts were made to determine the validity of the claims made for the manuscript. A recognized handwriting expert examined the pages of the codex. Two pages were removed at random, both of which had Laffite signatures. These were compared with two documents believed to have been written by Laffite in 1819. All four samples of handwriting had identical characteristics of letter formation. Again the journal was declared genuine.[10]

In 1975, Price Daniel, former governor of Texas, an able researcher and historian in his own right, acquired the collection. In 1980, he donated the entire set of Laffite materials and memorabilia to the Sam Houston Regional Library and Research Center in Liberty, Texas.[11]

Acceptance of the document, once it was available to researchers, in spite of its impressive array of supporters, has been far from universal. A New Orleans authority on graphology, Miriam Bethancourt, made a study of the codex. When John A. Laflin's handwriting was compared with the document, it was suggested that he may have been the author of the journal.[12] Another researcher concluded that "it can be proven beyond any reasonable doubt that the journal-memoir attributed to the privateer, Jean Laffite, was not, in fact, written by him."[13] A 1981 work by Charles Hamilton entitled *Great Forgers and Famous Fakes* listed the memoirs as "a forgery due to handwriting and other information."[14]

In spite of the skepticism regarding the authenticity of the journal, the document continued to have its supporters. Robert L. Schaadt, director-archivist of the Sam Houston Research Center, who has worked with the codex and believes it to be authentic, has pointed out that "Charles Hamilton never came to see the manuscript," and that some of his basic information, including the name of the institution that houses the document, is incorrect.[15] In 1981, Dr. Jane De Grummond, scholar and authority on Louisiana and Caribbean history, defended the authenticity of the memoirs in an article published in *The Laffite Study Group Newsletter*.[16]

Richard Santos proposed a multiple-author theory. He suggested that a portion of the journal was written by Laffite, while Laflin added other pages using old leaves of blank paper from antique book shops. A New Orleans newspaper article quoted Santos as stating that parts of the journal were genuine because "there is information in that collection that only Jean Laffite could have known." Other portions, particularly the later part, he conceded may have been forgeries.[17]

In the face of contradictory evaluations of the journal by the experts, what can be said about its authorship? In any documentary study, the best evidence of origin is that within a manuscript's pages. Content can be far more convincing than authentication based primarily upon external data.

Handwriting, especially flowing signatures, can be reproduced. It was customary in the early nineteenth century for persons of importance, particularly heads of state, and Laffite considered himself to be both, to employ amanuenses who would sign documents in their behalf developing a standard facsimile of their signatures. It is possible that the comparison signatures used by experts in the 1974 study were no more penned by Jean Laffite than those that appear in the disputed manuscript.

The argument that a portion of the journal is genuine based on the fact that it does contain some accurate information bears little weight. The contemporary clippings that are a part of the collection, along with the printed accounts available at the time, account for the verifiable data in the document. The age of the paper could be explained by the fact that antique writing materials can be purchased and could have been used to produce the codex.

There is one external argument for authenticity that cannot be easily explained: the aging of the ferrous ink. This fact would substantiate other evidence of the mid-nineteenth century origin of the memoirs. This would absolve John A. Laflin of having committed the forgery for which he has been accused.

Who, then, was the actual author? Is it conceivable that Laffite survived his years in Yucatan, lived until 1854, and actually penned this unique work?

Internal evidence would rule out this possibility. Dates and place names are often badly confused. While there are certain portions of the codex that are detailed and orderly, many sections are hopelessly jumbled, indicating that the author relied upon his own imagination when he was between source materials. The sense of confusion intensified about a third of the way through the journal with a change in the tenor of the document appearing with the manuscript entry dated May 4, 1846. This fact could argue for multiple authorship. But these are alterations in mood and not in style. Sentence structure remains much the

150

same throughout the memoir, indicating that the manuscript was written by a single person subject to pronounced psychological aberrations that took place over the five-year period in which the manuscript was produced.

This being the case, who was this single author? A careful consideration of even the more orderly content argues against authorship by Laffite. Although the writer had access to some of the details of the Battle of New Orleans, information that was easily available in the middle years of the nineteenth century, the author of the journal had a limited knowledge of the circumstances that preceded the publicized events. He knew nothing about the geography of the New Orleans area and southern Louisiana. He knew little about the coast where the Baratarian establishment flourished or of Galveston island. The journal contains geographical information that shows a greater familiarity with cities such as Charleston, South Carolina, and Baltimore, Maryland, than with the southern reaches of the Mississippi.

It is impossible to ascribe the document to the person whose name appears throughout its pages. Robert Vogel made an intensive study of Laflin's documents and came to the same conclusion. He noted that the "Journal" included "many glaring inaccuracies" and that the author "warped and mangled history almost beyond recognition."[18]

If the journal was written in the mid-nineteenth century, as external evidence would indicate, and the writer was not the privateer chieftain who died in the mid-1820s, who was the author? The available evidence points to only one conclusion: The document was composed by an ancestor of John Laflin, a gunpowder merchant named Mathew Laflin who lived from 1803 to 1854. Because of his trade, he was knowledgeable of nineteenth century seagoing vessels as well as the arms and explosives described in the journal. He was familiar with Charleston, South Carolina, and Baltimore where he had lived. The dates in the codex correspond to the available information about his final years. About 1845, he retired to Missouri. He was buried in Alton, Illinois, the site that John Laflin claimed as the grave of Jean Laffite.[19]

The cover page of the manuscript includes a signature of Mathew Laflin[20] that displays the same flourishes as those of the purported signature of Laffite. This page was a dedication of the book to "John Laffite . . . by your most obedient and humble servant."[21] It is significant that this page was not reproduced for the printed work.

A full-page, hand-drawn picture of Mathew Laflin is a part of the manuscript. This appears on leaf number 258. This, too, was excluded from the published volume. Beneath the picture, these words were written: "Mathew Laflin born 1803." This is clearly the same person portrayed in two portraits that were claimed as pictures of Laffite and were reproduced in the printed work, one said to be by an artist named Mañuel De Franca and the other by a granddaughter, Lois Ann Little. The hand-drawn picture included in the codex was perhaps Laflin's way of saying, in one of his more temperate moments, that he was the actual author of the journal.

While it has been claimed that Laflin was really Laffite, it is obvious that Laflin was Laflin and that he assumed what he believed to be the emotional ferment of Laffite as he pored over the documents in his possession until he finally convinced himself and some of his associates that he was actually his own alter ego.

Perhaps Mathew Laflin did not write the document as a deliberate fraud. By the time he moved to Missouri, he was subject to the delusion that he was Jean Laffite. He had assembled several pieces of early nineteenth century memorabilia including a collection of contemporary clippings about Laffite. These he used to put together the unique codex in the glass case in Liberty, Texas.

Others have had Napoleonic complexes. Laflin had a Laffite complex.

John A. Laflin believed that his ancestor, Mathew Laflin, was Laffite. At least he went to great lengths to prove this claim. He dutifully held the document until the allotted one hundred and seven years had expired and then had it published.

The journal of Jean Laffite is a document with no real value to the serious researcher and is of interest only to the antiquarian.

Capt. Dominique Youx's Company
December 23, 1814–March 16, 1815
Battery Number 3

Youx, Dominique, Captain
Beluche (Bluche), Renato, 1st Lt.
Marguerie, 2nd Lt.
Pelegrain, Sgt.**
Chairie, Christophle, Sgt.
Hulan, Jean, Sgt.
Sapia, Franciseque Fois, Sgt.
Allin, Jean
Allan, Jn. Jacque
Adrien, Jne
Baritau,
Belnaut, Francios
Bertrand, Pierre
Boutin, Josephe*
Bruleau, Pre.
Cannon
Caragome
Cassou, Jn.*
Ceressol, Andre
Dominique, Manuel
Ferrand, Pre.
Francois
Gamby, Vicent*
Isnard, Jean
Jean, Josephe

Laurend, Jean
Larrabas, Dominique
Laurin, Pre (?), Folis
Lissaunce, Raimond
Loustalot, Jean*
Merlle, Bte.
Mousson, Michel
Nerac
Page, Valentice
Passis (Lessier) Goivan (?)
Pervis, Josephe
Plochet, Baptiste
Sterlin
Suisee, Barthelemy
Tour, Ene.
Veauluisan, Francs
Verdois, Francois

* wounded in battle, January 8,
     1815
** died of wounds received on
     January 8, 1815

Source: *Louisiana In the War of
     1812,* Powell A. Casey, 1963,
     Baton Rouge

153

This structure was built in the 1870s over the foundation and wine cellar of Jean Laffite's Maison Rouge, or Red House, in Galveston, Texas. It still existed in 1996.

— Courtesy Nancy Dearing Johnson

154

Notes

Preface

1. A typescript in the Melrose Collection, Number 41, consisting of the Memoirs of Martha Martin of Nashville, Tennessee, Northwestern State University Library, Natchitoches, Louisiana.

2. Erskine Caldwell, *Deep Delta Country*, p. 43. A chapter by Harnett T. Kane cited a report of a Mrs. Johnson who gave an account of meeting Jean Laffite.

3. The Lamar Papers, Manuscript 1614, Texas State Archives, Austin, Texas.

4. Willis Pratt, editor, *Galveston Island, Or, A Few Months off the Coast of Texas: The Journal of Francis C. Sheridan, 1839–1840*, p. 55.

5. "Barataria and Lafitte," Manuscript, Texas State Archives, Austin, Texas.

6. Philip Grosse, *The History of Piracy*, p. 213.

7. A. Lacarriere Latour, *Historical Memoirs of the War in West Florida and Louisiana, 1814–1815*, p. clxxxvii.

8. Ray Thompson, *The Land of Lafitte the Pirate*, p. 30.

9. The surname was a common one among the French-speaking persons who migrated to Louisiana in the late eighteenth century, usually spelled with one "f" and two "t's." Documents that apparently originated with either Jean Laffite or his brother, Pierre, used a dissimilar spelling, one with two "f's" and a single "t."

10. Lyle Saxon, *Lafitte, the Pirate*, p. ix.

11. Winnie Allen and Corrie Walker Allen, *Pioneering In Texas*, p. 138.

Chapter 1

1. Jane Lucas De Grummond, *Renato Beluche, Smuggler, Privateer and Patriot, 1780–1860*, p. 35.

2. *Ibid.*, p. 36.

3. *Ibid.* De Grummond cited a contemporary account written in 1806 for the details of the transfer of the possession of Louisiana to the government of the United States: C. C. Robin, *Voyages dans l'interieur de la Louisiane*, II, 137–138.

4. De Grummond cited contemporary evidence that indicated the privateer captain was in New Orleans at the time of the transfer of the Louisiana territory to the United States. (De Grummond, *op. cit.*, p. 36)

5. Willis W. Pratt, editor, *Galveston Island, Or, A Few Months off the Coast of Texas: The Journal of Francis C. Sheridan, 1839–1840*, p. 63. A similar description appeared in the report of a Mrs. Johnson cited in Erskine Caldwell's *Deep Delta Country*, p. 43.

6. The Lamar Papers, Manuscript 1612, The Texas State Archives, Austin, Texas.

7. Rene Robert Cavelier, sieur de La Salle, laid claim to the entire region in behalf of the French Crown by exploring the Mississippi to its mouth early in the seventeenth century. In 1698, the British Navy sought to gain control of the northern coast of the Gulf of Mexico, but was thwarted by a French colony on the river's bank. Spain made her bid to extend empire to Louisiana in the following century. (De Grummond, *op. cit.*, p. 127; Grace King, *Jean Baptiste le Moyne Sieur de Bienville*, p. 257; Alexander DeConde, *This Affair of Louisiana*, pp. 14–19; Joe Gray Taylor, *Louisiana: A History*, pp. 9 ff.)

8. E. Wilson Lyon, *Louisiana in French Diplomacy, 1759–1804*, p. 172.

9. *Ibid.*, p. 128.

10. *Ibid.*

11. *Ibid.*, p. 151.

12. *Ibid.*, p. 163.

13. Donald Barr Chidsey, *The Great Conspiracy*, p. 7.

14. Rufus Blanchard, *Documentary History of the Cession of Louisiana to the United States Till it Became an American Province*, p. 27.

15. John Keats, *Eminent Domain: The Louisiana Purchase and the Making of America*, p. 341–349.

Chapter 2

1. DeConde, *op. cit.*, p. 31.

2. *Ibid.*, p. 62.

3. De Grummond, *op. cit.*, p. 18.

4. A. L. Dunn, Typescript, Folder 103, Melrose Collection, Northwestern State University Library, Natchitoches, Louisiana.

5. Cesar Poulenc, *Jean Laffite, Gentleman Pirate*, p. 4.

6. Robin Reilly, *The British at the Gates*, p. 193; Edward Lucie-Smith, *Outcasts of the Sea*, p. 238; Stanley Clisby Arthur, *Jean Lafitte, Gentleman Rover*, p. 9; Poulenc, *op. cit.*, p. 3.

7. Poulenc, *op. cit.*, pp. 5–7.

8. De Grummond, *op. cit.*, p. 39. Eli Whitney's invention of the saw-toothed cotton gin and Etienne de Bore's discovery of a method of producing sugar from Louisiana cane increased the importance of black laborers, some 300,000 of whom were available on the island of Jamaica. In spite of the congressional ban on the importation of slaves, little was done to stop the flow of human merchandise into the area. (Thompson, *op. cit.*, p. 20; B. W. Higman, *Trade, Government and Society in Caribbean History*, p. 5.)

9. Saxon, *op. cit.*, p. 22.

10. *Ibid.*, p. 41.

11. *Ibid.*, p. 22.

12. English efforts to claim the Mississippi valley were thwarted in 1755 when a powerful British force under Maj. Gen. Edward Braddock met defeat at Fort Duquesne.

13. *Ibid.*, p. 32.

Chapter 3

1. Ray Thompson described the area as "a great semi-liquid wilderness . . . [consisting of] a maze of streams and swamps . . . ideal for either habitation or hiding . . . an experienced boatman could make a hundred round trips to New Orleans and never exactly follow the same route twice." (Thompson, *op. cit.*, p. 5)

2. Saxon established 1809 as the year in which the Laffites became agents in New Orleans for smugglers, but added that it was "probable" they had visited New Orleans "as early as 1804." (Saxon, *op. cit.*, p. 16)

3. Manuscript 56, The Historic New Orleans Collection, New Orleans, Louisiana.

4. "Letter from Colonel Saml. M. Williams to Mirabeau Lamar," The Lamar Papers, Manuscript 1612, Texas State Archives, Austin, Texas.

5. Pierre Laffite declared himself to be a native of Bayonne, France in recording the baptism of his illegitimate daughter on January 16, 1811, according to the St. Louis Cathedral Register of Baptismal Records (Saxon, *op. cit.*, pp. 32, 33). Other sources indicated a possible connection between Jacques Laffitte of Bayonne, and Jean and Pierre, but there is no evidence of this relationship. *(Eminent Personages: Laffite,* a rare printed work in the Barker Library, Austin, Texas)

6. An anonymous printed article in the Louisiana State Museum, New Orleans, Louisiana; Charles Ellms, in his 1837 account of Laffite, gave St. Malo as Laffite's birthsite (Charles Ellms, *The Pirates Own Book,* or *Authentic Narratives of the Lives, Exploits and Executions of the Most Celebrated Sea Robbers,* p. 57).

7. The Lamar Papers, Manuscript 1614, Laffite's Texas State Archives, Austin, Texas.

8. J. Frank Dobie cited "an unpublished work" as his source of information as to the Spanish origin of Laffite, but commented that his evidence was "not wholly satisfactory." (J. Frank Dobie, *Coronado's Children,* p. 307).

9. *Lafitte, or the Baratarian Chief,* p. 67.

10. Jane De Grummond, *The Baratarians and the Battle of New Orleans,* p. 148.

11. Privateering was a means not only of contesting the passage of an enemy, but of gaining necessary supplies. "Letters of Marque" or "letters of reprisal" were issued by a nation against the vessels of another when there was no war. Commissions were granted when a merchant captain claimed he had been robbed at sea. He could then recoup losses by attacking another ship sailing under the flag of the nation that had inflicted harm upon his trade. Most European countries followed this practice when lacking a strong naval force. (Donald Macintyre, *The Privateers,* pp. 2–9)

157

12. Between the years 1689 and 1696, French vessels sailing from St. Malo took a total of 1,124 English prizes and ransoms, and, in the eighteenth century, large fleets operated from French ports against both the English and Spanish. (Patrick Crowhurst, *The Defense of British Trade, 1689–1815,* Table 1.1, p. 18 and Table 1.16, p. 41)

13. *Papers Relative to French Affairs,* pp. 17, 18.

14. Willis J. Abbot, *The Naval History of the United States,* p. 216. Armed licensed merchantmen outnumbered the novice Continental Navy by ten to one. During the War of 1812, the United States issued 515 letters of marque to vessels that reported the capture of 1,345 ships. (Edgar Slanton Maclay, *A History of American Privateers,* p. 507) One authority believed the United States would have had little chance against the British had it not been for American privateers. (George Coggeshall, *History of the American Privateers and Letters-of-Marque,* pp. vi-vii)

15. Earl Willis Crecraft, *Freedom of the Seas,* p. 15.

16. The Spanish originally claimed and settled the island in the sixteenth century calling it Española. (Kenneth Andrews, *The Spanish Caribbean,* p. 19) Spain found it difficult to prevent smuggling, and all ports were closed and inhabitants of coastal villages were forced inland. (Otto Schoenrich, *Santo Domingo,* p. 24) Island hunters who developed a method of cooking and preserving meat called "boucan," came to be called buccaneers. Many had originally been Europeans who found cruising against the Spanish most profitable than hunting. (James Burney, *History of the Buccaneers of America,* p. 48; John Esquemeling, *The Buccaneers of America,* p. 218)

17. Slaves were imported to work the fields. Before the end of the eighteenth century, nearly half a million black laborers were on St. Dominique providing rich returns for their French overlords. (Brian Weinstein and Aaron Segal, *Haiti: Political Failures and Cultural Successes,* p. 25.)

18. B. W. Higman, *Trade Government and Society in Caribbean History 1700–1920,* p. 11.

19. Weinstein and Segal, *op. cit.,* pp. 52–69.

20. W. Adolphe Roberts, *The French in the West Indies,* p. 62.

21. Cabildo Records in the Louisiana State Museum, New Orleans, Louisiana, Manuscript Document 9892.

22. Cabildo Records in the Louisiana State Museum, New Orleans, Louisiana, Document 373, File 3748.

23. Cabildo Records in the Louisiana State Museum, New Orleans, Louisiana.

24. Melrose Collection, Northwestern State University, Natchitoches, Louisiana, Manuscript Folder 545.

25. Photocopies of documents relating to the Lafitte family in the Sam Houston Library and Research Center, Liberty, Texas.

26. These documents described Aubry as a merchant, and indicated that he was involved in legal actions necessary to collecting sums of money ranging up to 550 pesos. Cabildo Records in the Louisiana State Museum, New Orleans, Document 1174, Box 44; Document 1174, File 2982; Document 1596, File 49; Document 1724, File 30; and document 1690, File 75.

27. Aubry married the widow of a "Juan Lafitte [who] did not possess any

properties when married nor after his death." This indicated she was a recent refugee from Santo Domingo. (Cabildo Records in the Louisiana State Museum, New Orleans, Document 1011, File 2979) At least for a time, she had lived in her father's home, a Don Enrique Roche. (Cabildo Records in the Louisiana State Museum, New Orleans, Document 2062, File 2334).

28. "The Birth of Juan Enrico," photocopy, Texas State Archives, Austin, Texas.

29. One researcher reported finding the record of a marriage that took place on December 5, 1777 in which a "J. Lafitte" wed a woman who may have been the Elizabeth Roche who later married Aubry. This identification is questionable. The account of the discovery in 1933 stated that the name of the bride was "not . . . easily determined" because of the condition of the record document. (Catherine B. Dillon, "The Parentage of Lafitte," a printed article in the Northwestern State University Library, Natchitoches, Louisiana)

30. "Barataria and Lafitte," Manuscript, Texas State Archives, Austin, Texas.

31. De Grummond, *Renato Beluche*, pp. 19–21.

32. *Ibid.*, pp. 27, 28.

33. *Ibid.*

34. *Ibid.*, p. 42.

35. Thompson, *op. cit.*, p. 122; Saxon, *op. cit.*, pp. 266, 267.

36. *Ibid.*, p. 18.

Chapter 4

1. Phillip Graham, "Mirabeau Buonaparte Lamar's First Trip to Texas," *Southwest Review*, July 1939, Volume 21, Number 4, p. 378.

2. Herbert Asbury, *The French Quarter*, p. 86.

3. De Grummond, *Renato Beluche*, p. 37.

4. Oliver Evans, *New Orleans*, p. 42.

5. Francois-Xavier Martin, *The History of Louisiana*, p. 347. Martin stated that in 1810, one third of the population of the territory, 24,552, was in the "precinct of New Orleans."

6. Reilly, *op. cit.*, p. 193.

7. Asbury, *op. cit.*, pp. 87 ff.

8. The St. Philip Theater opened in 1808 with an auditorium that could accommodate 700 persons. (Evans, *op. cit.*, p. 52) The Theater d'Orleans began business the following year. (Asbury, *op. cit.*, p. 91)

9. Evans, *op. cit.*, p. 52.

10. Asbury, *op. cit.*, p. 96.

11. In 1810, the quadroon balls were transferred to the more spacious arena of the St. Philips Theater.

12. Saxon, *op. cit.*, p. 55.

Chapter 5

1. De Grummond, *Renato Beluche*, p. 41.

2. After Burr left New Orleans, Wilkinson denounced him. He was ar-

rested and charged with treason but was later acquitted. (Donald Barr Chidsey, *The Great Conspiracy*, p. 55)

3. Thompson, *op. cit.*, p. 80.

4. Reilly, *op. cit.*, p. 194.

5. A typescript based on an article in the *Picayune*, dated August 20, 1871, in the Juanita Henry Collection, Folder 14, Northwestern State University Library, Natchitoches, Louisiana.

6. Ines Murat (Frances Frenaze, translator), *Napoleon and the American Dream*, p. 124

7. De Grummond, *Renato Beluche*, p. 43.

8. *Ibid.*, pp. 48, 49.

9. *Ibid.*, p. 48.

Chapter 6

1. A seaman who visited Grande Terre in 1844 described the island's unique isolation. (*Laffite Study Group Newsletter*, Volume VI, Number 2, Summer 1986) Gayarre gave a similar description in his nineteenth century account. (Charles Gayarre, *Historical Sketch of Pierre and Jean Lafitte*, p. I:4)

2. The *New Orleans Daily Picayune* of August 27, 1844, cited in *Laffite Study Group Newsletter*, Volume VI, Number 2, Summer 1986.

3. Asbury, *op. cit.*, p. 117.

4. Saxon, *op. cit.*, p. 37.

5. Thompson, *op. cit.*, p. 12.

6. De Grummond, *The Baratarians and the Battle of New Orleans*, p. 1.

7. Thompson, *op. cit.*, p. 24.

8. Gayarre's late nineteenth century account noted that a "forgerons" on Bourbon Street may have been used as a location for Laffite's clandestine enterprise, but that the buildings to which he referred in 1883 "have since disappeared." (Gayarre, *op. cit.*, p. I:2) An advertisement in an 1802 publication described the services of "Hearico & Lafitte, Forgerons and Taillandiers." (*The Life and Times of Jean Laffite*, December 1977) There were many Lafittes in Louisiana at this time, and there is no evidence that one of the proprietors of the Bourbon street blacksmith shop was either Pierre or Jean.

9. De Grummond, *Renato Beluche*, p. 53.

10. Cited by De Grummond, *Ibid.*, p. 54.

11. *Ibid.*, pp. 54, 55.

12. *Ibid.*, p. 55.

13. *Ibid.*, p. 57.

14. Reilly, *op. cit.*, p. 194.

15. *Ibid.*, p. 59; Stanley Faye suggested that Grand Isle, immediately west of the pass, was the base of the Baratarians. Both islands had been used by smugglers. Grande Terre, the larger of the two islands, was the center of operations during Laffite's day. (Faye, *Louisiana Historical Quarterly*, Volume 23, Number 3, July 1940, p. 16)

16. "Barataria and Lafitte," Manuscript, Texas State Archives, Austin, Texas.

Chapter 7

1. The M. B. Lamar Papers, Set II, #3011, Texas State Archives, Austin, Texas.

2. Saxon suggested that Pierre may have had a stroke in 1810, which would explain his more passive role after that date. (Saxon, *op. cit.*, p. 32) Stanley Faye proposed a much more likely theory believing that Pierre chose to remain in New Orleans since he possessed an "orderly and disciplined mind," while Jean established himself as "a daring smuggler boss in a region the more romantic for being so near the town." (Faye, *op. cit.*, p. 23)

3. Gayarre, *op. cit.*, p. I:3.

4. De Grummond, *Renato Beluche*, p. 53.

5. Reilly, *op. cit.*, p. 195.

6. "Barataria and Lafitte," Manuscript, Texas State Archives, Austin, Texas.

7. Gayarre, *op. cit.*, p. I:2.

8. *Ibid.*

9. *Ibid.*, p. I:3.

10. De Grummond, *Renato Beluche*, p. 62.

11. Thompson, *op. cit.*, p. 32; Ellis P. Bean reported encountering "Captain Dominic, a Frenchman" commanding the schooner, *Tiger,* sailing under Laffite off the Texas coast in 1814. (*The Life and Times of Jean Laffite,* Volume IX, Number 3, p. 4 citing "The Memoir of Ellis P. Bean" originally published in 1856 in Henderson Yoakum's *History of Texas,* Volume I, pp. 447–448).

12. "Youx" appears as a surname in documents in the Archives Nationales in Paris. This brings into question the tradition that Dominique received his appellation when, as a cabin boy sailing out of St. Dominique, he was hailed by the name of the Caribbean island followed by the French word, "vous!"

13. Sayulvie Feuillie, "Dominique Youx and La Superbe," *The Life and Times of Jean Laffite,* Volume IX, Number 1, Spring 1989, p. 2. Feuillie's article includes a photographic reproduction of the document.

14. A photocopy of a ten-page manuscript in the Rosenberg Library, Galveston (Miscellaneous Collection of Papers and Documents relating to Jean Laffite) claimed that Dominique Youx was a brother of Jean and Pierre. The location of the original is unknown, and there is no reason to believe that the document contains authentic information.

15. Francois-Xavier Martin, *op. cit.*, p. 347.

16. *Ibid.*, p. 349.

17. Reilly, *op. cit.*, p. 195.

18. Gayarre gave March 15, 1812, as the date of Claiborne's proclamation. (Gayarre, *op. cit.*, p. I:3) The wording of the statement, however, would indicate that this was issued after Louisiana had been fully incorporated into the Union, an event which did not occur until November 1812. Niles gave March 1813 as the month in which the governor's denouncement of Barataria was issued. (*Niles' Weekly Register,* Volume IV, p. 142)

19. Saxon, *op. cit.*, p. 65.

20. Thompson, *op. cit.*, p. 80.

21. *La Courrier de la Louisiane,* May 4, 1812, Page 3, Column 5, Louisiana State Museum, New Orleans.

Chapter 8

1. The United States entered the war with an army of less than 3,500 men and a greatly reduced navy. (Reginald Horsman, *The War of 1812,* pp. 12–14)

2. De Grummond, *Renato Beluche,* p. 63.

3. Cited by De Grummond, *Ibid.,* p. 64. For years, New England's ship-building industry had produced some of the finest vessels afloat, many of which had been purchased by Europeans. In the final months before war was declared, frantic efforts were made to build up the American navy, but the nation would need more than a skeletal naval force in a war with Great Britain.

4. Edgar Slanton Maclay, *A History of American Privateers,* p. 323.

5. Manuscript 56, Folder 3, Historic New Orleans Collection, New Orleans, Louisiana.

6. Cited by De Grummond, *Renato Beluche,* p. 64.

7. U.S. District Court, "Synopses of Cases," 1806–1831, Case #552, Louisiana State Museum, New Orleans, Louisiana.

8. De Grummond, *Renato Beluche,* p. 64.

9. *Laffite Study Group Newsletter,* Spring 1987, Volume VII, Number 1.

10. "John R. Grymes Petition, dated November 10, 1812," Manuscript, Parsons Collection, Humanities Research Center, University of Texas, Austin, Texas.

11. "Holmes Manuscript, dated November 19, 1812," Parsons Collection, Humanities Research Center, University of Texas, Austin, Texas.

Chapter 9

1. Registration certificate number 3, 1813, was issued by the Port De La Nouvelle-Orleans to *Le Brig Goelette la Diligente.* Throughout this document, the surname for both brothers was spelled with two "f's" and one "t." (Manuscript file Number 56, Folder 2, Historic New Orleans Collection, New Orleans, Louisiana)

2. *Ibid.*

3. *Ibid.*

4. One researcher suggested that Laffite's *La Diligente* was granted a letter of marque by the French consul in New Orleans since the source of the documents now in the Historic New Orleans Collection "seems to be the office of the French consul." (Robert C. Vogel, "Jean Laffite, the Baratarians, and the Historical Geography of Piracy in the Gulf of Mexico," *Maritime History of the Gulf Coast,* Volume 5, Number 2, Spring 1990, p. 74) Laffite, however, never claimed a French commission, and there is no documentation to substantiate this supposition.

5. Gayarre, *op. cit.,* p. I:4.

6. Saxon, *op. cit.,* p. 67.

7. *Ibid.,* p. 79.

8. "Letter dated April 22, 1813," Manuscript, Parsons Collection, Humanities Research Center, University of Texas, Austin, Texas.

9. Manuscript 194, Historic New Orleans Collection, New Orleans, Louisiana.

10. *Niles' Weekly Register,* Volume IV, p. 142.

11. U.S. District Court "Synopses of Cases, 1806–1817," Louisiana State Museum, New Orleans, Louisiana.

12. A letter addressed to "Captain Garrison," was signed "per Laffite." Some researchers have concluded this was a letter from Pierre. Since the abbreviation for the name of Jean's older brother was usually written either as "P." or as "Pre.," the use of "per" before the name Laffite may have meant the document was written by a secretary or an amanuensis for, or in behalf of, Jean. ("Manuscript letter, April 22, 1813," Parsons Collection, Humanities Research Center, University of Texas, Austin, Texas.)

Chapter 10

1. Gayarre, *op. cit.,* p. I:6.

2. "Hall Manuscript," Parsons Collection, Humanities Research Center, University of Texas, Austin, Texas.

3. Gayarre, *op. cit.,* p. I:5.

4. *Ibid.,* p. I:6.

5. De Grummond cited a letter written by Walker Gilbert to Thomas Freeman, dated February 18, 1814, as evidence of the counter offer for the arrest of Claiborne that was reported to be ten times that of the governor's reward for Laffite. (De Grummond, *The Baratarians and the Battle of New Orleans,* p. 21) Saxon, who based his information on another tradition, reported that the counter reward was $1,500. (Saxon, *op. cit.,* p. 103)

6. This was an undated letter that appears to have been written at some time during 1814. "Laffite letter to Claiborne," Manuscript, Parsons Collection, Humanities Research Center, University of Texas, Austin, Texas.

7. Thompson, *op. cit.,* p. 50.

8. Saxon, *op. cit.,* p. 91.

9. *Ibid.,* pp. 114–117.

10. Gayarre, *op. cit.,* p. I:7. cit.

11. Robert Vogel cited the *St. Louis Missouri Gazette & Illinois Advertiser* of June 11, 1814, for his report. (Vogel, *op. cit.,* p. 66)

12. Gayarre, *op. cit.,* pp. I:8, 9.

13. *Ibid.,* p. I:9.

14. *Ibid.,* p. I:10.

15. Poulenc, *op. cit.,* p. 25.

16. Gayarre, *op. cit.,* p. I:11.

17. Gayarre stated that Grymes and Livingston both received fees of $20,000 as retainers for their services in securing Pierre Laffite's release, believing that the district attorney was "seduced out of the path of professional honor and duty by the bloodstained gold of pirates." *(Ibid.)* It is doubtful, however, that sums of this size were offered or paid to either man.

18. Saxon cited a document in the Pelletier Collection dated August 10, 1814, as the source of this information. (Saxon, *op. cit.,* p. 122)

19. *Laffite Study Group Newsletter,* Volume VII, Number 1, Spring 1987.

Chapter 11

1. Gayarre's account stated that the British sloop anchored six miles from the Barataria pass. (Gayarre, *op. cit.*, p. 2)

2. Latour, *op. cit.*, p. 17.

3. *Ibid.*, p. 18. Latour's *Memoirs* was originally published in 1816.

4. John Sugden, "Jean Lafitte and the British Offer of 1814," *Louisiana History,* Spring 1979, p. 165.

5. Manuscripts 196, Number 55, Historic New Orleans Collection, New Orleans, Louisiana.

6. "Percy Manuscripts," Parsons Collection, Humanities Research Center, University of Texas, Austin, Texas.

7. *Ibid.*

8. "Nicholls to Laffite, August 31, 1814," Manuscript, Parsons Collection, Humanities Research Center, University of Texas, Austin, Texas.

9. "Proclamation by Lt. Col. Nicholls," Parsons Collection, Humanities Research Center, University of Texas, Austin, Texas. Nicholls' August 31 letter to Laffite included the statement "I herewith enclose you a copy of my proclamation to the inhabitants of Louisiana which will I trust point out to you the honorable intentions of my government." (Manuscripts 196, Folder 1, Historic New Orleans Collection, New Orleans, Louisiana)

10. Frank Lawrence Owsley, *Struggle for the Gulf Borderlands,* p. 126.

11. Latour stated that the British offered Laffite $30,000 as an additional enticement for joining their ranks. (Latour, *op. cit.*, p. 19) Samuel Williams declared that the offer included a gift of "75 thousand pounds and a commission in the British navy." (The Lamar Papers, Manuscript 1612)

12. A photocopy of the letter of Nicholls to Laffite, August 31, 1814, is a part of the holdings of the Manuscript Department, William R. Perkins Library, Duke University. The same letter, written in a different hand, is in the Historic New Orleans Collection, New Orleans, Louisiana. (Manuscripts 196, Folder 1)

13. Photocopy of a manuscript letter from Laffite dated September 4, 1814, Manuscript Department, William R. Perkins Library, Duke University, Durham, North Carolina.

14. "Laffite Letter to Lockyer, Captain of the Brig *Sophia,* September 4, 1814," Manuscript, Parsons Collection, Humanities Research Center, University of Texas, Austin, Texas.

15. Niles printed Laffite's letter in an issue dated November 19, 1814, as a justification for Patterson's raid on Barataria. *(Niles' Weekly Register,* Volume VII, p. 166)

16. Duplicate contemporary manuscripts exist of the communications from Nicholls and Percy to the Baratarians of August 30, August 31, and September 1, 1814. The documents in the Parsons Collection, the Humanities Research Center, University of Texas, Austin, Texas, appear to be the original papers. Identical manuscript copies are among the holdings of the Historic New Orleans Collection, New Orleans, Louisiana. Contemporary copies were made in case the originals were lost or destroyed. It is unclear whether Laffite sent the originals or the copies to Blanque.

17. De Grummond, *Renato Beluche,* p. 84.

18. "Laffite Letter to Wm. C. C. Claiborne, September 4, 1814," Manuscript, Parsons Collection, Humanities Research Center, University of Texas, Austin, Texas. Translations of the French manuscripts in this series are those provided by the staff of the Humanities Research Center.

19. "Laffite letter to Jean Blanque, September 7, 1814," Manuscript, Parsons Collection, Humanities Research Center, University of Texas, Austin, Texas.

20. *La Courrier de la Louisiane,* September 26, 1814, page 4, column 3, Louisiana State Museum, New Orleans, Louisiana.

21. Reilly, *op. cit.,* p. 201.

22. Gayarre, *op. cit.,* p. II:2.

23. "Manuscript dated September 10, 1814," Parsons Collection, Humanities Research Center, University of Texas, Austin, Texas.

24. *Niles' Weekly Register,* November 5, 1814, pp. 134, 135.

25. De Grummond, *Renato Beluche,* p. 87.

Chapter 12

1. "Barataria and Lafitte," Manuscript, Texas State Archives, Austin, Texas.

2. Gardner W. Allen, *Our Navy and the West Indian Pirates,* p. 8.

3. Patterson reported that his opposition included a force of up to 1,000 men. Other accounts gave 400 to 500 as the total number of inhabitants of the island. (Juanita Henry Collection, Folder 14, Typescript in the Northwestern State University Library, Natchitoches, Louisiana) It is doubtful that even as many as 400 men would have been on Grande Terre at any one time.

4. Patterson later reported capturing "six fine schooners, one felucca, cruisers and prizes" on the morning of September 16. (*Niles' Weekly Register,* Volume VII, p. 166) One of the prizes was probably an armed schooner.

5. De Grummond, *Renato Beluche,* p. 86.

6. Thompson, *op. cit.,* p. 100.

7. De Grummond, *Renato Beluche,* pp. 86, 87.

8. *Ibid.,* p. 87.

9. *Niles' Weekly Register,* Volume VII, p. 111.

10. *Ibid.,* p. 166.

11. *Ibid.,* p. 133.

12. Poulenc, *op. cit.,* p. 26.

13. De Grummond, *Renato Beluche,* footnote to page 62.

14. Typescript, the Juanita Henry Collection, Folder 14, The Northwestern State University Library, Natchitoches, Louisiana.

15. "Testimony of John Oliver," Manuscript, Parsons Collection, Humanities Research Center, University of Texas, Austin, Texas.

16. *Ibid.*

17. Typescript, the Juanita Henry Collection, Folder 14, The Northwestern State University Library, Natchitoches, Louisiana. A manuscript letter relating to this case from Joseph Martinot, dated September 30, 1814, is a part of the Parsons Collection, Humanities Research Center, University of Texas, Austin, Texas.

18. "Sales in the Case of Danl. T. Patterson and others," Manuscript, The Parsons Collection, Humanities Research Center, University of Texas, Austin, Texas.

Chapter 13

1. Cited by Gayarre, *op. cit.,* pp. II:3, 4.
2. "Laffite Letter to Wm. C. C. Claiborne, September 4, 1814," Manuscript, Parsons Collection, Humanities Research Center, University of Texas, Austin, Texas.
3. De Grummond cited the St. Louis Cathedral Archives Marriage Book 3, 1806–21, p. 117b. for evidence of the relationship between Beluche and Claiborne's wife. (De Grummond, *Renato Beluche,* pp. 84, 85)
4. John Spencer Bassett, *The Life of Andrew Jackson,* p. 147.
5. De Grummond, *Renato Beluche,* p. 85.
6. Gayarre, *op. cit.,* p. II:3.
7. John Spencer Bassett, editor, *Correspondence of Andrew Jackson,* Volume II, pp. 57–58.
8. Bassett, *The Life of Andrew Jackson,* p. 130.
9. *Ibid.,* p. 153.
10. "Barataria and Lafitte," Manuscript, Texas State Archives, Austin, Texas.
11. Bassett, editor, *Correspondence of Andrew Jackson,* Volume II, p. 100.
12. *Ibid.,* p. 92.
13. Bassett, *The Life of Andrew Jackson,* p. 127.
14. Philo A. Goodwin, *Biography of Andrew Jackson, President of the United States, Formerly Major General in the Army of the United States,* p. 122.
15. Owsley, *op. cit.,* p. 128.
16. Herman J. Viola, *Andrew Jackson,* p. 16.
17. De Grummond, *Renato Beluche,* p. 90.
18. Bassett, *The Life of Andrew Jackson,* p. 153.
19. One account stated Latour arranged the meeting between Laffite and Jackson at the general's headquarters at 106 Royal. The general was surprised to find Laffite to be a cultivated and refined gentleman. Jackson offered Laffite sherry as the two men instantly became staunch admirers. (Poulenc, *op. cit.,* p. 37) Gayarre reported that "from that time on Jackson trusted to the utmost Lafitte and his 'bandits.'" (Gayarre, *op. cit.,* p. II:5)
20. One account reported Laffite and Jackson met on December 3 at which time they "joined forces." (Typescript, Louisiana State Museum, New Orleans, Louisiana) This seems unlikely since on this date Jackson was touring the area to determine the invasion route. The future president did not agree to confer with Laffite until after he had discovered the inadequacy of the city's defenses and had received information about the arrival of the British fleet on Lake Borgne.
21. Bassett, *The Life of Andrew Jackson,* p. 153.

Chapter 14

1. Viola, *op. cit.,* p. 14.
2. J. Mackay Hitsman, *The Incredible War of 1812,* p. 232.

3. Latour commented that it was widely believed the reason the British army invaded Louisiana was nothing other than the age-old quest for "beauty and booty." Although he could not authenticate the charge, he declared, for the honor of Great Britain, there should be a "demand that it be refuted, if capable of refutation." (Latour, *op. cit.*, p. 256)

4. Owsley, *op. cit.*, p. 129.

5. "The Journal of Major C R. Forrest," p. 44.

6. De Grummond, *Renato Beluche*, p. 89. The Journal of Major C. R. Forrest listed a total of 5,349 men in the initial attack force consisting of Dragoons, Royal Artillery, Infantry and a Rocket Brigade. ("The Journal of Major C. R. Forrest," p. 24)

7. Owsley, *op. cit.*, pp. 126, 127.

8. Owsley stated that Jackson was so enamored with Laffite that "he made him an aide." (*Ibid.*, footnote, p. 148)

9. [McAfee, Robert], *History of the Late War in the Western Country*, p. 504. A detailed account of the battle is extant in a volume published less than two years after the conclusion of the conflict by a participant. This work carries no author's name, but has been attributed to Robert B. McAfee, an American officer who served under Jackson.

10. "The Journal of Major C. R. Forrest," pp. 24, 25.

11. Marquis James, *Andrew Jackson: The Border Captain*, p. 235; Forrest listed the 93rd Highlanders' strength at 907 men. The regiment was supported by two West India units under the command of Major General Keane. ("The Journal of Major C. R. Forrest," p. 24)

12. *Niles' Weekly Register*, Volume VII, p. 231.

13. De Grummond, *Renato Beluche*, p. 97.

14. Latour, *op. cit.*, pp. xxxiii–xxxv. Originally written in French, Latour's *Historical Memoirs* was translated into English and published in 1816. This is an important source of information about the seventeen-day battle both because Latour was a participant and because he included copies of documents and correspondence as appendices to his work.

15. "The Journal of Major C. R. Forrest," p. 25.

Chapter 15

1. De Grummond, *Renato Beluche*, pp. 101, 102.

2. Bernard Marigny, "Reflections on the Campaign of General Andrew Jackson," *Louisiana Historical Quarterly*, Volume 6, p. 65.

3. [McAfee, Robert], *op. cit.*, p. 507.

4. De Grummond, *Renato Beluche*, p. 103.

5. Goodwin, *op. cit.*, p. 132.

6. *Letters and Other Writings of James Madison, Fourth President of the United States.* Published by Order of Congress, Volume III, p. 599.

7. Stanislaus Murray Hamilton, editor, "Letter to Judge Hugh L. White, Jan. 26th, 1827," *The Writings of James Monroe Including a Collection of His Public and Private Papers and Correspondence Now for the First Time Printed*, Volume VII, p. 94.

8. "Andrew Jackson Letter to Major Michael Reynolds, December 22,

1814," Manuscript, Parsons Collection, Humanities Research Center, University of Texas, Austin, Texas.

9. *The New Orleans Bulletin,* August 29, 1874, page 1, The Louisiana State Museum, New Orleans, Louisiana.

10. Robert Vogel cited John S. Bassett's *Correspondence of Andrew Jackson* (3:339) for Jackson's recollection that his army procured from the Baratarians 7,500 flints for pistols and boarding pieces which was solely the supply of flints for all my militia." (Vogel, *op. cit.,* p. 75)

11. De Grummond, *Renato Beluche,* p. 102.

12. "The Journal of Major C. R. Forrest," p. 29; Goodwin, *op. cit.,* p. 132.

13. "The Journal of Major C. R. Forrest," pp. 30, 31.

14. Latour, *op. cit.,* p. 95.

15. "The Journal of Major C. R. Forrest," pp. 31, 32.

16. [McAfee, Robert], *op. cit.,* p. 511.

17. "The Journal of Major C. R. Forrest," p. 33.

18. James, *op. cit.,* p. 245.

19. "Edward Livingston to Jackson, New Orleans, December 25, 1814," John Spencer Bassett, editor, *Correspondence of Andrew Jackson,* Volume II, p. 125.

20. "The Journal of Major C. R. Forrest," p. 33.

21. De Grummond, *Renato Beluche,* pp. 108, 109.

22. [McAfee, Robert], *op. cit.,* p. 513.

23. *Ibid.;* Forrest's Journal reported the destruction of the *Carolina* as having occurred on December 26. ("The Journal of Major C. R. Forrest," p. 33)

24. [McAfee, Robert], *op. cit.,* p. 514.

25. Latour, *op. cit.,* p. 122.

26. *Ibid.,* p. 148.

27. De Grummond, *Renato Beluche,* p. 113; James, *op. cit.,* p. 253.

28. Marigny, *op. cit.,* p. 67; Latour, *op. cit.,* p. 121.

29. Latour, *op. cit.,* p. 123.

30. *Ibid.,* p. 1.

31. [McAfee, Robert], *op. cit.,* p. 514.

32. James, *op. cit.,* p. 249; Marigny, *op. cit.,* p. 65.

Chapter 16

1. Latour, *op. cit.,* p. 134.

2. De Grummond, *Renato Beluche,* pp. 114, 115.

3. Gayarre, *op. cit.,* II:5,6.

4. James, *op. cit.,* p. 257.

5. Latour, *op. cit.,* p. 133.

6. "The Journal of Major C. R. Forrest," p. 38.

7. Forrest's report stated that the assault did not take place at this time because of the ineffectiveness of the British artillery. (*Ibid.*)

8. [McAfee, Robert], *op. cit.,* p. 514.

9. De Grummond, *Renato Beluche,* p. 118.

10. [McAfee, Robert], *op. cit.,* p. 515.

11. *Ibid.,* p. 516.

12. *Ibid.,* p. 515.

13. James, *op. cit.*, p. 260.

14. [McAfee, Robert], *op. cit.*, p. 516.

15. *Ibid.*

16. James, *op. cit.*, p. 261. Gayarre recorded another legend. During the battle, Jackson noticed the Baratarian battery had ceased firing. He asked Dominique Youx why. He was told "The powder is good for nothing — fit only to shoot blackbirds with, and not red-coats!" Jackson turned to an aide and said: "Tell the ordnance officer that I will have him shot in five minutes as a traitor, if Dominique complains any more of his powder." He then galloped off. When he returned, Dominique was blazing away. "Ha! Ha! friend Dominique, I see you are hard at work." "Pretty good work, too!" replied Dominique with a chuckle, "and I guess that the British have discovered by this time that there has been a change of powder in the battery." (Gayarre, *op. cit.*, p. II:6) There is probably no basis in fact for either legend, but both tales illustrate Jackson's appreciation for the former cannoneers of Grande Terre.

17. [McAfee, Robert], *op. cit.*, p. 517.

18. De Grummond, *Renato Beluche*, p. 123.

19. [McAfee, Robert], *op. cit.*, p. 517.

20. *Ibid.*, p. 518.

21. Latour, *op. cit.*, p. 159.

22. James, *op. cit.*, pp. 266, 267.

23. [McAfee, Robert], *op. cit.*, pp. 519, 520.

24. *Ibid.*, p. 523.

25. Owsley, *op. cit.*, p. 162.

26. Bassett, *The Life of Andrew Jackson*, p. 151.

27. *Ibid.*

28. Latour described Jackson's "Address" as one that was "to be read at the head of each of the corps composing the line below New Orleans, Jan. 21, 1815." (Latour, *op. cit.*, pp. clxxxii-cxc)

29. *Ibid.*, p. clxxxii.

30. *Ibid.*, p. clxxxvii. Gayarre gave an identical account of Jackson's General Orders, probably having taken his information from the appendix of Latour's work. (Gayarre, *op. cit.*, p. II:6)

Chapter 17

1. Bassett, editor, *Correspondence of Andrew Jackson*, Volume II, p. 150.

2. Latour, *op. cit.*, p. 199.

3. *Niles' Weekly Register*, Volume VIII, Supplement, p. 163.

4. Niles' account gave January 24 as the day of the celebration (*Ibid.*, Volume VIII, Supplement, p. 163) Latour listed January 23 as the date of the public thanksgiving. (Latour, *op. cit.*, p. 199)

5. Marquis James cited a letter dated January 21, 1814 in the Louisiana State Museum, New Orleans, for a description of the celebration. (James, *op. cit.*, p. 274)

6. Latour, *op. cit.*, p. 199.

7. *Niles' Weekly Register*, Volume VIII, Supplement, p. 163.

8. *Ibid.*

9. Latour, *op. cit.*, pp. 199–200.

10. *Ibid.*, Appendix Number XXXV, p. lxxiii.

11. *Niles' Weekly Register,* Volume VIII, Supplement, p. 163; Latour, *op. cit.,* p. 200.

12. Asbury, *op. cit.,* p. 126; Saxon, *op. cit.,* p. 190; Thompson, *op. cit.,* p. 110; Latour's detailed account of the day of celebration made no mention of an evening social gathering. (Latour, *op. cit.,* pp. 197–200)

13. The tradition of a late evening celebration included a legend that it was at this time Laffite was introduced to General Coffee who snubbed him because of his reputation, an experience which resulted in his decision to leave Louisiana. (Asbury, *op. cit.,* p. 126) Laffite, however, was known to Coffee at least a month before the public celebration, for it was the Tennessee commander who commended Laffite for his "personal courage in action" during the battle of December 23. ("Letter of Andrew Jackson to Jean Laffite," photocopy in the Manuscript Department, William R. Perkins Library, Duke University, Durham, North Carolina)

14. De Grummond, *The Baratarians and the Battle of New Orleans,* p. 147.

15. *Ibid.,* p. 147.

16. [McAfee, Robert], *op. cit.,* p. 528.

17. De Grummond, *The Baratarians and the Battle of New Orleans,* p. 148.

18. Marigny, *op. cit.,* p. 74.

19. *Ibid.,* p. 70.

20. De Grummond, *The Baratarians and the Battle of New Orleans,* p. 152.

21. James, *op. cit.,* p. 283.

22. De Grummond, *Renato Beluche,* p. 128.

23. *Niles' Weekly Register,* Volume VII, p. 380.

24. *Ibid.*

25. "Andrew Jackson to Jean Laffite," Photocopy in the Manuscript Department, William R. Perkins Library, Duke University, Durham, North Carolina.

26. "Jean Blanque Manuscript, "Parsons Collection, Humanities Research Center, University of Texas, Austin, Texas.

Chapter 18

1. De Grummond, *The Baratarians and the Battle of New Orleans,* pp. 153–155.

2. De Grummond, *Renato Beluche,* p. 131.

3. *Ibid.*

4. *Ibid.,* pp. 133, 134

5. *Ibid.,* pp. 70–74

6. *Ibid.,* pp. 140 ff.

7. *Ibid.,* p. 160.

8. A photostat of an article by Edith Elliott Long dated August 20, 1965, in the Louisiana State Museum, New Orleans, Louisiana.

9. De Grummond, *Renato Beluche,* pp. 171–184.

10. *Ibid.,* p. 275.

11. *Ibid.,* pp. 277–279.

12. Gayarre, *op. cit.,* p. II:7.

13. Asbury, *op. cit.,* p. 128. According to Saxon, Napoleon's death oc-

curred three days before Dominique Youx's ship was to leave New Orleans to attempt the rescue. (Saxon, *op. cit.*, p. 269)

14. Stanley Clisby Arthur included a reproduction of the funeral notice of Dominique Youx in his work, *Jean Laffite, Gentleman Rover*, p. 233.

15. *Ibid.*, p. 235.

16. The full text of the original epitaph was the following: *"Intrépide Guerrier sur la terre et sur lónde, Qui sut dans cent combats signaler sa valeur, Et ce nouveau Bayard sans reproche et sans peur, Aurait pu, sans trembler Voir s écrouler le monde!"* Thompson recorded that Dominique Youx's burial site was located in St. Louis Cemetery Number One. (Thompson, *op. cit.*, p. 117) Current records that were confirmed by National Park Rangers, Lafitte National Park, New Orleans Unit, indicate that the tomb is located in what today is designated as St. Louis Cemetery Number Two which is separated from Number One by a housing project. A 1989 publication included a photograph of the site within the bounds of Cemetery Number Two. (Mary Louise Christovich, editor, *New Orleans Architecture: the Cemeteries*, Volume III)

17. Thompson, *op. cit.*, p. 34.

18. Gayarre, *op. cit.*, pp. II:7, 8.

19. Faye, *op. cit.*, p. 23.

20. Gayarre, *op. cit.*, p. II:7.

21. *Life and Times of Jean Laffite*, December 1977, Number 3.

22. Saxon, *op. cit.*, p. 198.

23. "Testimony of John Oliver," Manuscript, Parsons Collection. This document and the accompanying correspondence between Laffite and the British and the letters forwarded to Blanque were originally filed with the court records, but according to Saxon, disappeared only to turn up in a New Orleans curio shop and eventually pass into the hands of E. A. Parsons. The collection is now located in the Humanities Research Center, Austin, Texas.

24. "Sales in the Case of Danl T. Patterson and others," Manuscript, Parsons Collection, Humanities Research Center, University of Texas, Austin, Texas.

25. Saxon, *op. cit.*, p. 198.

26. *Ibid.*, p. 211.

27. Stanley Faye, *op. cit.*, Number 3, p. 24.

28. *Ibid.*, p. 34.

29. Stanley Faye cited "Jn Laffite to the president," Madison Correspondence, Library of Congress, Manuscript, for the text of the petition. (Faye, *op. cit.*, p. 22)

Chapter 19

1. Saxon, *op. cit.*, p. 213.

2. *Southwestern Historical Quarterly*, October 1941, Volume XLV, #2.

3. Harris Gaylord Warren, "Documents Relating to the Establishment of Privateers at Galveston, 1816–1819," *Louisiana Historical Quarterly*, Volume 21, Number 4, p. 5.

4. Correspondence between the Vice Consul, Diego Morphy in New Orleans and the Captain General in Cuba designated Pierre as "No. 13-uno" and

Jean as "No. 13-dos." ("Correspondence of the Vice Consul in New Orleans, Diego Morphy, with the Captain General of the Island of Cuba, 1817–1819.")

5. Faye, *op. cit.*, pp. 32, 33.

6. David G. McComb, *Galveston: A History*, p. 34.

7. Carlos A. Ferro, *Vida de Luis Aury*, p. 42.

8. T. Fredrick Davis, *MacGregor's Invasion*, pp. 33, 34.

9. Ray Miller, *Ray Miller's Galveston*, pp. 45, 47.

10. *State Papers and Publick Documents of the United States*, Volume XI, p. 354.

11. Faye, *op. cit.*, p. 33.

12. "Correspondence of the Vice Consul in New Orleans, Diego Morphy, with the Captain General of the Island of Cuba, 1817–1819," p. 16. Latour and Jean Laffite accompanied a Louis Bringier into Arkansas in 1816 on an espionage mission "dispatched by the Spanish secret service to gather intelligence on Anglo-American encroachment on New Spain." *The Life and Times of Jean Laffite* (Volume X, No. 1, Spring 1990) cited an article by W. D. Williams, *Arkansas Historical Quarterly*, XLVIII, No. 2, Summer 1989, for information relating to this early effort by the Laffites to convince Spain of their reliability.

13. Warren, *op. cit.*, p. 5.

14. *Ibid.*, p. 14.

15. *Ibid.*

16. "Correspondence of the Vice Consul in New Orleans, Diego Morphy, with the Captain General of the Island of Cuba, 1817–1819," pp. 11, 12.

17. *Ibid.*, pp. 21–25.

18. Faye, *op. cit.*, p. 37.

19. "Correspondence of the Vice Consul in New Orleans, Diego Morphy, with the Captain General of the Island of Cuba, 1817–1819," pp. 18, 19.

20. Faye, *op. cit.*, p. 38.

21. "Correspondence of the Vice Consul in New Orleans, Diego Morphy, with the Captain General of the Island of Cuba, 1817–1819, p. 21.

22. *Ibid.*

Chapter 20

1. Surveyors had mapped much of the Gulf Coast under orders from a Spanish governor of Louisiana, Bernardo de Galvez, whose surname was entered on the maps as the designation for the largest bay in the survey. (Ray Miller, *op. cit.*, p. 43) Some early records referred to the island as "Snake Island." (Alfred George Course, *Pirates of the Western Sea*, p. 187)

2. McComb, *op. cit.*, p. 34.

3. Davis, *op. cit.*, p. 34. The United States' ban on slaving had added economic incentive to the illicit importation of field hands. The price of an able-bodied black, once brought to American shores, was sometimes as much as forty times the purchase price on the African coast. (Asbury, *op. cit.*, p. 119)

4. "Correspondence of the Vice Consul in New Orleans Diego Morphy, with the Captain General of the Island of Cuba, 1817–1819," p. 23.

5. Ray Miller, *op. cit.*, p. 47.

6. Davis, *op. cit.*, p. 33.

7. "Information derived from James Campbell now resident on the Galves-

ton Bay 10th June 1855," Manuscript, The Lamar Papers, Manuscript 2492, Texas State Archives, Austin, Texas, pp. 1, 2.

8. *Ibid.,* p. 11.

9. Vogel, *op. cit.,* p. 69.

10. "Correspondence of the Vice Consul in New Orleans, Diego Morphy, with the Captain General of the Island of Cuba, 1817–1819," p. 21.

11. *Ibid.,* p. 68.

12. The Lamar Papers, Manuscript 1614, Texas State Archives, Austin, Texas.

13. Faye, *op. cit.,* p. 39.

14. A letter signed "Jn. Laffite" dated May 14, 1817, cited by Stanley Faye from Notas Diplomaticas, V. 2, Cienfuegos to Apodaca. *(Ibid.)*

15. "Letter dated Galveston, July 23, 1817" cited by Stanley Faye who believed this document was written by Pierre during his stay on the island. The authorship is unclear since this and an accompanying document were dispatched from Galveston to New Orleans under the Spanish code name "Number 13." *(Ibid.,* pp. 43, 44)

16. A letter from Beverly Chew to William Crawford dated August 1, 1817, cited by E. R. Snow in *True Tales of Pirates and their Gold,* p. 20. Excerpts from Chew's letter were included in an article in *The Life and Times of Jean Laffite* (Volume IX, Number 2, pp. 4–7) that cited *The American State Papers, Foreign Relations,* Volume IV, pp. 134–135.

17. *State Papers and Publick Documents of the United States,* Volume XI, p. 365.

18. Ray Miller, *op. cit.,* p. 47.

19. *State Papers and Publick Documents of the United States,* Volume XI, p. 354.

20. Davis, *op. cit.,* p. 27.

21. *Ibid.,* p. 54.

22. *State Papers and Publick Documents of the United States,* Volume XI, p. 398.

23. *The Debates and Proceedings in the Congress of the United States,* Volume XXXII, p. 1803.

24. *Ibid.,* pp. 1801–1812.

Chapter 21

1. "A Visit to Galveston Island, J. Randall Jones 1818," a typescript in the Rosenberg Library, Galveston, which was copied from the original manuscript prior to the document's destruction in the Galveston hurricane of 1900.

2. McComb, *op. cit.,* p. 35.

3. Faye, *op. cit.,* p. 32.

4. David McComb recorded a legend in which Satan offered to build the Maison Rouge in return for a promise from Laffite that the Ruler of Hades could claim the first living creature he saw the following morning. Laffite agreed, and the Devil built the house. The crafty privateer, however, outwitted Satan the next day by throwing a mongrel dog into his path. The Devil took revenge by painting the house he had constructed for Laffite blood red. (McComb, *op. cit.,* p. 36)

5. *Ibid.*

6. Amelia Barr lived in a building on Galveston Island that was believed to

be the renovated Maison Rouge at some time between the years 1856 and 1868. (Paul Adams, "Amelia Barr in Texas," *Southwestern Historical Quarterly*, XLIX, Number 3, p. 371.

7. Course, *op. cit.*, p. 189.

8. *Ibid.*

9. *Ibid.*, p. 185.

10. *Laffite Study Group Newsletter*, Volume VIII, Number 2, Summer 1988 cited *Biographical and Historical Memoirs of Louisiana*, Volume I, pp. 410–411, a work published in 1892.

11. Names on the privateering commission were in Spanish in order to maintain the fiction that this was a patent issued in behalf of the revolutionary Republic of Mexico.

12. "Le Brave Documents," Manuscript, Historic New Orleans Collection, New Orleans, Louisiana. The original manuscripts are in French. Citations used here are from the English translations of the documents provided by the staff of the Historic New Orleans Collection.

13. *Ibid.*

14. Faye, *op. cit.*, p. 42.

15. Faye cited "Fatio to the captain-general, March 1, 1818." (*Ibid.*, p. 56)

16. *Ibid.*, p. 53.

17. *Ibid.*, p. 69.

18. The Lamar Papers, Manuscript 1612, Texas State Archives, Austin, Texas.

19. Faye, *op. cit.*, p. 41.

20. *Ibid.*, p. 45.

21. *Ibid.*, pp. 73, 74.

22. "Correspondence of the Vice Consul in New Orleans, Diego Morphy, with the Captain General of the Island of Cuba, 1817–1819," p. 75.

23. Stanley Faye cited Notas Diplomaticas, V. 2, Cienfuegos to Apodaca, July 17, 1818. (Faye, *op. cit.*, p. 78)

24. Warren, *op. cit.*, p. 4.

25. Faye, *op. cit.*, p. 74.

Chapter 22

1. *The Life and Times of Jean Laffite* (December 1977) cited the February 6, 1818, issue of *The Courier of Louisiana*, p. 3., column 1.

2. John R. Spears, *The American Slave-Trade*, p. 127.

3. *Ibid.*, p. 128.

4. Throughout the second decade of the nineteenth century, Congress continued to debate means for putting an end to the abuses of the slave traffic. Some modifications were made to the 1818 law in an act passed on March 3, 1819. Another revision to the law was enacted on May 15, 1820, but it was not until January 30, 1823, that an effective measure passed both houses. (Spears, *op. cit.*, pp. 129–133)

5. "A Visit to Galveston Island, J. Randall Jones, 1818," Rosenberg Library, Galveston, Texas.

6. McComb, *op. cit.*, p. 35.

7. Asbury, *op. cit.*, p. 133.

8. McComb, *op. cit.*, p. 35.

9. Evelyn Brogan gave South Carolina as the site of the birth of James Bowie. (Evelyn Brogan, *James Bowie, a Hero of the Alamo*, p. 9) Others believed he was born either in Georgia or Kentucky. (Asbury, *op. cit.*, p. 132)

10. Raymond Thorp, *Bowie Knife*, p. 121.

11. *Ibid.*, p. 120.

12. *Ibid.*, pp. 121, 122.

13. *Ibid.*, p. 23.

14. According to Raymond Thorp, reports of the nature of the contest were greatly exaggerated. The legend of the battle, however, demonstrates the fact Bowie was considered by his contemporaries to be a man of extreme violence. (*Ibid.*, pp. 6–8)

15. Mody C. Boatright and Donald Day, *From Hell to Breakfast*, p. 199.

16. The Bowie legend has been tarnished by information uncovered by Edward S. Sears that was reported in a documented work by Mody Boatright and Donald Day who believed Bowie married into the Beramendi family "largely because he knew the land fraud case in Arkansas upon which he based his claims to fortune would soon go against him." (Boatright and Day, *op. cit.*, p. 178) Bowie's promised dowry to the father of Ursula Beramendi was never paid. After his death, his estate was appraised at $33.11 consisting of saws, old clothes, and two cranks. (*Ibid.*, p. 198)

17. Asbury, *op. cit.*, p. 132.

18. Thorp, *op. cit.*, p. 122, 123.

19. Asbury, *op. cit.*, pp. 132, 133; Boatright and Day, *op. cit.*, p. 176; Thorp, *op. cit.*, p. 123.

20. Eugene C. Barker, "African Slave Trade in Texas," *Quarterly of the Texas State Historical Association*, Volume VI, Number 2, October 1902, p. 149.

21. *La Courier de la Louisiane*, May 22, 1818, p. 3, Louisiana State Museum, New Orleans, Louisiana.

22. Poulenc, *op. cit.*, pp.. 44, 45.

23. *La Courrier de la Louisiane*, May 22, 1818, p. 3, Louisiana State Museum, New Orleans, Louisiana.

24. Ed Kilman, *Cannibal Coast*, p. 175.

25. *Ibid.*, p. 176.

26. Harbert Davenport and Joseph K. Wells, "The First Europeans in Texas," *Southwestern Historical Quarterly*, Volume XXII, Number 1, October 1918, pp. 137, 138. Another account of the battle stated the Indians lost "about thirty men." (Albert S. Gatschet, "The Karankawa Indians," *Peabody Museum of American Archaeology and Ethnology Papers*, I, cited in *The Life and Times of Jean Laffite* (Volume IX, Number 2, p. 7)

27. W. W. Newcomb, Jr., *The Indians of Texas*, p. 341; Basil Fuller, *Pirate Harbors and their Secrets*, p. 119.

28. "A Visit to Galveston Island, J. Randall Jones, 1818," Rosenberg Library, Galveston, Texas.

29. "Notes and Documents," *Southwestern Historical Quarterly*, Volume LXXIII, Number 1, July 1969, p. 58.

30. Saxon, *op. cit.*, p. 222.

31. Faye, *op. cit.*, p. 66.

32. Saxon, *op. cit.*, p. 223.

33. Basil Fuller, *Pirate Harbors and their Secrets*, p. 119.

34. Warren, *op. cit.*, p. 7.

35. Charles Gayarre's printed work, *The Famous Lafittes at Galveston*, included the Graham-Laffite correspondence. The originals of these letters are in the Department of State Manuscript collection in the Library of Congress, Washington, D.C. (*Life and Times of Jean Laffite*, June 1982, Number VI)

36. Charles Francis Adams, editor, *Memoirs of John Quincy Adams*, Volume IV, pp. 175-176.

37. An outlaw nation organized by the Madagascar pirates flourished in the seventeenth and eighteenth centuries off the coast of Africa. (Frank Sherry, *Raiders and Rebels*, pp. 85 ff.)

38. The Lamar Papers, Manuscript 2492, Texas State Archives, Austin, Texas, p. 7.

39. *Laffite Study Group Newsletter*, Number 5, 1981.

40. Cited by David McComb, *op. cit.*, p. 36.

Chapter 23

1. In July 1839, two decades after the visit of members of the crew of the *Enterprise* to Galveston, an article appeared in the *United States Magazine and Democratic Review* entitled "The Cruise of the Enterprise, A Day with La Fitte." The length of time between the event and the writing would invalidate the accuracy of some of the details of the visit including quoted statements cited by the writer. The date, "in year of our Lord, 1819," was probably incorrect. (*United States Magazine and Democratic Review*, July 1839, Volume VI, Number XIX, p. 33)

2. *Ibid.*, pp. 33–36.

3. *Ibid.*, pp. 37, 38.

4. *Ibid.*, pp. 38, 39.

5. *Ibid.*, p. 40.

6. *Ibid.*, p. 42.

7. *Ibid.*, pp. 40, 41.

8. *Ibid.*

9. *Ibid.*, p. 40.

10. *Ibid.*, p. 42.

11. *Ibid.*, p. 38.

12. Joe B. Frantz, *Texas. A History*, p. 44.

13. After Lallemand's plans were known to Spanish authorities, Luis de Onis called upon John Quincy Adams in his Washington office to discuss the French invasion of Texas. The secretary of state assured him the United States had no intention of supporting the colony on the Trinity River. George Graham was sent to Galveston to convey to both Laffite and Lallemand the information that French settlement would not be tolerated between "the Sabine and the Rio Grande," (Faye, *op. cit.*, p. 65)

14. David Nevin, *The Texans*, p. 20.

15. Stanley Faye recorded two letters from Pierre to Jean Laffite under the date February 17, 1818, taken from a "contemporary Spanish translation made

in Havana . . . [which] appears incompetent." (Faye, *op. cit.*, pp. 55–57) The transcript of these Spanish documents in the Rosenberg Library does not give the full text of either letter. ("Correspondence of the Vice Consul in New Orleans, Diego Morphy, with the Captain General of the Island of Cuba, 1817–1819," p. 76)

16. "Correspondence of the Vice Consul in New Orleans, Diego Morphy, with the Captain General of the Island of Cuba, 1817–1819," p. 76.

17. Naiveness, *op. cit.*, p. 20.

18. Faye, *op. cit.*, p. 56.

19. Julia Kathryn Garrett, *Green Flag Over Texas,* pp. 141–225.

20. George P. Garrison, *Texas: A Contest of Civilizations,* p. 122.

21. Frantz, *op. cit.*, p. 44.

22. Faye, *op. cit.*, p. 82.

23. Garrison, *op. cit.*, p. 123.

24. The Lamar Papers, Document Number 19, Texas State Archives, Austin, Texas. A photocopy of the original manuscript along with a typescript of Laffite's letter to Long is in the Rosenberg Library, Galveston, Texas. Document Number 24 appears to be further correspondence between Laffite and Long.

25. Lois Garver, "Benjamin Rusk Milam," *Southwestern Historical Quarterly,* October 1934, Volume 38, Number 2, p. 84.

26. *Ibid.*

27. *Niles' Weekly Register* of January 29, 1820 declared: "We learn that Lafitte has lately received a commission from Gen. Long." (*Niles' Weekly Register,* Volume XVII, p. 376)

28. *Ibid.*, February 5, 1820, Volume XVII, p. 396.

29. Saxon cited a letter in the National Archives of Mexico (*Historia, Notas, Diplomaticas,* Volume Four), from Laffite to Juan Mañuel de Cagigal, Spanish governor of Havana, Cuba, dated December 11, 1819, in which Laffite referred to a communication he had written on October 7. (Saxon, *op. cit.*, pp. 231–232)

30. *Southwestern Historical Quarterly,* October 1934, Volume 38, Number 2, p. 84.

31. Frantz, *op. cit.*, p. 45.

32. Anne Brindley, "Jane Long," *Southwestern Historical Quarterly,* LVI, 217.

33. *Southwestern Historical Quarterly,* October 1957, Volume LXI, Number 2, p. 300.

34. *Niles' Weekly Register,* November 18, 1820, Volume XIX, p. 191.

35. Frantz, *op. cit.*, p. 45.

36. James A. Creighton, *A Narrative History of Brazoria County,* p. 8.

37. Garrison, *op. cit.*, p. 123.

38. Adele Looscan, "Life and Service of John Birdsall," *Southwestern Historical Quarterly,* XXVI, 1, p. 46; The Lamar Papers, Numbers 351 and 397, Texas State Archives, Austin, Texas.

Chapter 24

1. Saxon included the full text of the account of the robbery which appeared in the October 22, 1819, issue of *The Louisiana Courier.* (Saxon, *op. cit.*, pp. 233–234)

2. Niles referred to the leader of the raiders as William Brown (*Niles' Week-*

177

ly Register, February 5, 1820, Volume VII, p. 396) while other accounts gave his name as George Brown. (*The Louisiana Courier* of November 24, 1819, cited in *Life and Times of Jean Laffite,* December 1977)

3. Stanley Faye stated that "by signing the Florida treaty the United States government had recognized Galveston as lying beyond its own limits. So privateersmen at Galveston felt that their port had nothing to fear from American warships." (Faye, *op. cit.,* p. 82)

4. Niles reported the correspondence between Laffite and the captain of the *Lynx* in the February 5, 1820, issue of the journal. (*Niles' Weekly Register,* Volume XVII, p. 395)

5. *Niles' Weekly Register,* February 5, 1820, Volume XVII, p. 396.

6. The *Lynx* was a vessel of 150 tons built during the War of 1812. In 1820, the ship was lost at sea when bound for Jamaica. (*Laffite Study Group Newsletter,* Volume V, Number 2, Summer 1985)

7. *Niles' Weekly Register,* January 29, 1820, Volume XVII, p. 376.

8. *Ibid.,* February 5, 1820, Volume XVII, p. 396.

9. *Ibid.*

10. *Ibid.* A fanciful account ("A Visit to Lafitte," *The Knickerbocker,* March 1847, Volume XXIX, Number 1, p. 254) of the visit was published twenty-eight years after the event, probably based on Niles' report.

11. The November 24, 1819, issue of *The Louisiana Courier.* (Cited in *Life and Times of Jean Laffite,* December 1977)

12. *Niles' Weekly Register,* February 5, 1820, Volume XVII, p. 395.

13. Allen, *op. cit.,* p. 16.

14. "Le Brave Documents," Manuscript, Historic New Orleans Collection, New Orleans, Louisiana.

15. Asbury, *op. cit.,* p. 127.

16. Saxon, *op. cit.,* p. 241.

17. "Le Brave Documents," Manuscript, Historic New Orleans Collection, New Orleans, Louisiana.

18. Asbury, *op. cit.,* p. 127.

Chapter 25

1. "Pierre Laffite to Commodore D. F. Patterson, New Orleans, January 3, 1820," Manuscript, Parsons Collection, Humanities Research Center, University of Texas, Austin, Texas.

2. *Niles' Weekly Register,* January 8, 1820, Volume XVII, p. 309.

3. *Ibid.,* February 5, 1820, Volume XVII, 395.

4. McComb, *op. cit.,* p. 36.

5. The Lamar Papers, Manuscript 2492, Texas State Archives, Austin, Texas, p. 18.

6. *Ibid.,* p. 21.

7. *Ibid.,* p. 23.

8. Andrew Forest Muer, editor, *Texas in 1837,* Endnotes to page 180.

9. "A Veteran Gone: Chas. Cronea, Who Fought Under Jean Lafitte," typescript in the Library of Northwestern State University, Natchitoches, Louisiana.

10. The account of Kearny's visit to Laffite, written years after the event,

was dated 1819. Some authorities have followed Saxon in dating Kearny's contact with the island chieftain as "early in 1821," assuming that Laffite left Galveston soon afterwards. (Saxon, *Lafitte, the Pirate*, p. 247) However, internal evidence would argue for an earlier date for the visit, but one later than 1819. The aide to Kearny recalled that a body was hanging on the gallows on the beach. ("The Cruise of the Enterprise, A Day with La Fitte," *United States Magazine and Democratic Review*, July 1839, Volume VI, Number XIX, p. 40) Since the execution took place in the winter of 1819–1820 (*Niles' Weekly Register*, January 29, 1820, Volume XVII, p. 376), it would have been impossible for the body to have survived as recognizable human remains beyond the warm months of 1820. One other clue to the exact date of the visit exists in the description of the weather indicating spring-like conditions. (*Ibid.*, p. 33) In all probability, Kearny made his contact with Laffite in April or May of 1820. The letter of Laffite to Patterson in the Parsons Collection, May 24, 1820, would confirm this dating.

11. "Laffite Letter to Commodore Patterson, May 24, 1820," Manuscript, Parsons Collection, Humanities Research Center, University of Texas, Austin, Texas.

12. "The Cruise of the Enterprise, A Day with La Fitte," *United States Magazine and Democratic Review*, July 1839, Volume VI, Number XIX, p. 39.

13. Spears, *op. cit.*, pp. 130–133.

14. Niles reported convictions of persons who were guilty of procuring slaves in 1820. (*Niles' Weekly Register*, December 2, 1820, Volume XIX, pp. 215, 216)

15. Typescript, Sam Houston Regional Library and Research Center, Liberty, Texas.

16. *Niles' Weekly Register*, January 20, 1821, Volume XIX, p. 352.

17. *Ibid.*, December 16, 1820, Volume XIX, pp. 251, 252; January 8, 1821, Volume XVII, p. 320; January 20, 1821, Volume XIX, p. 352.

18. Niles quoted the *New Orleans Advertiser* as the source of this account. (*Ibid.*, September 30, 1820, Volume XIX, p. 80)

19. Macum Phelan recorded an account of a woman who claimed to have been a "wife" of Laffite "from early womanhood to middle age" who had followed him to Galveston Island. In 1839 she "repented" of her relationship to the privateer commander and became a Methodist convert. (*Laffite Study Group Newsletter*, Number 4, December 1978 cited Macum Phelan's *History of Methodism in Texas*, p. 111)

20. Stanley Faye accepted May 7, 1820, as the date upon which Laffite quit Galveston. (Faye, *op. cit*, p. 93) The fact that privateers continued to sail from Galveston as late as September 1820 would indicate that a remnant remained on the island until late in the year or early in 1821. (*Niles' Weekly Register*, September 30, 1820, Volume XIX, p. 80)

21. Saxon, *op. cit.*, p. 256.

22. Poulenc, *op. cit.*, p. 49.

23. *The Journal of Jean Laffite*, p. 119. The legend of the burning of the colony is a part of Laffite tradition. (J. S. Thrasher, *Early History of Galveston*, p. 2)

24. "A Veteran Gone: Chas. Cronea, Who Fought Under Jean Lafitte," Typescript in the Library of Northwestern State University, Natchitoches, Louisiana.

25. Garrett, *op. cit.*, p. 233.

Chapter 26

1. *Niles' Weekly Register,* Volume XXII, March, April, and June, 1822, pp. 34–264.

2. *History of the Lives and Bloody Exploits of the Most Noted Pirates; their Trials and Executions,* pp. 256 ff. [This work was originally printed in 1825 and reprinted with some additions in 1836]

3. *Niles' Weekly Register,* December 22, 1821, Volume XXI, p. 258.

4. *Ibid.,* June 1, 1822, Volume XXII, p. 222.

5. Saxon accepted the Niles report of December 22, 1821, as accurate. (Saxon, *op. cit.,* p. 258, 259) James Campbell, in the information he provided Mirabeau Lamar, mentioned an encounter in which Laffite was wounded. Campbell, however, had no independent knowledge of this event. (The Lamar Papers, Manuscript 2492, Texas State Archives, Austin, Texas, p. 18) It is doubtful that Laffite would have been in command of a corsair at the time.

6. The Lamar Papers, Manuscript 2492, The Texas State Archives, Austin, Texas, pp. 18, 19.

7. *Niles' Weekly Register,* June 22, 1822, Volume XXII, p. 265.

8. Robert Greenhalgh Albion and Jennie Barnes Pope, *Sea Lanes in Wartime: The American Experience, 1775–1942,* pp. 141–142.

9. *Niles' Weekly Register,* December 25, 1819, Volume XVII, p. 287.

10. *Ibid.,* May 19, 1821, Volume XX, p. 192.

11. *Ibid.,* June 2, 1821, Volume XX, p. 224. Niles first reported the capture of the *Valiente Guaricuru* on May 5, 1821. (*Ibid.,* p. 154)

12. *Niles' Weekly Register* reported accounts of sea raiding in most of the issues printed between March 16, 1822, and March of the following year. (*Ibid.,* Volume XXII, pp. 34–359 and Volume XXIII, pp. 64–401). Several executions of convicted pirates were announced during the period of March through September 1823. (*Ibid.,* Volume XXIV, pp. 4–340).

13. A. B. Whipple, *Pirate: Rascals of the Spanish Main,* p. 239.

14. Alan Westcott, editor, *American Sea Rovers Since 1775,* p. 93.

15. Aaron Smith's work was originally published in London in 1824 under the title: *The Atrocities of the Pirates;* being a faithful narrative of the unparalleled suffering endured by the author during his captivity among the pirates of the island of Cuba with an account of the excesses and barbarities of those inhuman freebooters.

16. Aaron Smith claimed that during his career as a pirate, he and his fellow raiders were entertained in Cuba and that on one occasion he danced with a Spanish magistrate's daughter. (*Ibid.,* p. 23)

17. *La Courrier de La Louisiane,* November 29, 1822.

18. *Ibid.*

19. Charles Gayarre, "The Famous Lafittes at Galveston," photocopy of a printed work in the Louisiana State Museum.

20. The author of the *Journal* claimed he lived "for almost a year" at Charleston, South Carolina, and visited other cities on the North American continent after which he journeyed to Yucatan because of a "skin irritation and a sore throat." (*The Journal of Jean Laffite,* p. 123)

21. J. H. Kuykendall, "Reminiscences of Early Texans," *The Quarterly of the Texas State Historical Association,* Volume VI, October 1902, Number 2, p. 252.

22. Albion and Pope, *op. cit.,* p. 145.

23. Daniel Collins, *Narrative of the Shipwreck of the Brig Betsey, of Wiscasset, (Maine) and Murder of Five of Her Crew, By Pirates on the Coast of Cuba, Dec. 1824,* pp. 9–25.

24. Albion and Pope, *op. cit.,* p. 144; *History of the Lives and Bloody Exploits of the Most Noted Pirates; their Trials and Executions,* pp. 257–265.

25. *Ibid.,* p. 271.

26. Albion and Pope, *op. cit.,* p. 146.

27. *History of the Lives and Bloody Exploits of the Most Noted Pirates; their Trials and Executions,* p. 279.

28. *Ibid.,* p. 272; Albion and Pope, *op. cit.,* p. 146.

29. Sanford Sternlicht and Edwin M. Jameson, U.S.F. *Constellation: "Yankee Racehorse,"* pp. 60–144.

30. *Niles' Weekly Register,* March 13, 1824, Volume XXVI, p. 32.

31. Albion and Pope, *op. cit.,* p. 146.

32. Sternlicht and Jameson, *op. cit.,* p. 144.

33. Saxon, *op. cit.,* p. 261.

34. Hyatt A. Verrill, *The Real Story of the Pirates,* p. 355. Philip Grosse wrote a similar account. (*The Pirate's Who's Who: Giving the Particulars of the Lives and Deaths of the Pirates and Buccaneers,* pp. 187–188)

35. Charles Ellms, *op. cit.,* p. 80. Other accounts such as D. M. Kelsey's *Wild Heroes of the Sea* accepted Ellms' report on Laffite's death. (Kelsey, *Wild Heroes of the Sea,* p. 660)

36. *Ibid.,* p. 81.

37. Saxon based his conclusion that Laffite spent his last days on or near the eastern coast of Yucatan on two documents in the Lamar Papers (Document numbers 680 and 719) and on a letter dated May 1843, Galveston, from Thomas M. Duke to Ferdinand Pinchard. (Saxon, *op. cit.,* pp. 262–263) Other confirming evidence would include the statement of the "old Portuguese sailor" recorded by J. H. Kuykendall (*The Quarterly of the Texas State Historical Association,* Volume VI, October 1902, Number 2, p. 252) and the testimony of John L. Stephens, who in 1841 and 1842 visited sites where Laffite spent his final days. (J. L. Stephens, *Incidents of Travel in Yucatan,* Volume II, pp. 412 ff.)

Chapter 27

1. C. Bruce Hunter, *A Guide to Ancient Maya Ruins,* p. 303; William M. Ferguson, *Maya Ruins of Mexico,* p. 212.

2. J. L. Stephens, *Incidents of Travel in Yucatan,* p. 412.

3. Thomas Gann, *Ancient Cities and Modern Tribes,* p. 138. Late twentieth century maps of Isla Mujeres vary considerably from earlier accounts of the island. Hurricanes and heavy seas may have produced some variation in the dimensions of Mujeres.

4. *Ibid.,* p. 139.

5. The author saw evidence of the presence of sharks in 1983 on the leeward side of Isla Mujeres. In spite of this sighting, a scuba party entered the

water soon afterward with some members of the group encountering sharks. Although no one experienced difficulty, the diving director discounted the theory that these creatures were uniquely lethargic and warned all divers to take every possible precaution.

6. Stephens, *Incidents of Travel in Yucatan,* pp. 412, 413.

7. *Ibid.*

8. A record in the Merida archives recorded the burial of a "Pedro Lafite" by "the priest Jose Gregorio Cervera," November 10, 1821 "in the town of Dzilam." (*Laffite Study Group Newsletter,* Volume VIII, Number 1, Spring 1988, p. 5) Since James Campbell had agreed to meet Laffite on Mujeres (The Lamar Papers, Manuscript 2492, Texas State Archives, Austin, Texas, p. 18), possibly the two brothers had planned a similar rendezvous.

9. Stanley Faye cited Major Harry A. Davis, Washington, D.C. as the source for the information that the census of 1830 listed Pierre Laffite as a resident of Louisiana. (Faye, *op. cit.,* p. 96)

10. Stanley Faye concluded his study of Pierre Laffite with these words: "Pierre Laffite died, an elderly man in poor circumstances . . . Visitors today in New Orleans view the tomb of Dominique You and inquire about Jean Laffite. Few of them think to ask where Pierre Laffite was buried." (Faye, *op. cit.,* p. 96) A copy of a letter signed by a Eugene Laffite who claimed to be Pierre's son, stated his father was in St. Louis in 1837 and that he died several years later. Only a copy of this letter is extant making it impossible to assess the authenticity of the original. ("Eugene Laffite Letter," Miscellaneous Collection, Rosenberg Library, Galveston, Texas)

11. Robert Vogel (*op. cit.,* p. 71) cited J. Ignacio Rubio Mañe (*Los Piratas Laffite,* pp. 27–30) who noted a record of the death of a Pierre Laffite in Merida's Notarias Publicas.

12. Faye, *op. cit.,* p. 95.

13. The Lamar Papers, Manuscript 2492, Texas State Archives, Austin, Texas, p. 19.

14. Stephens, *Incidents of Travel in Yucatan,* p. 413.

15. The Lamar Papers, Manuscript 680, Texas State Archives, Austin, Texas.

16. The Lamar Papers, Manuscript 719, Texas State Archives, Austin, Texas.

17. Stephens, *Incidents of Travel in Yucatan,* p. 412.

18. *The Quarterly of the Texas State Historical Association,* Volume VI, October 1902, Number 2, p. 252.

Epilogue

1. Creighton, *op. cit.,* p. 157.

2. Willis W. Pratt, editor, *The Journal of Francis C. Sheridan,* pp. 54, 55.

3. Hobart Huson, *El Copaño: Ancient Port of Bexar and La Bahia,* p. 10.

4. Asbury, *op. cit.,* p. 158.

5. Simone de la Souchere Delery, *Napoleon's Soldiers in America,* pp. 26, 27, and p. 196.

6. Thompson, *op. cit.,* p. 118.

7. "Cruise of the Enterprise," *United States Magazine and Democratic Review,* July 1839, p. 38.

8. Howells cited one account that described Laffite as "tall" and another that stated he was at least "six feet, two inches" in height. (John Howells, *Life and Times of Jean Laffite,* May 1980) A near-contemporary gave his height as "six feet." (The Lamar Papers, Manuscript 1614)

9. J. Stielow, *The Life and Times of Jean Laffite,* June 1982.

10. Pratt, editor, *The Journal of Francis C. Sheridan,* p. 63; Asbury, *op. cit.,* p. 119; Caldwell, *op. cit.,* p. 43.

11. A Louisiana State Museum publication reproduced the painting in 1938. (Louisiana State Museum, *The Story of Jean and Pierre Lafitte, the Pirate-Patriots,* p. 8)

12. Driscoll, *op. cit.,* pp. 78, 79.

13. Thompson, *op. cit.,* p. 76.

14. Pratt, editor, *The Journal of Francis C. Sheridan,* p. 54. Detailed maps of sites where treasure may have been buried on Galveston Island appeared in a 1966 publication. (Carroll Lewis, *The Treasures of Galveston Bay,* pp. 10 ff.)

15. A clipping in the Cammie G. Henry Scrapbook, Melrose Collection, Northwestern State University Library, Natchitoches, Louisiana.

16. Dobie, *op. cit.,* pp. 306–332.

17. Dobie, *op. cit.,* p. 330; *Laffite Study Group Newsletter,* Volume VIII, Number 1, Spring 1988, p. 3.

18. A typescript in the Juanita Henry Collection, Folder 14, Northwestern State University Library, Natchitoches, Louisiana.

19. Ariane Dewey, *Laffite the Pirate,* pp. 41 ff.

20. Lyle Saxon, compiler, *A Collection of Louisiana Folk Tales: Gumbo Ya-Ya,* p. 258.

21. Carroll Lewis, *op. cit.,* p. 27.

22. *Ibid.,* p. 275. Stanley Faye concluded "The brothers lacked chest fulls of doubloons to bury in sandbanks." (Faye, *op. cit.,* p. 92)

23. Driscoll, *op. cit.,* p. 64.

24. E. R. Snow, *True Tales of Pirates and their Gold,* p. 1.

25. Charles Finger, *The Distant Prize: A Book About Rovers, Rangers and Rascals,* p. 321.

26. A publication dated April 1925 entitled *New Orleans Life* in the Melrose Collection in the Library of Northwestern State University Library, Natchitoches, Louisiana.

27. *Lafitte, or the Baratarian Chief, A Tale Founded on Facts.* No author's name appeared on the cover page of this printed work, but one cataloger believed it was penned by Joseph Holt Ingraham.

28. Charles Ellms, *op. cit.,* pp. 57–82. Engravings appear on pages 61, 71, and 82.

29. D. M. Kelsey, *Wild Heroes of the Sea,* p. 649.

30. Saxon, *op. cit.,* p. viii; Course, *op. cit.,* p. 185.

31. Asbury, *op. cit.,* p. 118.

32. Andrew Forest Muer, Editor, *Texas in 1837,* Endnotes of p. 180; Saxon, *Lafitte, the Pirate,* p. 271.

33. Leslie A. Marchant, editor, *The Selected Poetry of Lord Byron,* p. 557.

34. *Ibid.*, p. 506.

35. *Lafitte; or The Baratarian Chief, A Tale Founded on Facts.*

36. The holdings of the Wilson Library, University of North Carolina, Chapel Hill, include a copy of the London edition of Ingraham's work that was published under the title *The Pirate: or Lafitte of the Gulph of Mexico.* Later editions were entitled *Pirate of the Gulf* and *Lafitte the Pirate of the Gulf.*

37. Card Catalogue of The Library of Congress, Washington, D.C.

38. J. V. Ridgely, Foreword to the 1970 reprinting of *Lafitte, The Pirate of the Gulf,* p. iv.

39. Card Catalogue of the Library of Congress, Washington, D.C.

40. Charles Gayarre, *Historical Sketch of Pierre and Jean Lafitte, the Famous Smugglers of Louisiana,* pp. I:1, 2. Originally printed in 1883, Gayarre's work was reprinted in 1938 by the Louisiana State Museum in New Orleans and again reproduced in a limited edition in 1964.

41. French's work was reprinted in 1943. (The Card Catalogue of the Library of Congress, Washington, D.C.)

42. A number of works about Laffite are no longer available. The Card Catalogue of the Library of Congress listed several volumes of fiction that could not be found by the Library staff. J. Frank Dobie's list of suggested reading related to Laffite contained novels, probably written in the early twentieth century, that no longer appear on library shelves. ("The Mystery of Jean Laffite and His Treasure," a lecture by J. Frank Dobie, January 8, 1929)

43. Alan Le May, *Pelican Coast.*

44. Saxon, *Lafitte the Pirate,* p. ix.

45. J. Ignacio Rubio Mañe, *Los Piratas Lafitte,* pp. 228 ff.

46. Hervey Allen, *Anthony Adverse,* pp. 1086 ff.

47. Ralph T. Ward, *Pirates in History,* p. 151.

48. David Mitchell, *Pirates,* p. 172.

49. Philip Grosse, *The History of Piracy,* p. 213. Grosse wrote extensively about piracy publishing a bibliography on the subject. (Grosse, *My Pirate Library*)

50. *De Bow's Review,* New Orleans, 1851, pp. 372.

51. Muer, *op. cit.,* p. 6.

52. E. Alexander Powell, *Gentlemen Rovers,* p. 92.

53. Gayarre, *Historical Sketch of Pierre and Jean Laffite,* p. I:10.

54. *Ibid.,* p. II:8.

55. *Ibid.,* p. I:11.

56. Ray Miller, *op. cit.,* p. 49.

57. Owsley, *op. cit.,* p. 108.

58. Hyatt A. Verrill, *The Real Story of the Pirates,* pp. 345 ff.

59. Allen, *op. cit.,* p. 6.

60. Ray Thompson, *op. cit.,* p. 28.

61. Latour, *op. cit.,* p. 71.

62. "Information derived from Col. S. M. Williams respecting Lafitte," The Lamar Papers, Manuscript 1612, Texas State Archives, Austin, Texas.

63. "A statement affirmed by Edward Livingston and John R. Grymes," a typescript in the Louisiana State Museum, New Orleans, Louisiana.

64. Pratt, editor, *The Journal of Francis C. Sheridan,* p. 61.

65. *Ibid.*, p. 56.

66. *Ibid.*, p. 61; Latour, *op. cit.*, p. 71; a typescript in the Louisiana State Museum, New Orleans.

67. Edward Teach, known as Blackbeard, and Calico Jack Rackam were early eighteenth century pirates who were noted for cruelty to their victims. (Frank Sherry, *Raiders and Rebels: The Golden Age of Piracy*, pp. 235 ff.)

68. The case of the *Golden Rocket* technically ended the age of privateering under American law. Evidence was presented to the courts that a merchant vessel had been captured by a raider, the *Sumter*, which had sailed under a Confederate States of America Letter of Marque. The *Golden Rocket* was insured by Merchants' Mutual Marine Insurance Company against "perils of the seas, fire, enemies, pirates." The plaintiffs sought reimbursement for loss claiming entitlement to recovery under the piracy clause of the insurance contract. The case was argued before the Supreme Court of Maine in April 1862. The court ruled in favor of the plaintiffs declaring "the act of the *Sumter* was piratical" and the crew of the Confederate vessel were pirates who were punishable by death. (Richard H. Dana and Horace Gray, *Argument of the Plaintiff in the Case of the Golden Rocket before the Supreme Court of Maine*, pp. 4 ff.)

69. J. M. Kenworthy and George Young, *Freedom of the Seas*, p. 19.

70. Barry Hart Dubner, *The Law of International Sea Piracy*, pp. 12.

71. Earl Willis Crecraft, *Freedom of the Seas*, p. 116.

72. Dubner, *op. cit.*, p. 45.

73. *Ibid.*, p. 22.

74. "Le Brave Documents," Manuscript, Historic New Orleans Collection, New Orleans, Louisiana.

Appendix A

1. Robert C. Vogel, "Research Summary — 'The Journals of Jean Laffite,'" p. 6. (Typescript in the Rosenberg Library, Galveston, Texas)

2. *Laffite Study Group Newsletter*, Volume VIII, Number 1, Spring 1988.

3. Stanley Arthur stated in the preface to his biography of Laffite that the subject "remains a baffling mystery" (p. ii) but he was basing his work on "seemingly unquestioned evidence" that included letters and documents made available to him. (Stanley Arthur, *Jean Laffite, Gentleman Rover*, p. iii)

4. The author secured the aid of a French linguist in comparing copies of portions of the manuscript with the English version. Although the printed work conveyed the account recorded in the original with reasonable accuracy, it was not a precise translation.

5. *The Journal of Southern History*, February 1960, Volume XXVI, Number 1, pp. 138, 139.

6. *Laffite Study Group Newsletter*, Volume VIII, Number 2, 1988.

7. John L. Howells, "The Journal of Jean Laffite," *Life and Times of Jean Laffite*, Volume I, Number 1, p. 6.

8. John L. Howells reported two letters in his possession relative to the age of the codex: one from David Means, Manuscript Division, Library of Congress, dated September 5, 1956, affirming the authenticity of the paper; the other a letter from L. E. Harris of Harris Laboratories dated June 2, 1955,

substantiating the age of the ink. (Howells, *op. cit.*, p. 7) A copy of the Harris report is among the sheets of the manuscript, and was probably used by Laflin to convince Simpson of the authenticity of the codex. The Harris letter concluded with this statement: "After making the above indicated examinations of the three samples, it is our opinion that all of them are more than 75 years old."

9. Howells, *op. cit.*, p. 7.

10. *Ibid.*, pp. 8, 9.

11. Letter dated August 13, 1986, from Robert L. Schaadt describing the Jean Laffite Collection.

12. Photocopy of article entitled "Lafitte," in the Sam Houston Regional Library and Research Center, Liberty, Texas.

13. *Laffite Study Group Newsletter,* Volume I, Number 3, 1981.

14. *Ibid.*

15. Interview with Robert L. Schaadt in Liberty, Texas, in 1987.

16. *Laffite Study Group Newsletter,* Volume 1, Number 4, 1981.

17. *The Times-Picayune,* New Orleans, June 8, 1980.

18. Vogel, *op. cit.*, p. 9.

19. A memo from the Sam Houston Regional Library and Research Center, Liberty, Texas, stated that a grave exists in Alton, Illinois, where it is believed Laffite was buried in May 1854.

20. The name "Mathew Laflin" appears on both the first page of the manuscript journal and beneath the full page picture.

21. "The Journal of Jean Laffite," Manuscript, Sam Houston Regional Library and Research Center, Liberty, Texas.

Bibliography

Abbot, Willis J. *American Merchant Ships and Sailors*. New York: Dodd, Meade and Company, 1902.

———. *The Naval History of the United States*. New York: Dodd, Meade and Company, 1896.

Adams, Charles Francis, editor. *Memoirs of John Quincy Adams Comprising Portions of his Diary From 1795 to 1848*. Volume IV. Philadelphia: P. Lippincott and Company, 1875.

Albion, Robert Greenhalgh, and Jennie Barnes Pope. *Sea Lanes in Wartime: The American Experience, 1775-1942*. New York: W. W. Norton and Company, Inc., 1942.

Allen, Gardner W. *Our Navy and the West Indian Pirates*. Salem, Massachusetts: Essex Institute, 1929.

Allen, Hervey. *Anthony Adverse*. New York: Farrar and Rinehart, Inc., 1933.

Allen, Winnie, and Corrie Walker Allen. *Pioneering in Texas*. Dallas: Southern Publishing Company, 1935.

Andrews, Kenneth R. *The Spanish Caribbean: Trade and Plunder*. New Haven: Yale University Press, 1978.

Arthur, Stanley Clisby. *Jean Laffite, Gentleman Rover*. New Orleans: Harmanson, Publisher, 1952.

———. *Old New Orleans: A History of the Vieux Carre, Its Ancient and Historical Buildings*. New Orleans: Harmanson, Publisher, 1962.

———. *The Story of the Battle of New Orleans*. New Orleans: Louisiana Historical Society, 1945.

Asbury, Herbert. *The French Quarter*. New York: Alfred A. Knopf, 1936. [Reprinted by Mockingbird Books, Inc., 1987]

Auchinleck, G. A. *History of the War Between Great Britain and the United States of America*. Toronto: Maclear and Company, 1855.

Barskett, James. *History of the Island of St. Domingo*. London: Frank Cass, First Edition, 1818. Reprint, 1972.

Bassett, John Spencer, editor. *Correspondence of Andrew Jackson*. Washington: The Carnegie Institute of Washington, 1926. (two volumes)

————. *The Life of Andrew Jackson*. New York: The Macmillan Company, 1925.

Bazant, Jan. *A Concise History of Mexico from Hidalgo to Cardenas, 1805-1940*. Cambridge: Cambridge University Press, 1977.

Blanchard, Rufus. *Documentary History of the Cession of Louisiana to the United States Till it Became an American Province*. Chicago: R. Blanchard, 1903.

Blond, Georges. *Moi, Laffite Dernier Roi Des Flibusters*. Paris: Albin Michel, 1985.

Boatright, Mody C., and Donald Day, editors. *From Hell to Breakfast*. Dallas: University Press, Southern Methodist University, 1944.

Bollaert, William. *Life of Jean Lafitte: The Pirate of the Mexican Gulf*. September 1930.

Borel, Raymond C. *Le Revolté de la Louisiane*. Paris: Stock, 1978.

Bradlee, Francis B. C. *Piracy in the West Indies and its Suppression*. Salem, Massachusetts: The Essex Institute, 1923.

Brogan, Evelyn. *James Bowie, A Hero of the Alamo*. San Antonio: Theodore Kunzman, Printer and Publisher, 1922.

Brown, Wilburt S. *The Amphibious Campaign For West Florida and Louisiana, 1814-1815*. University of Alabama Press, 1969.

Burney, James. *History of the Buccaneers of America*. London: George Allen and Unwin, Ltd. [reprinted from the edition of 1816], 1912.

Caldwell, Erskine, editor. *Deep Delta Country*. New York: Duell, Sloan and Pierce, 1944.

Calvert, Peter. *Mexico*. New York: Praeger Publishers, 1973.

Carmer, Carl. *The Pirate Hero of New Orleans*. New York: Harvey House, Publishers, 1975.

Carroll, John M. *Galveston and the Gulf, Colorado and Santa Fe Railroads*. Galveston: Center for Transportation and Commerce, 1985.

Carse, Robert. *The Age of Piracy*. New York: Rinehart and Company, Incorporated, 1957.

Casey, Powell A. *Louisiana at the Battle of New Orleans*. Originally Published by the Battle of New Orleans, 150th Anniversary Committee of Louisiana, 1965. Reprinted by Eastern National Park and Monument Association, 1987.

Charnley, Mitchell V. *Jean Lafitte: Gentleman Smuggler*. New York: Viking Press, 1934.

Chatterton, Edward Keble. *The Romance of Piracy*. Philadelphia: J. P. Lippincott Company, 1915.

Chidsey, Donald Barr. *The Great Conspiracy*. New York: Crown Publishers, Inc., 1967.

Christian, Marcus. *Negro Ironworkers of Louisiana, 1718-1900*. Gretna, Louisiana: Pelican Publishing Company, 1972.

Christovich, Mary Louise, editor. *New Orleans Architecture,* Volume III. Gretna, Louisiana: Pelican Publishing Company, 1989.

Coggeshall, George. *History of the American Privateers, and Letters-of-Marque.* New York: Published by the Author, 1861.

Coles, Harry L. *The War of 1812.* Chicago: The University of Chicago Press, 1965.

Collins, Daniel. *Narrative of the Shipwreck of the Brig Betsey, of Wiscasset, (Maine,) and Murder of Five of Her Crew, By Pirates on the Coast of Cuba, Dec. 1824.* Wiscasset: Printed by John Dorr, 1825.

Course, Alfred George. *Pirates of the Western Sea.* London: Frederick Muller, 1969.

Crassweller, Robert D. *The Caribbean Community.* New York: Praeger Publishers, 1972.

Crecraft, Earl Willis. *Freedom of the Seas.* New York: D. Appleton-Century Company, 1935.

Creighton, James A. *A Narrative History of Brazoria County,* n. d.

Crowhurst, Patrick. *The Defence of British Trade 1689-1815.* Kent, England: Wm. Dawson and Sons, Ltd., 1977.

Dana, Richard H., and Horace Gray. *Argument for the Plaintiffs in the case of the Golden Rocket before the Supreme Court of Maine. Taking by Rebels on the High Seas is Piracy, not Capture, Seizure or Detention; by the Law of Insurance.* Boston: Press of John Wilson and Son, 1862.

Davis, T. Frederick. *MacGregor's Invasion of Florida, 1817, Together With An Account of His Successors Irwin, Hubbard and Aury On Amelia Island, East Florida.* The Florida Historical Society, 1928.

Debates and Proceedings in the Congress of the United States With an Appendix Containing Important State Papers and Public Documents and all the Laws of a Public Nature. Fifteenth Congress — First Session. Volume XXXII. Washington: Gales and Seaton, 1854.

DeConde, Alexander. *This Affair of Louisiana.* New York: Charles Scribner's Sons, 1976.

De Grummond, Jane Lucas. *The Baratarians and the Battle of New Orleans.* Baton Rouge: Louisiana State University Press, 1961.

————. *Renato Beluche: Smuggler, Privateer and Patriot, 1780–1860.* Baton Rouge and London: Louisiana State University Press, 1983.

Delery, Simone de la Souchere. *Napoleon's Soldiers in America.* Gretna, Louisiana: Pelican Publishing Company, 1972.

De Leeuw, Hendrick. *Crossroads of the Buccaneers.* Philadelphia: J. P. Lippincott Company, 1937.

Devereux, Mary. *Lafitte of Louisiana,* Boston: Little, Brown and Company, 1902.

Dewey, Ariane. *Laffite the Pirate.* New York: Greenwillow Books, 1985.

Dobie, J. Frank. *Coronado's Children.* Dallas, Texas: The Southwest Press, 1930.

Driscoll, Charles B. *Doubloons: The Story of Buried Treasure.* New York: Farrar and Rinehart, Incorporated, 1930.

———. *Pirates Ahoy.* New York: Farrar and Rinehart, Incorporated, 1941.

Dubner, Barry Hart. *The Law of International Sea Piracy.* The Hague: Martinus Nijhoff Publishers, 1980.

Ellms, Charles. *The Pirates Own Book, or Authentic Narratives of the Lives, Exploits and Executions of the Most Celebrated Sea Robbers.* Salem, Massachusetts: Marine Research Society, 1924, a reproduction of the original printed in Boston, 1837.

Esquemeling, John. *The Buccaneers of America.* London: George Routhledge and Sons, Ltd. (Second Impression, rendered into English with facsimilies of all the original engravings, maps, etc., 1684-5), 1928.

Evans, Oliver. *New Orleans.* New York: Macmillan Company, 1959.

Ferguson, William M. *Maya Ruins of Mexico.* Norman: University of Oklahoma Press, 1977.

Ferro, Carlos A. *Vida de Luis Aury.* Buenos Aires: Editorial Cuarto Poder, 1976.

Finger, Charles J. *The Distant Prize: A Book About Rovers, Rangers and Rascals.* New York: D. Appleton-Century Company, 1935.

Fortier, James J. A., editor. *The Story of Jean and Pierre Lafitte.* New Orleans: The Louisiana State Museum [1938].

Frank, Doctor. *Negrolana.* Boston: Christopher Publishing House, 1924.

Frantz, Joe B. *Texas: A History.* New York: W. W. Norton and Company, 1984.

French, Joseph Lewis. *Great Pirate Stories.* New York: Tudor Publishing Company, 1922.

Fuller, Basil. *Pirate Harbors and their Secrets.* London: S. Paul and Company, Ltd., 1935.

Gambrell, Herbert. *Anson Jones, The Last President of Texas.* Austin: The University of Texas Press, 1964.

Gann, Thomas. *Ancient Cities and Modern Tribes.* London: Duckworth, 1926.

Garrett, Julia Kathryn. *Green Flag Over Texas.* Austin: The Pemberton Press, 1939.

Garrison, George P. *Texas: A Contest of Civilizations.* New York: Houghton, Mifflin and Company, 1903.

Gayarre, Charles Etienne Arthur. *Historical Sketch of Pierre and Jean Lafite.* Austin: Pemberton Press, 1964. [This was a reprint of the original printed in 1883]

Gibbs, George. *The Shores of Romance.* New York: D. Appleton and Company, 1928.

Gollomb, Joseph. *Pirates Old and New.* New York: Macaulay, 1928.

Gonzales, Catherine Troxell. *Lafitte the Terror of the Gulf.* Burnet, Texas: Eakin Press, 1981.

Goodwin, Philo A. *Biography of Andrew Jackson, President of the United States, Formerly Major General in the Army of the United States.* Hartford: Silas Andrus and Son, 1849.

Graham, Philip. *The Life and Poems of Mirabeau B. Lamar.* Chapel Hill: University of North Carolina Press, 1938.

Grant, Neil. *Buccaneers.* London: Angus and Robertson, 1976.

Grosse, Philip. *My Pirate Library.* New York: Burt Franklin, 1926 [reprinted in 1970].

————. *The History of Piracy.* New York: Tudor Publishing Company, 1946.

————. *The Pirates Who's Who: Giving Particulars of the Lives and Deaths of the Pirates and Buccaneers.* Boston: Charles E. Lauriat Company, 1924.

Gulick, Charles Adams, Jr., and Katherine Elliott, editors. *Texas State Library: The Papers* of *Mirabeau Buonaparte Lamar.* Six volumes. Austin: Von Boechmann-Jones, Company, 1921-1927.

Hamilton, Charles. *Forgers and Famous Fakes.* New York: Crown Publishers, 1980.

Hamilton, Stanislaus Murray, editor. *The Writings of James Monroe Including a Collection of His Public and Private Papers and Correspondence Now for the First Time Printed.* Seven volumes. New York: G. P. Putnam's Sons, 1903.

Hart, Francis Russell. *Admirals of the Caribbean.* Boston and New York: Houghton Mifflin Company, 1922.

Heinl, Robert Debs, and Nancy Gordon Heinl. *Written in Blood: The Story of the Haitian People, 1942-1971.* Boston: Houghton Mifflin Company, 1978.

Higman, B. W. *Trade Government and Society in Caribbean History, 1700-1920.* Kingston, Jamaica: Heinemann Educational Books, Ltd., 1983.

History of the Lives and Bloody Exploits of the Most Noted Pirates; their Trials and Executions. Including a correct account of the late piracies committed in the West Indies, and the expeditions of Commodore Porter; also those committed on the Brig Mexican who were tried and executed at Boston in 1835. Hartford: S. Anderson and Son, 1836. [An earlier printing of this work was dated 1825]

Hitsman, J. Mackay. *The Incredible War of 1812.* Toronto: University of Toronto Press, 1965.

Hogan, William Ransom. *The Texas Republic.* Norman: University of Oklahoma Press, 1946.

191

Holland, Rupert Sargent. *The Pirate of the Gulf.* Philadelphia: J. P. Lippincott Company, 1929.

Horsman, Reginald. *The War of 1812.* New York: Alfred A. Knopf, 1969.

Hunter, C. Bruce. *A Guide to Ancient Maya Ruins.* Norman: University of Oklahoma Press, 1974.

Hunter, Theresa Moore. *Saga of Jean Laffite.* San Antonio: Naylor, 1940.

Huson, Hobart. *El Copaño: Ancient Port of Bexar and La Bahia.* Refugio, Texas: The Refugio Timely Remark, 1935.

Ingraham, Joseph Holt. *The Pirate: or, Lafitte of the Gulph of Mexico.* London: J. Cunningham, 1839.

———. *Pirate of the Gulf.* New York: Pollard and Moss, 1889.

———. *Lafitte the Pirate of the Gulf.* [with a new foreword by J. W. Ridgely] New York: Garrett Press, Inc., 1970.

Ingraham, Prentiss. *Lafitte's Lieutenant.* Cleveland, Ohio: The Arthur Westbrook Company, 1931.

James, Marquis. *Andrew Jackson: The Border Captain.* Indianapolis: The Bobbs-Mewrrill Company, 1933.

Jerrmann, Ludwig. *Claribelle Lafitte.* Hamburg: Richard Hermes Verlag, 1913.

Karraker, Cyrus Harreld. *Piracy was a Business.* Rindge, New Hampshire: Richard R. Smith Publisher, Inc., 1953.

Kauffman, Reginald Wright. *Pirate Jean.* New York: The Macaulay Company, 1930.

Keats, John. *Eminent Domain: The Louisiana Purchase and the Making of America.* New York: Charterhouse, 1973.

Kelsey, D. M. *Wild Heroes of the Sea.* St. Louis: Scammell and Company, 1892.

Kenamore, Jane A., and Michael E. Wilson, editors. *Manuscript Sources in the Rosenberg Library.* College Station: Texas A&M University Press, 1983.

Kent, Madeleine Fabiola. *The Corsair.* New York: Doubleday and Company, 1955.

Kenworthy, J. M., and George Young. *Freedom of the Seas.* New York: Horace Liveright, n.d.

Kilman, Ed. *Cannibal Coast.* San Antonio: The Naylor Company, 1959.

King, Grace. *Jean Baptiste Le Moyne Sieur de Bienville.* New York: Dodd, Mead and Company, 1892.

Korn, Bertram Wallace. *The Early Jews of New Orleans.* Waltham, Massachusetts: American Jewish Historical Society, 1969.

[Laffite, Jean]. *Journal of Jean Laffite.* New York: Vantage Press, 1958.

Lafitte, or the Baratarian Chief, A Tale Founded on Facts. New York, 1828.

Latour, A. Lacarriere. *Historical Memoirs of the War in West Florida and*

Louisiana, 1814-1815. Written originally in French and translated for the author by H. P. Nugent. Philadelphia: Published by John Conrad and Company, J. Maxwell, Printer, 1816.

Le May, Alan. *Pelican Coast.* New York: Doubleday, Doran and Company, Inc., 1929.

Lewis, Carroll. *The Treasures of Galveston Bay.* Waco, Texas: Texian Press, 1980.

Lucie-Smith, Edward. *Outcasts of the Sea: Pirates and Piracy.* New York and London: Paddington Press, Ltd., 1978.

Lyon, E. Wilson. *Louisiana In French Diplomacy, 1759-1804.* Norman: University of Oklahoma Press, 1974.

[McAfee, Robert]. *History of the Late War in the Western Country.* Lexington, Kentucky: Worsley and Smith, 1816.

McComb, David. *Galveston: A History.* Austin: The University of Texas Press, 1986.

Macintyre, Donald. *The Privateers.* London: Paul Elek, Ltd., 1975.

Maclay, Edgar Slanton. *A History of American Privateers.* New York: D. Appleton and Company, 1899.

Madison, James. *Letters and Other Writings of James Madison, Fourth President of the United States.* Published by Order of Congress. Four volumes. New York: R. Worthington, 1884.

Marchant, Leslie A., editor. *The Selected Poetry of Lord Byron.* New York: The Modern Library, 1951.

Martin, Francois-Xavier. *The History of Louisiana.* New Orleans: James A Gresham, Publisher, 1882.

Miller, John Chester. *The Wolf By the Ears: Thomas Jefferson and Slavery.* New York: The Free Press, 1977.

Miller, Ray. *Ray Miller's Galveston.* Austin: Capital Printing, 1983.

Mitchell, David. *Pirates.* New York: The Dial Press, 1976.

Mueller, G. O. W., and Freda Adler. *Outlaws of the Ocean.* New York: Hearst Marine Books, 1985.

Muer, Andrew Forest, editor. *Texas in 1837.* Austin: The University of Texas Press, 1958.

Murat, Ines. Frances Frenaze, translator. *Napoleon and the American Dream.* Baton Rouge and London: Louisiana State University Press, 1976.

Nevins, David. *The Texans.* New York: Time-Life Books, 1975.

Newcomb, W. W., Jr. *The Indians of Texas.* Austin: The University of Texas Press, 1961.

Owsley, Frank Lawrence. *Struggle for the Gulf Borderlands: The Creek War and the Battle of New Orleans 1812-1815.* Gainesville: University Presses of Florida, 1981.

Parsons, Edward Alexander. *Jean Laffite in the War of 1812.* Worcester, Massachusetts: American Antiquarian Society, 1941.

Phelan, Macum. *History of Methodism in Texas,* 1924.

Poulenc, Cesar. *Jean Laffite, Gentleman Pirate.* Privateer Press, 1987.

Powell, E. Alexander. *Gentlemen Rovers.* New York: Charles Scribner's Sons, 1913.

Pratt, Willis W., editor. *Galveston Island, Or, A Few Months off the Coast of Texas: The Journal of Francis C. Sheridan, 1839-1840.* Austin: The University of Texas Press, 1954.

Reilly, Robin. *The British at the Gates.* New York: G. P. Putnam's Sons, 1974.

Remini, Robert V. *Andrew Jackson and the Course of American Empire, 1767 -1821.* New York: Harper and Row, 1977.

Ritchie, Robert C. *Captain Kidd and the War against the Pirates.* Cambridge, Massachusetts: Harvard University Press, 1986.

Roberts, W. Adolphe. *The French in the West Indies.* Indianapolis: The Bobbs-Merrill Company, 1942.

Rubio Mañe, J. Ignacio. *Los Piratas Lafitte.* Mexico: Editorial Polis, 1938.

Rutland, Lucile, and Rhoda Cameron. *Lafitte. A Play in Prologue and Four Acts.* [No publisher listed], 1899.

Sabin, Edwin L. *Wild Men of the Wild West.* New York: Thomas Y. Crowell Company, 1929.

Saxon, Lyle. *A Collection of Louisiana Folk Tales, Gumbo Ya-Ya.* New York: Bonanza Books, 1945.

———. *Laffite the Pirate.* New York and London: The Century Company, 1930.

Schmitz, Joseph William. *Thus They Lived: Social Life of the Republic of Texas.* San Antonio: The Naylor Company, 1935.

Schoenrich, Otto. *Santo Domingo.* New York: The Macmillian Company, 1918.

Schwarz, Ted. *Forgotten Battlefield of the First Texas Revolution.* Austin: Eakin Press, 1985.

Seitz, Don C. *Under the Black Flag.* New York: The Dial Press, 1925.

Shaw, Ronald E., editor. *Andrew Jackson, 1767-1845.* Dobbs Ferry, New York: Oceana Publications, Inc., 1969

Smith, Aaron. *The Atrocities of the Pirates; being a faithful narrative of the unparalleled suffering endured by the author during his captivity among the pirates of the island of Cuba with an account of the excesses and barbarities of those inhuman freebooters.* Waltham Saint Lawrence, Berkshire: The Golden Cockerel Press, 1929 [a reprint of the original published in London in 1824].

Smith, R. P. *Lafitte or the Baratarian Chief.* Auburn, New York: Oliphant and Skinner, Printers, 1834.

Smither, Harriet. *Texas Library and Historical Commission: The Papers of*

194

Mirabeau Lamar. Volume V. Austin: Von Boechmann-Jones Company, 1927.

Snow, Edward Rowe. *True Tales of Pirates and their Gold.* New York: Dodd, Meade and Company, 1953.

Spears, John R. *The American Slave Trade.* Williamstown, Massachusetts: Corner House Publishers, 1970.

Sperry, Armstrong. *Black Falcon.* Philadelphia: The John C. Winston Company, 1949.

Sprague, Marshall. *So Vast, So Beautiful A Land.* Boston: Little, Brown and Company, 1974.

Stephens, John L. *Incidents of Travel in Central America, Chiapas and Yucatan.* Volume I. New Brunswick: Rutgers University Press, 1949. [A reprint of the 1841 edition]

Stephens, John L. *Incidents of Travel in Yucatan.* Volume II. New York: Harper and Brothers, 1843.

————. *Viaje A Yucatan, 1841-1842.* Trans. al Castellaño de Justo Sierra O'Reilly, Mexico, 1937.

Sternlicht, Sanford, and Edwin M. Jameson. U.S.F. *Constellaion: "Yankee Racehorse."* Cockeysville, Maryland: Liberty Publishing Company, 1981.

Synopeses of Cases, 1806–1831, U.S. District Court, New Orleans [a WPA project, 1941], Cases 552, 573, 574 and 608.

Tallant, Robert. *The Pirate Lafitte and the Battle of New Orleans.* New York: Random House, 1951.

Tarbell, Ida M. *A Short Life of Napoleon Bonaparte.* New York: Doubleday and McClure Company, 1898.

Taylor, Joe Gray. *Louisiana: A History.* New York: W. W. Norton and Company, 1984.

Thompson, Ray M. *The Land of Lafitte the Pirate.* New Orleans: Jefferson Parish Yearly Review, 1943.

Thorp, Raymond W. *Bowie Knife.* Albuquerque: The University of New Mexico Press, 1948.

Townsend, Tom. *Powderhorn Passage.* Austin: Eakin Press, 1988.

Verrill, A. Hyatt. *The Real Story of the Pirates.* New York: D. Appleton and Company, 1927.

Viola, Herman J. *Andrew Jackson.* New York: Chelsea House Publications, 1986.

Ward, Ralph T. *Pirates in History.* Baltimore: York Press, 1974.

Weinstein, Brian, and Aaron Segal. *Haiti: Political Failures and Cultural Successes.* New York: Praeger Special Studies, 1984.

Westcott, Allan, editor. *American Sea Rovers Since 1775.* New York: J. P. Lippincott Company, 1947.

Wheeler, Richard. *In Pirate Waters.* New York: Thomas Y. Crowell Company, 1969.

Whipple, Addison Beecher. *Pirate: Rascals of the Spanish Main.* New York: Doubleday and Company, Incorporated, 1957.

Wilkinson, Elizabeth. *Monsieur Lafitte (Jean Lafitte) Pirate-Patriot, South Louisiana, 1808-1815.* New Orleans: [no publisher listed], 1924.

Williams, Neville. *Contraband Cargoes: Seven Centuries of Smuggling.* London: Longmans, Green and Company, 1959.

JOURNALS, DOCUMENTS, AND STUDY PAPERS

Adams, Paul. "Amelia Barr in Texas," *Southwestern Historical Quarterly,* Volume XLIX, Number 3, January 1946.

"Antonio Martinez, Spanish Governor of Texas," *Southwestern Historical Quarterly,* Volume LXI, Number 2, October 1957.

Barker, Eugene C. "African Slave Trade in Texas," *Quarterly of the Texas State Historical Association,* Volume VI, Number 2, October 1902.

Biesele, R. L. "Book Reviews," *Southwestern Historical Quarterly,* Volume XLV, Number 2, October 1941.

Brindley, Anne A. "Jane Long," *Southwestern Historical Quarterly,* Volume LVI, 1952-1953.

"Cruise of the Enterprise," *United States Magazine and Democratic Review,* July 1839, pp. 33-42.

Davenport, Harbert, and Joseph K. Wells. "The First Europeans in Texas," *Southwestern Historical Quarterly,* Volume XXII, Number 2, October 1918.

Dyer, J. O. "Jean Lafitte in Galveston 1818 -1820," *Galveston News,* May 7, 14, and 21, 1922.

Eminent Personages: Laffitte. [A biography of James or Jacques Laffitte, a rare printed work in the Barker Library, Austin, Texas, c. 1838]

Faye, Stanley. "The Great Stroke of Pierre Laffite." *The Louisiana Historical Quarterly,* Volume 23, Number 3, July 1940.

Forrest, Major C. R. "The Journal of Major C. R. Forrest," *The Battle of New Orleans: A British View,* Introduction and Annotations by Hugh F. Rankin. New Orleans: The Hauser Press, 1961.

Fortier, James J. A., editor. *The Story of Jean and Pierre Lafitte, the Pirate-Patriots.* A publication of the Louisiana State Museum, March 20, 1938.

Garver, Lois. "Benjamin Rush Milam," *Southwestern Historical Quarterly,* Volume 38, Number 2, October 1934.

Howells, John L. "The Journal of Jean Laffite," *Life and Times of Jean Laffite,* Volume I, Number 1.

Huff, Millicent, and H. Bailey Carroll. "Hurricane Carla at Galveston," *Southwestern Historical Quarterly,* Volume LXV, Number 3, January 1962.

Journal of Southern History, Volumes VIII, IX, and XXVI.

Kuykendall, J. H. "Reminiscences of Early Texans," *The Quarterly of the Texas State Historical Association.* Volume VI, Number 2, October 1902.

"Locations of Early Spanish Missions," *Southwestern Historical Quarterly,* Volume XLI, Number 3, January 1938.

Looscan, Adele B. "Life and Service of John Birdsall," *Southwestern Historical Quarterly,* Volume XXVI, Number 1, July 1922.

Louisiana Historical Quarterly, Volumes XX–XXIV, XXXIX, and LIV.

Louisiana History, Volume 1, Number 1, 1960.

Marigny, Bernard, "Reflections on the Campaign of General Andrew Jackson," *Louisiana Historical* Quarterly. Volume 6.

Mayfield, Robert B. An article on Laffite in the *Times Picayune,* August 23, 1925.

Mora, Isidro A. Beluche. "Privateers of Cartagena," *The Louisiana Historical Quarterly,* Volume XXXIX, Number 1, January 1956.

Niles, H., editor. *Niles' Weekly Register.* Baltimore: The Franklin Press, Volumes IV, VII, XVII, XIX, XX, XXI, XXII, XXIII, XXIV, XXV, XXVI.

"Notes and Documents," *Southwestern Historical Quarterly,* Volume LXXIII, Number 1, July 1969.

Papers Relating to French Affairs. [Printed copies of documents dated July 7, 1807 to December 17, 1807, no publisher listed.]

The Southern Bivouac, New Series, Volume II, Louisville, Kentucky, 1886, 1887.

State Papers and Publick Documents of the United States. Volume XI, Boston: Thomas B. Wait, 1819.

Sugden, John. "Jean Lafitte and the British Offer of 1814," *Louisiana History,* Spring 1979.

"Visit to Lafitte," *The Knickerbocker,* March 1847, Volume XXIX, No. 3, pp. 254-261.

Vogel, Robert C. "Jean Laffite, the Baratarians, and the Historical Geography of Piracy in the Gulf of Mexico," *Maritime History of the Gulf Coast,* Volume 5, Number 2, Spring 1990.

———, editor. *The Laffite Study Group Newsletter [The Life and Times of Jean Laffite],* Volumes I through X.

Warren, Harris Gaylord, translator and editor. "Documents Relating to the Establishment of Privateers at Galveston, 1816, 1817," *Louisiana Historical Quarterly,* Volume 21, Number 4, October 1938.

Williams, Amelia. "A Critical Study of the Seige of the Alamo," *Southwestern Historical Quarterly,* Volume 37, Number 2, October 1933.

MANUSCRIPTS AND PAPERS IN THE SAM HOUSTON
REGIONAL LIBRARY AND RESEARCH CENTER,
LIBERTY, TEXAS

The Journal of Jean Laffite, Manuscript.

Laffite family records from two Bibles dated 1820 and 1839 containing handwritten data, photocopies.

Letters and documents relating to the authenticity of the manuscript, Journal of Jean Laffite.

Papers relating to Jean and Pierre Laffite, photocopies.

MANUSCRIPTS AND DOCUMENTS IN THE LOUISIANA STATE
MUSEUM, 400 ESPLANADE, NEW ORLEANS, LOUISIANA

Cable, George W. "Plotters and Pirates of Louisiana," *The Century Magazine,* Volume XXV.

De Bow's Review, New Orleans, 1851.

La Courrier de la Louisiane, 4 Mai 1812, 26 Septiembre 1814, 22 Mai 1818, 29 Novembre 1822.

Louisiana State Museum papers relating to Laffite, untitled typescripts.

Morrison, Andrew, Editor. "The Island Home of the Corsair Chief," *The Industries of Galveston,* Galveston, 1887.

New Orleans Bulletin, August 29, 1875.

Printed articles relating to Jean and Pierre Laffite, early nineteenth century, photocopies.

"Re Barataria Settlement," a manuscript note.

"A Visit to Lafitte," a photocopy of a work dated March 1847, in the Louisiana State Museum papers.

HISTORIC NEW ORLEANS COLLECTION, 533 ROYAL STREET,
NEW ORLEANS, LOUISIANA

Certificate of Inspection at New Orleans for a vessel to sail to New York, Manuscript, March 2, 1813, file number 56, Folder 2, Historic New Orleans Collection.

Edwards Nicholls document, August 13, 1814, Manuscript, file number 55, Historic New Orleans Collection.

Henry Percy Letters, August 30, 31, and September 1, 1814, Manuscript, file number 196, Historic New Orleans Collection.

James Stirling documents, March 17, 1813, Manuscript, file number 194, Historic New Orleans Collection.

Jean Laffite letter, February 1813, Manuscript, Historic New Orleans Collection.

Le Brave Documents, Manuscripts, Historic New Orleans Collection.

Papers and letters relating to the authenticity of the Journal of Jean Laffite, typescripts, Historic New Orleans Collection.

"Roll of Ship Diligente," Manuscript, file number 56, Historic New Orleans Collection.

NORTHWESTERN STATE UNIVERSITY LIBRARY, NATCHITOCHES, LOUISIANA

Juanita Henry Collection of papers relating to Laffite.

Melrose Collection, including typescripts relating to Laffite prepared as a part of the Federal Writers Project.

Papers and articles relating to the Laffite family history including a copy of an article entitled "Parentage of Lafitte" (photocopies).

Smith, Mary Fay. "A Family of Pirates," typescript.

"A Veteran Gone: Chas. Cronea, Who Fought Under Jean Lafitte," photocopy of a typescript.

HUMANITIES RESEARCH CENTER, THE UNIVERSITY OF TEXAS, AUSTIN, TEXAS

John R. Grymes Petition, November 10, 1812, Manuscript, Parsons Collection.

Holmes document, November 19, 1812, Manuscript, Parsons Collection.

Laffite letter to Captain Garrison, April 22, 1813, Manuscript, Parsons Collection.

Dominique Hall order for arrest of Jean Lafite, July 24, 1813, Manuscript, Parsons Collection.

Laffite letter to Wm. C. C. Clayborne, Manuscript, Parsons Collection.

Testimony of John Oliver in trial of Lafitte, Manuscript, Parsons Collection.

Nicholls Proclamation to the people of Louisiana, August 26, 1814, Manuscript, Parsons Collection.

Edwards Nicholls letter, August 31, 1814, Manuscript, Parsons Collection.

Percy documents, August 30 and September 1, 1814, Manuscript, Parsons Collection.

Laffite to Lockyer, Captain of the Brig Sophia, September 4, 1814, Manuscript, Parsons Collection.

Laffite letter to Wm. C. C. Clayborne, September 4, 1814, Manuscript, Parsons Collection.

Laffite letter to Jean Blanque, September 7, 1814, Manuscript, Parsons Collection.

Laffite document, September 10, 1814, Manuscript, Parsons Collection.

Joseph Martinot document, September 30, 1814, Manuscript, Parsons Collection.

Daniel T. Patterson sales of cargoes of the Schooner General Bolivar and other vessels taken at Barataria, November 12, 1814, Manuscript, Parsons Collection.

John Oliver document, December 3, 1814, Manuscript, Parsons Collection.

Godfrey Williams document, December 3, 1814, Manuscript, Parsons Collection.

Edward Williams document, December 3, 1814, Manuscript, Parsons Collection.

Andrew Jackson letter to Major Michael Reynolds, December 22, 1814, Manuscript, Parsons Collection.

Jean Blanque documents, April 22, 1815, Manuscript, Parsons Collection.

Daniel T. Patterson letter, April 24, 1816, Manuscript, Parsons Collection.

Laffite letter to Commodore D. F. Patterson, January 3, 1820, Manuscript, Parsons Collection.

Laffite letter to Commodore Patterson, May 24, 1820, Manuscript, Parsons Collection.

Miscellaneous Laffite papers and autographs, various dates, Manuscript, Parsons Collection.

ROSENBERG LIBRARY, TEXAS HISTORICAL COLLECTION, GALVESTON, TEXAS

Correspondence of the Vice Consul in New Orleans, Diego Morphy, with the Captain General of the Island of Cuba, 1817-1819, typescript, the location of the original is unknown.

Crozier, Harry Benge. "Lafitte, 'Lord of Galveston Island,' Reigned here in 1817," mounted photocopies.

Dyer, Joseph Osterman. "Jean Laffite, Buccaneer," photocopy.

Hunter, Theresa. "Blood and Booty — the Story of Laffite," mounted newspaper clippings.

James Brown Letter to Hon. James Monroe, October 1, 1814, photocopy of manuscript.

Jean Laffite letter to Mr. James Young [Long], General of the Army, Galveston, July 7, 1819.

Jean Stephen Edward Laffite letter, November 1837, photocopy of manuscript.

Livingston letter to the President of the United States, James Madison, October 24, 1814, photocopy of manuscript.

Miscellaneous collection of papers and documents relating to Jean Laffite.

Mitchell, Edward Page. "A Romance of American History, the Story of Laffite, the Pirate of Genius and the Baratarians," photocopy.

200

Rhodes, William Henry. *The Indian Gallows and Other Poems*. New York: E. Walker, 1846.

Stuart collection of papers and scrapbooks relating to Jean Laffite.

"The Three Trees," radio script broadcast on KLUF, June 27, 1946.

Thrasher, J. S. A collection of clippings from the *Galveston Tribune* relating to Laffite and Galveston.

"A Visit to Galveston, J. Randall James, 1818," typescript of the notes of Philip Crosby Tucker, the original of which was lost in the 1900 Galveston storm.

Vogel, Robert C. "Research Summary: The Journals of Jean Laffite," typescript.

TEXAS STATE ARCHIVES, AUSTIN, TEXAS

"Barataria and Lafitte," MS, a fourteen-page unnumbered manuscript in the Texas State Archives.

"The Birth of Juan Enrico," photocopy.

The Lamar Papers, Manuscripts 19, 24, 351, 397, 680, 719, 1611, 1612, 1613, 1614, 2492 and 2800.

The Lamar Papers II, Document Numbers 2926 and 3011.

Wharton, C. R. *The Baron of Bastrop*. n. d., a rare pamphlet.

LAFFITE MATERIALS IN THE PERKINS LIBRARY,
   DUKE UNIVERSITY, DURHAM, NORTH CAROLINA

Andrew Jackson letter to Laffite, 1815, photocopy.

Edward Nicholls letter to Laffite, August 31, 1814, photocopy.

Laffite's letter of response to Edward Nicholls, September 18, 1814, photocopy.

1000 piastres de récompense

SERONT payées à quiconque arrêtera PIERRE LAFITTE qui, la nuit dernière, a forcé la prison de paroisse et s'est évadé. Ledit Pierre Lafitte est de la taille de 5 pieds 10 pouces, fortement constitué, a un beau teint et les yeux un peu de travers. On croit inutile d'en donner une plus ample description, ledit Lafitte étant très-connu en cette ville.

Ledit Lafitte a emmené avec lui trois nègres, savoir : Sam jadis la propriété de Mr. Sawza ; Cézar, appartenant à Mr. Lefebvre ; et Hamilcar, appartenant à Mr. Jarnand La récompense ci dessus sera donnée à quiconque délivrera ledit Lafitte au soussigné, qui payera aussi cinquante piastres pour chacun desdits nègres.

J. H. Holland,
7 Septembre.——— Geôlier.

Etat de la Louisiane.—Cour de

Copy of poster announcing reward of "1000 piastres de recompense"
for the arrest of Jean Laffite.
— Courtesy Institute of Texan Cultures

Index

A

Adams, President, 113
  Secretary, 108
Alabama, 119
Allen, Gardner W., 142
  Hervey, 140
Alton, Illinois, 151
Amelia Island, 97
American Forces Radio and Television Services, 141
American Revolution, 11
Arthur, Stanley Clisby, 148
Asbury, Herbert, 138
Atascosito, 112
Attakopas Canal, 87
Aubry, Don Pedro, 12
Aurilla, 126
Aury, Louis-Michel, 90-92, 93-97, 108
Austin, Stephen F., 123
Aux Cayes, 86

B

Balize, 54, 123
Baltimore, Maryland, 63, 151
Baptista, Captain, 95
Barataria, 23-24, 27, 28-33, 36-37, 39, 40, 41, 42-46, 48, 53-55, 56-57, 65, 82, 84, 87, 96, 124, 125, 140
Baratarians and the Battle of New Orleans, The, 140
Baton Rouge, Louisiana, 7, 68
Battalion d'Orleans, 61
Bay of Bengal, 138
Bayonne, France, 10
Bayou Lafourche, 30, 141
Bayou Teche, 30
Bell, Sollie Lee, 140
Beluche, Renato, 2, 14, 20, 21, 22, 25-26, 27, 29, 30, 36, 40, 58, 59, 69, 71, 77, 81, 84-86, 95, 101, 132
Beluche family, 14, 16

Besson, Baptiste, 26, 27
Bethancourt, Miriam, 149
Betsey, 128
Blackbeard, 23-24, 142
Black Falcon, 140
Blanque, Jean, 27, 30, 45, 46, 51, 52, 53, 56, 65, 83
Blanques, 14, 16
Blond, George, 140
Bolivar, Simon, 85-86
Bolivar Peninsular, 104, 106
Bonaparte, Napoleon, 136
Bordeaux, France, 10, 39
Borel, Raymond, 140
Bowie, James, 105-106, 122
  Resin, 105, 106, 122
  Ursula Beramendi, 105
Brazoria, 115
Brest, France, 10
Brown, William (George), 116, 117, 118
Brugman, Pierre, 25
Buccaneer, The, 141
Buenos Aires, 127
Burr, Aaron, 21, 128
  Theodosa, 128
Butler, Mr., 102
Byron, Lord, 138-139

C

Cabildo, 12, 46
Calico Jack, 142
Campbell, James, 94-95, 108, 121, 125, 131
  Mrs. James, 108
Campeche, 90
Campo Santo of Merida, 133
Carmer, Carl, 141
Carolina, 54, 61, 69, 70, 71
Carroll, William, 68

203

Cartagena, 30, 36, 40, 43, 85, 90, 101, 124
Catahoula Parish, Louisiana, 105
Cat Island, 42, 65
Champlin, Mr., 95
Charleston, South Carolina, 35, 127, 151
Charnley, Mitchell Vaughn, 140
Chartres Street ballroom, 17, 18-19
Chew, Beverly, 91, 96, 97, 103
Chighizola,———, 87
Cienfuegos, Captain General, 91
  Jose, 102
Claiborne, Cornelia Tennessee, 16
  Eliza, 16
  Susana, 59
  William C. C., 2, 4, 6, 7, 14, 16, 17, 22, 26, 30, 32-33, 40, 43, 45, 51, 58-59, 60, 61, 67, 83, 144
Claribelle Lafitte, 140
Clement, Joseph, 54
Cleopatra, 85, 92
Cochrane, Alexander, 65-66, 69, 70, 80
Coffee, John, 68, 74, 82
Committee of Defense, 81
Committee for the Defense of New Orleans, 65
Congreve Rocket, 72
Constellation, 95, 128-129
Constitution, 95, 129
Corsair, The, 138-139, 140
Crawford, William, 96
Cronea, Charles, 121, 123

D

Daniel, Price, 149
Debon, Stephen, 36
De Mille, Cecil B., 141
Desfarges, Jean, 118-119, 120, 144
  Juan, 100
Devereux, Mary, 139
Devorador, 92
Dewey, Ariane, 141
Dobie, J. Frank, 137
Dubourg, Reverend Abbé, 78, 79, 81
Duc de Montebello, 26, 27

E

Ellms, Charles, 129, 138, 139, 142, 144
Embargo Act, 22, 35
Enterprise, 110, 111, 121-122
Evans, Lawton Bryan, 140

F

Fatio, Felipe, 91-92, 94, 102
Faye, Stanley, 88, 101
Firebrand, 85
Fisher, S. Rhoads, 133
Floriant, Madame, 79
Flournoy, Major General, 60
Forment, Dr. Felix, 99-100
Forrest, C. R., 66, 69-70, 71, 74
Fort Bowyer, 52, 59, 80
Fort St. John, 69, 71
Fort St. Philip, 76
Forty-fourth Infantry Regiment, 53-54
Franca, Mañuel De, 152
Francais le Pandoure, 35
French, Joseph Lewis, 140

G

Galveston Island, 90, 93-97, 107, 118, 136, 137
Galveston, Texas, 92, 98, 101, 102, 103, 108, 123
Gambi, Vincent, 44, 84, 85
Gambis, 99
Garrison, Captain, 41
Gayarre, Charles, 39, 42, 45, 46, 52, 87, 127, 139, 141-143
General Bolivar, 54, 56
George III, 49
Ghent, Belgium, 71, 80
Gibbs, George, 140
Gilbert, Walker, 42-43
Girod, Nicholas, 60
Gonzales, Catherine Troxell, 141
Graham, George, 108
Grande Isle, x, 23, 46, 87, 137
Grande Terre, x, 23, 27, 29, 30, 31, 37, 40, 47, 50, 53, 54, 56, 59, 61, 64, 67, 69, 82, 87, 93, 101, 117, 136
Grand Lake, 137

204

Great Forgers and Famous Fakes, 149
Great Pirate Stories, 140
Grosse, Philip, 141
Grummond, Jane De, 54, 140, 149
Grymes, John R., 14, 37, 46, 56, 132
Guichard, Magloire, 72

H
Haiti, 12, 124
Hall, Dominick, 57, 61, 67, 81
   Warren D. C., 114
Hamilton, Alexander, 3
   Charles, 149
Havana, Cuba, 20, 91, 124, 126, 127
Henley, J. D., 97
   John, 69
Herrera, Mañuel de, 90
Hinds, Thomas, 69
Hispanola, 10
*Historical Sketch of Pierre and Jean
   Lafitte,* 139
Holland, J. H., 51
   Rupert Sargent, 140
Holmes, Andrew, 37
Holquin, Cuba, 125
Houston, Sam, 115
Humbert, Jean Robert Marie, 39,
   112-113

I
Ingraham, Joseph, 139, 142, 144
Isle of Muger, 121
Ix Chel, 130

J
Jackson, Andrew, viii, 58, 59-62, 63,
   64, 65, 67-72, 74-77, 78-82, 86,
   87, 113, 132
Jamaica, 64, 65
Jane, 36
Jarvis, J. W., 136
Jean Laffite: Gentleman Rover, 148
Jean Lafitte, Gentleman Smuggler, 140
Jefferson, Thomas, 3, 4, 7, 35
Jenny, 35
Jerrmann, Ludwig, 140
Johnson, Robert, 118-119, 120, 144
Jones, J. Randall, 98, 104
   Thomas A. C., 66
Journal of Jean Laffite, The, 148

Jupiter, The, 121

K
Karankawas, 93, 107
Kauffman, Reginald Wright, 140
Kearny, Lt. Larry, 110-111, 121-123,
   128
Kent, Madeline Fabiola, 140
Kentucky militia, 81
Kingston, Jamaica, 128

L
La Bahia, 114, 115
La Caridad, 85
La Courrier de la Louisiane, 33, 51,
   106
La Courrier de La Louisiane, 127
Lacroix, Jacques, 122
Laffite, Jean: adopts Galveston as
   base, 92, 94, 95-97, 98-102;
   adopts Havana as base, 124-125,
   126; adopts Yucatan as base,
   130-134; aids French settlers,
   112; as ally of Jackson, viii, 61-
   62, 65, 67, 68-72, 77, 132; arrives
   in Louisiana, 6, 9; birth of, 9-10,
   12, 14, 39, 134; business acumen
   of, 100-101, 104-105, 142; as captain of *Diligente,* 38-40; charged
   with violating revenue law, 37,
   39, 42-46; children of, 10, 89,
   99; death of, 132-134; described,
   vii-viii, 2, 28, 33, 39, 44, 62, 82,
   91-92, 98, 106, 109, 111, 132,
   136, 138, 142-143, 145; escapes
   prison, 127; as fugitive, 127-128,
   130-134; imprisoned, 127; journal of, 147-152; and Karankawas, 107; knowledge of bayou
   country, 13; leaves Galveston,
   123; leaves Havana, 127; and
   Longs, 113-115; legends about,
   135-145; loses support, 116, 118-
   119, 120, 121, 122-123, 127; as
   merchandiser, 28, 83, 145; mistresses of, 18-19, 21, 32-33, 44,
   89, 111, 131, 137; movies about,
   141; national park named for,
   viii; offered position in Royal

Navy, 48-57, 65, 83; pardoned,
82, 88, 138, 144; as pirate, 39-40,
43, 55, 82, 101, 102, 108, 111,
118-119, 121, 122, 125, 138, 142,
143-145; reported dead, 121,
129; reports of his whereabouts,
127-128; and slave trade, 103-
106, 111, 132; as smuggler, 13,
24, 28-29, 31-32, 33, 37, 39, 40-
41, 42-46, 56-57, 96, 101, 103-
109, 118, 121, 125, 132; social
life of, 17-18, 19, 21, 33; spelling
of his name, viii, 12; as spy, 90,
91, 94, 102, 112; sues for recompense, 88, 90; threatened by
storms, 107-108, 109; threatened
by U.S. to leave Galveston, 108,
110-111, 116-119, 121-123; town
named for, viii, 136; treasure
stories about, 136-137; in war,
46, 48-52, 68-72, 77, 81, 137,
142; warehouse of, 21, 24; writings about, 137-142; as youth,
13-14
Marie Josephe, 10
Pierre, 6, 7, 10, 13, 19, 24, 28-29,
32, 37, 38, 40-41, 44, 45-46, 51-
52, 55-56, 58, 87, 88, 90, 101-
102, 112, 120, 131, 142
Laffite the Pirate, 141
Laffite Study Group Newsletter, The,
149
Lafitte, Baptiste, 12
Bruno, 12
Jean, Sr., 12
Juan, 12
P., 12
Pierre, 12
Pierre, Jr., 12
Sylvestre, 12
Lafitte, the Terror of the Gulf, 141
Lafitte, Louisiana, 136
Lafitte of Louisiana, 139-140
Lafitte the Pirate, 140
*Lafitte: A Play in Prologue and Four
Acts,* 141
Laflin, John A., 147-148, 149, 150,
151, 152

Mathew, 151-152
La Invecta España, 27
La Isla de las Mujeres, 130-134
Lake Borgne, 65, 67, 70, 73, 75
Lake Pontchartrain, 69
Lake Sabine, 104
Lallemand, Charles, 112
Lamar, Mirabeau, 115, 133, 142
La Popa, 85, 86
Laportes, 14, 16
Lara, Jose Bernardo Gutiérrez de,
114
Lasbocas, Yucatan, 133
La Soeur Cherie, 6, 7
Lassy, Louise Moreau de, 14
La Superbe, 31
Latour, Lacarriere, 30, 48, 50, 61,
65, 91, 142
Laussat, Governor, 2
Lavaca River, 136
League of Nations, 143
Le Brave, 100, 118-119
Lebrequet, Michel, 122
Le Brig Goelette la Diligente, 38, 40
Le May, Alan, 140
L'Epine, 26-27
Le Revolte De La Louisiana, 140
Liberty, Texas, 112, 147, 149, 152
Library of Congress, 149
L'Insurgente, 129
L'Intrepide, 25-26, 27
Little, Lois Ann, 152
Livingston, Edward, 14, 27, 46, 60,
61, 65, 70, 80
Robert, 4, 14
Lockyer, Nicholas, 48, 49, 50, 64, 66
Long, James, 113-115
Jane, 114-115
Los Piratas Lafitte, 140
Los Pirates Del Golfo, 139
Louaillier,————,81
Louise, Marie, 32
Louisiana, 61, 69, 71, 72, 74
Louisiana Courier, 118
Louisiana Gazette, 35, 36
Louisiana militia, 81
Louisiana Purchase, 1-4, 14, 66
Louisiana, statehood of, 34

206

Lusitania, 143
Lynx, 117, 118
Lyons, John, 116, 117-118

M

McWilliams, Captain, 48
Madagascar, 108
Madison, J. R., 117-118
  James, 7, 34, 68, 82, 84
Magee, Augustus W., 113
Maison Rouge, 98-100, 107
Malheureux Islands, 66
Mañe, J. Ignacio Rubio, 140
Manique, Governor, 60
Marcel Armand, A Romance of Old Louisiana, 140
Marigny, Bernard, 81
Marott,————,95
Marsh Island, x
Martin, Martha, vii
Martínez, Antonio, 114
Mary, 128
Mayan ruins, 130-131
Mendonca, Henrique Lopez De, 139
Merida, Yucatan, 133
Milam, Ben, 114
Miller, Ray, 142
Miña, Francisco Xavier, 91, 92, 93-95, 112
Miro, Governor, 18
Mississippi militia, 81
Mississippi River, 5, 7, 8, 40, 135
Missouri Historical Society, 148
Mobile, Alabama, 47
Moi, Laffite Dernier Roi Des Flibusters, 140
Monroe, James, 3-4, 68, 76, 97
Monsieur Lafitte, 141
Monsieur Lafitte, Pirate-Patriot, 140
Morales, Juan Ventura, 3

N

Nacogdoches, Texas, 113, 114
Napoleon, 3, 11, 15, 86, 99, 112
Natchitoches, Louisiana, 12, 113
New Enterprise, 112
New Orleans, Battle of, 13, 67-77, 81, 87, 138, 141, 142, 151
New Orleans, Louisiana: British forces attack, viii, 8, 47, 50, 52, 53-55, 63-77; celebrations in, 78-80, 81; described, 1-2, 5-6, 15-16; growth of, 7, 16-17, 22; and Louisiana Purchase, 1-4; piracy trial in, 119; as principal port, 20, 21, 22; residents of, 6, 7-8, 13-14, 18; smuggling in, 3, 24, 30-33, 37, 41, 45; social life in, 17-19, 20; under France, 1, 2, 3, 4, 8; under Spain, 1, 3, 4, 5, 8; under U.S., 2-3, 4, 7, 8, 14, 29, 45
Nicholls, Edward, 48, 49, 50, 59, 64
Niles' Weekly Register, 40, 52, 55, 66, 79, 82, 114, 118, 120-121, 125-126, 129
Ninety-third Scottish Highlanders, 66

O

octoroon castes, 18
Oliver, John, 56
Onis, Don Luis de, 102
Orduna, Spain, 10
Os Piratas Do Norte, 139
Owsley, Frank Lawrence, Jr., 142

P

Pakenham, Sir Edward, 70-72, 73, 74-76
Palacio, Vincente Riva, 139
Patterson, Daniel, 50, 53-55, 56-57, 59, 61, 64, 66, 67, 69, 72, 74, 76, 87, 88, 96, 110, 117, 118, 120, 121, 123
Pensacola, Florida, 47, 52
Percy, William Henry, 48, 49
Perez, Igñacio, 114
Perry, Henry, 91, 92, 93, 94, 95, 112
Picornell, Mariano, 90
piracy, defined, 143-144; increase of, 125-129
Pirate of Barataria, The, 140
Pirate of the Gulf, The, 140
Pirate Hero of New Orleans, The, 141
Pirate Jean, 140
Pirate Laffite and the Battle of New Orleans, The, 141
"Pirate of New Orleans, The," 141
Place d'Armes, 1, 2, 6, 8, 79, 119

Plauche, J. P., 61, 69, 79
Point Bolivar, 114, 115
Port-au-Prince, 11, 127
Porter, David, 26-27, 128
Powderhorn Passage, 140
Pride, The, 99
privateering, 11, 12, 20, 25-26, 29-33,
    39, 85, 95-97, 100-102, 121, 122,
    124, 125, 126-127, 143

Q
quadroon castes, 18-19
Quixote, Don, 24

R
Ramírez, Alexandro, 91, 102
Rapides, Louisiana, 105
Ravenswaay, Charles van, 148
Reynolds, Michael, 68
Rigaud, Madeline, 89
Robertson, Thomas, 30, 32
Roeny, James, 122
Rome, 143
Ross, Colonel, 54, 56
Rush, Attorney General, 58

S
Sabine River, 137
St. Barthélemy, 25
St. Charles Parish, 55
St. Dominique, 10, 11-12, 13, 64, 124
St. Geme, 87
St. Helena, 86, 136
St. John the Baptist Parish, 31
St. Louis Cathedral, 2
St. Louis Cemetery, 16
St. Louis Cemetery Number Two, 87
St. Louis, Missouri, 106, 131
St. Louis sanctuary, 78
St. Malo, France, 10
St. Martin, 25
St. Philip Theater, 17
Sam Houston Regional Library and
    Research Center, 147-148, 149
Santo Domingo, 10, 13, 31
Santos, Richard, 149-150
Sauvinet, Joseph, 25, 46, 56, 88
Saxon, Lyle, 44, 140, 141
Schaadt, Robert L., 149

Scottish Ninety-third Highlanders, 76
Sedella, Antonio de, 89, 90, 91, 94
Sheridan, Francis C., 142
Shores of Romance, The, 140
Sibley, Dr. John, 106, 107
Silan, Yucatan, 133
Simpson, William, 148-149
slaves, importation of, 22, 29-30, 92,
    94, 103-106, 122
Smith, Aaron, 126-127
Sophia, 48
Soto de la Marina, 92, 94
Sperry, Armstrong, 140
Spy, 36
Stephens, J. L., 130, 131, 133

T
Tallant, Robert, 141
Tallyrand-Perigord, Charles Maurice
    de, 4
Temple, 32, 44, 59
Tennessee militia, 81
Theater d'Orleans, 17
The Two Sisters, 20
Thompson, Charles, 69
    Ray, 148
    Sue, 148
Tousard, Louis de, 11
Townsend, Tom, 140
Trespalacios, Jose Felix, 114
Trinity River, 112, 121, 122
Tucker, John, 119

U
United Nations Conference on the
    Law of the Sea, 143

V
Valiente Guaricuru, 126
Vera Cruz, 20
Verrill, Hyatt A., 142
Vidalia Sandbar, battle at, 105
Villars, Catherine, 44, 89
    Marie Louise, 32, 44, 89
Villere Canal, 69
Vinton, Iris, 141
Vogel, Robert, 151

W
War of 1812, 11, 34-37, 42, 47-57, 60-
    77, 95

War with the Barbary States, 129
Washington, D.C., 63, 66, 88, 101-
102
Washington Hall, 101
Wellington, duke of, 66, 70
Westchester, New York, 10
West Indies, 125, 126, 128-129
*We Were There With Jean Lafitte at
New Orleans*, 141
Wild Heroes of the Sea, 138
Wilkinson, Elizabeth, 140, 141

James, 2, 21
Williams, —, 39
Samuel, 102, 142
Wilson, Woodrow, 143

Y
yellow fever, 15, 16
Youx, Dominique, 31, 35, 54, 55, 57,
58, 69, 71, 73, 75, 77, 81, 86-87,
88, 101, 136, 144, 153
Frederick, 35
Yucatan, 127, 128, 130, 133